# Preface



## Aim

The aim of this book is to provide a new kind of compleme
young adult learners – one that *actively* involves the learn
and form before providing practice.

It is principally intended to be used as support for teacher-directed courses at Elementary level. However, because of the active-learning approach, it can be used for independent study.

It is the first in a series ranging from Elementary to Advanced.

## Need

Most 'grammars' are either purely for reference, or reference with practice. This book actively guides the learner towards discovering the language for themselves – thus making it more memorable and engaging. Then the language point is consolidated with meaningful practice.

Used as a complementary support to a coursebook, this book can help learners to 'fill the holes' in their knowledge, consolidate, or preview important aspects of English grammar.

## Approach

The book has forty six Units, each covering a grammatical concept found in coursebooks at Elementary level. Each Unit is based on the same format – reflecting the way a teacher in the classroom would focus on meaning and form before going on to give practice.

- **Meaning and form.** The learner actively *discovers* meaning and form for him/herself through motivating activities. Examples of what is required are given to help overcome the difficulty, at this level, of understanding written instructions. Answers and explanations are provided (Appendix 4) – providing the learner with a clear reference. The answers the student is expected to give are shown in accessible *handscript.*

- **Practice.** Varied and meaningful practice activities help confirm understanding and give plenty of opportunity for consolidation. A key is provided (Appendix 5). *Note: an edition is available without a key to practice and further-practice (see below) exercises to suit teacher preference.* In addition to controlled written practice there are 'Practise with a friend' activities providing the opportunity for communicative oral practice.

- **'Test-yourself' exercises.** For each 'Part' (see Contents) a set of self-testing exercises is included. A combined answer and study/revision guide (Appendix 3) enables the learner to identify weak areas requiring further study or revision.

- **'Further-practice' exercises.** 'Further-practice' exercises are provided for each *Unit* to enable the learner to 'revisit' areas of difficulty. A key is provided (Appendix 6).

# Teachers' notes

- **Complementary use with any general English coursebook.** The contents of this book cover, comprehensively, grammar areas included in coursebooks at Elementary level. Having presented an element of grammar in your own way you may use this book for consolidation, revision or recycling. Alternatively, especially with *mixed ability groups* you may choose to ask students to preview material *before* dealing with it in class.
- **Organisation.** Most Units are independent of others and could be used in any order. Those Units making use of prior knowledge to convey meaning and form only do so within a logical teaching sequence (for example, past simple before present perfect).
- **Self-study.** The active-learning approach encourages learner autonomy, giving plenty of support for self-study.
- **Pairwork.** The activities under the heading 'Practise with a friend' could be used for in-class consolidation of homework or outside class in independent study.

# Students' notes

**Is this book for me?** This book is intended for you if you are beyond the 'Beginner' level i.e. you have a little English which you want to improve.

**How do I use it?** You can start at the beginning and work through, or pick out areas you find difficult (using the Map of the book (page vi) or Index (page 202). If you are not sure what you need to work on you can do the 'Test-yourself' exercises (page 94) to find out where your weak areas are. Alternatively, your teacher may direct you to Units which will help you. Working at home, this book will help and guide you like a teacher.

# Contents

# Map of the book

# Unit 1: Present tense of the verb 'to be' (am/is/are) She *is* a student

talking about **people, places and objects**

## Meaning

**Complete the gaps with 'am' 'is' or 'are'**

| *Example:* I am Susan |
| --- |

I ___ from London

His name ___ Carlos
He___ from
Mozambique

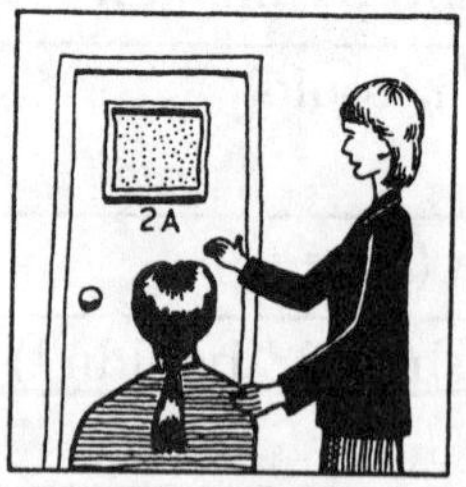


You ___ in class 2a

They___from Rome
They ___ Italian

I___John
My name___ Steve
We____ friends

This ___ the International School
It____ in Manchester

This _____ Claire
She _____ a student

## Form

Usually we don't say **'I am** Susan' – we say **'I'm** Susan' – this is a *contraction*.
**Write these sentences again with *contractions***

| *Example:* | |
| --- | --- |
| **I am** from London | I'm from London |

**You are** in my class ______________________
**She is** from Poland ______________________
**He is** a student ______________________
**It is** in London ______________________
**We are** German ______________________
**They are** from Denmark ______________________

### *Negative*

**Make the sentences *negative* (in *two* different ways)**

| *Examples* |
| --- |
| You're in my class |
| You're not in my class |
| You aren't in my class |

She's from Poland
______________________
______________________

He's a student
______________________
______________________

It's in London
______________________
______________________

We're German
______________________
______________________

They're from Denmark
______________________
______________________

I'm from London
______________________
(only one possibility here)



Answers and Explanations ➤page 147➔

# Unit 1: Practice

> ***Example:***
> "My name 's Susan Smith.
> I 'm a teacher. I 'm
> 27 years old and I 'm not
> married (yet!).
> Here are some photographs of my friends and
> family..."

**1. Match with the photographs and complete the gaps.**

A. This _______ my brother. He _______ very tall and thin. He _______ a teacher too so he _______ very rich.

B. My mother and father _______ quite young. They _______ both photographers. At the moment they _______ in England, they _______ on holiday in Africa.

C. My boyfriend _______ called Tom. He _______ very tall but we _______ very happy together!

D. My house _______ in London. It _______ quite old, but it _______ very big.

**2. Write full sentences about Susan's friends and family.**

| ***Example:*** | |
|---|---|
| Catherine/my sister. | Catherine's (Catherine is) my sister |
| very beautiful | She's (She is) very beautiful |
| doctor | She's (She is) a doctor. |

My father's name/John
photographer
from Ireland

Mary and Claudia/my friends
very intelligent
not very rich
actresses

My mother/called Hilary
photographer
49 years old

**3. Find the mistakes in these sentences and correct them.**

| ***Example:*** | |
|---|---|
| She're 27 years old ✗ | She's 27 years old. |
| I'm a doctor ✓ | |

(a) They from England
(b) My house it's quite old
(c) We're actresses
(d) He's not very tall
(e) I'm not a student, I are a teacher.
(f) She's very intelligent
(g) He's called Stephen.
(h) His name Peter.

**4. Practise with a friend. Talk to a friend about your family. You could use these words to help you:**

my brother
my mother
my parents
my sister
my father

is/are

beautiful
a teacher
quite goodlooking
Italian
very intelligent
from Poland

# Unit 2: Verb 'to be': questions (am I?/are you? is he?) *Is* he French?

**Asking questions about people, places and objects**

## Meaning

This is a party at the International School of English.
**Match each *question* with a suitable *answer*:**

| *Example:* |
|---|
| (a) 'Is he French?' 3 No, he isn't |

(b) 'Are we friends now?' ______
(c) 'Where are you from?' ______
(d) 'What's your name?' ______
(e) 'Is she from Japan?' ______
(f) 'Are you a model?' ______

## Form

**Complete these other conversations at the party**

| *Examples* | |
|---|---|
| **I/you** | |
| 'Am I boring?' | 'No, you aren't/you're not' |
| 'Are you tired?' | 'Yes, I am.' |

**He/She/It**
'Is she your sister?' 'Yes, ____ ____'
'____ ____ from Venezuela?' 'No, he isn't/he's not'

**We**
'____ ____ late?' 'No, we aren't/we're not'

**They**
'Are they married?' 'Yes, ____ ____'

**Complete the rules with these words:** *negative (x2) positive before after*

Normally we put the verb 'to be' ______ the subject, but to make questions with the verb 'to be' we put the verb ______ the subject

| | Subject + Verb | | Verb + Subject |
|---|---|---|---|
| *Example:* | You're Polish | = | **Are** you Polish? |

To make ______ short answers we *contract* but to make ______ short answers we do NOT *contract*

| *Example:* No, **I'm not**/Yes, **I am** |
|---|

______ short answers can contract two different ways (except 'No, I'm not')*

| *Example:* No, **he's not** or No, **he isn't** |
|---|

*see Unit 1


Answers and Explanations ➤page 147➤

**Question words – We can ask questions *with* or *without* a question word [who/what/why/how/when/where/which].**

> *Example*
> Are you a model? — Yes, I am.
> Why are you a model? — Because the money is good!

**Make questions *with* and *without* question words to match the answers.**

1. She's very rich.
   a) ______? Yes, she is.
   b) Why ______? Because she's a supermodel.
2. Warsaw is in Poland
   a) ______? Yes, it is.
   b) Where ______? In Poland
3. They're both 16
   a) ______? Yes, they are.
   b) How old ______? They're both 16!
4. We're late
   a) ______? Yes, we are.
   b) Why ______? I forgot the time.

# Unit 2: Practice

**1.** Rosa is a student at the International School of English, in London. In Brazil, she is a doctor. She is thirty two years old. She is married with two children – Juliana is six and Pedro is three. Her husband's name is Paulo. He's a teacher. He's not in London now. It isn't the holidays so Paulo and the children are at school.

**Write questions and *short* answers about Rosa and her family**

> *Example:*
> Rosa/student? — Is Rosa a student? Yes, she is.
> **Where**/Rosa/student? — Where is Rosa a student? In London.

a) Rosa/teacher? ______? ______
b) the International School of English/in France? ______? ______
c) **Where**/Rosa/doctor? ______? In ______
d) Rosa/forty years old? ______? ______
e) **How old**/Rosa? ______? ______
f) Rosa/married? ______? ______
g) Juliana/six? ______? ______
h) Pedro/six? ______? ______
i) **How old**/the children? ______? ______ and ______
i) **What**/her husband's name? ______? ______
j) Paulo/in London now? ______? ______
k) **Where**/Paulo and the children? ______? ______

**2. Read these conversations and correct any mistakes you find.**

> *Example:*
> Susan: 'Hello. My name **are** Susan' — ✗ My name's Susan.

John: Pleased to meet you. My name's John.
Susan: Sorry, are you my brother's friend?
John: No, I aren't. I'm Catherine's boyfriend.
Susan: You are a doctor?
John: No, it isn't!
Susan: Sorry!

Catherine: Who's that over there?
Jonathan: That's Michael. He are very famous.
Catherine: Why he is famous?
Jonathan : He's a singer.

Mark: Susan's my sister.
Jane: What her boyfriend's name?
Mark: Tom. He's a teacher too.
Jane: They is married?
Mark: No, not yet.

Susan: Are where Catherine and Jonathan?
Mark: In the kitchen.
Susan: Are they hungry?

# Unit 3: This/that/these/those

## *this* is your room and *that's* ours

Near or far?

**Meaning 1:** this/that

Maria-Jose is going to stay with her Englisl penfriend, Amanda.

(1)  (2) 

Is **that** your bag?
**This** is my husband John
**This** is **your room**
**That** is our room


**Look at the photographs and match the words with the pictures.**

(a) This = (1) or (2)? __________

(b) That = (1) or (2)? __________

**Meaning 2:** these/those

(1) 

(2) 

Are **these** your children?
**Those** are your towels
**These** books are in English. **Those** are in Portuguese


**Look at the photographs and match the words with the pictures.**

(c) These = (1) or (2)? __________

(d) Those = (1) or (2)? __________

**Form**

**Complete the form with *is* or *are***

*Examples:*
This is the bathroom
That 's the kitchen

This room ___ beautiful
That bag ___ mine.
(So, are this/that *singular* or *plural*?) _______

*(NB Only 'that's' normally contracts).*

*Examples:*
These are my children
Those are my bags

These apples ____ green
Those chairs ____ uncomfortable!
(So, are these/those *singular* or *plural*?) _______

**Make *negative statements* and *questions* from the following:**

| *Example* | | |
|---|---|---|
| This is your room | This isn't your room. | Is this your room? |

That's your daughter ________ ________
These are his keys ________ ________
Those are our bicycles ________ ________
This room is beautiful ________ ________
That room is John's ________ ________
These curtains are very nice ________ ________
Those chairs are uncomfortable ________ ________



Answers and Explanations ➤page 148➔

# Unit 3: Practice

1. Amanda has a dinner party for her friends and Maria-Jose.

**a) Complete with *this* or *these***

**b) Complete with *that* or *those***

**2.** Maria Jose and Amanda are in a music shop. **Put the words in the correct order to make their dialogue.**

> *Example*
> MJ: /'REM' CD/new/is/the/this = This is the new 'REM' CD

A: /that/your/is/band/favourite/?/ = ____________
MJ: /is/yes/it/,/ = ____________
A: /that/their/best/CD/is/?/ ____________
MJ: /it/no/,/isn't/./ = ____________
/is/this/ = ____________
A: /'s/very/expensive/that/ = ____________

**3.** Maria Jose and Amanda are in a clothes shop. **Complete the dialogue with [this/these/are/is]**

> *Example*
> MJ: This is a good shop.

MJ: ________ shoes ______ lovely!
A: Well, I think ______ ______ better.
MJ: But ______ ______ brown. ______ shirt ______ the same colour.
A: O.K. Try them on.
MJ: Ahh. ______ ______ uncomfortable.
A: So ______ ______ better! And ______ ______ a lovely colour.

**4. Complete the sentences under these pictures using *this/that/these/those* and *is/are/isn't/aren't*.**

How much are those?

This isn't very good

This is very cheap!

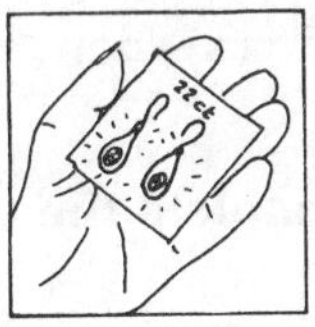
How much ________?

________ the last one!

________ very fashionable

________ the new REM CD?

________ fresh!

Why ____ ____ so expensive!

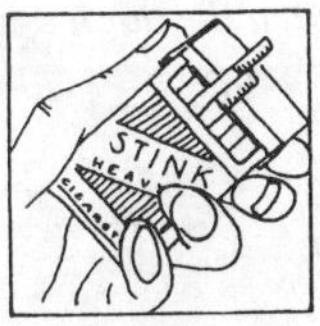

________ good for you.

________ English newspapers

**A:** ____ shoes ____ lovely!
**MJ:** No, I think ____ ____ nicer

**5. Practise with a friend.**
See page 127.

# Unit 4: Singular and plural nouns

**child/children, desk/desks**

**One or more than one?**

## Meaning

**(a)**

**(b)**

**Find twelve differences between the pictures and complete the sentences with '*a*' or a number *2–10***

1. In picture **(a)** there is _a_ dictionary. In picture **(b)** there are _two_ dictionaries
2. In picture **(a)** there is ____ teacher. In picture **(b)** there are ___ teacher**s**.
3. In picture **(a)** there are ___ key**s**. In picture **(b)** there is ____ key.
4. In picture **(a)** there are _____ desk**s**. In picture **(b)** there is ___ desk.
5. In picture **(a)** there are ____ **people**. In picture **(b)** there are ____ **people**.
6. In picture **(a)** there is ____ pen. In picture **(b)** there are ____ pen**s**.
7. In picture **(a)** there are ____ bus**es**. In picture **(b)** there is ____ bus.
8. In picture **(a)** there are ____ wom**en**. In picture **(b)** there are ____ wom**en**.
9. In picture **(a)** there is _____ m**a**n. In picture **(b)** there are ____ m**e**n.
10. In picture **(a)** there are ____ sandwich**es**. In picture **(b)** there is ___ sandwich.
11. In picture **(a)** there is _____ book (not the dictionary). In picture **(b)** there are ___ book**s** (not the dictionaries).
12. In picture **(a)** there are _____ child**ren**. In picture **(b)** there are ______child**ren**.

## Form **Complete the table with the nouns in singular and plural forms**

| | SINGULAR | | PLURAL |
|---|---|---|---|
| a) | book | ←→ | books |
| | desk | ←→ | desks |
| | table | ←→ | ______ |
| | ______ | ←→ | teachers |
| | pen | ←→ | ______ |

*RULE: Most nouns add ______ in the plural.*

| | | | |
|---|---|---|---|
| b) | ______ | ←→ | buses |
| | sandwich | ←→ | ______ |

*RULE: When the last SOUND of the noun is /s/ /S/ /tS/ /dz/ we add ______ in the plural.*

| | SINGULAR | | PLURAL |
|---|---|---|---|
| c) | dictionary | ←→ | ______ |

*RULE: When the noun ends consonant + y the 'y' changes to ______.*

| | | | |
|---|---|---|---|
| d) | ______ | ←→ | keys |

*RULE: When the noun ends vowel + y the 'y' does NOT change to -ies , we add ______ (like Rule a).*

| | | | |
|---|---|---|---|
| e) | man | ←→ | ______ |
| | ______ | ←→ | women |
| | person | ←→ | ______ |
| | child | ←→ | ______ |

*RULE: Some nouns (not only these four) are irregular.*



**Answers and Explanations ➤page 148➔**

# Unit 4: Practice

**1. Complete with *is* or *are***

(a) There are ten children
(b) There _____ a teacher
(c) There _____ two balls
(d) There _____ a dog
(e) There _____ a sandwich
(f) There _____ a bus
(g) There _____ two houses
(h) There _____ five girls
(i) There _____ a book
(j) There _____ two pens

**2. Complete the information about Britain today**

> ***Example***
> There are 57,800,000 [person] people

There are 23,628,000 [woman] __________
There are 22,472,000 [man] __________
There are 5,967,000 [girl] __________
There are 5,7333,000 [boy] __________
There are 11,700,000 [child] __________
There are 28,150 [church] __________
There are 23,000,000 [house] __________
There are 20,700,000 [car] __________
There are 71,000 [bus] __________
There are 2,000,000 [lorry] __________
There are 160,400 [factory] __________

**3. Read these sentences and correct the mistakes you find.**

> ***Example***
> a) There is 23,628,000 women in Britain ✗ are

b) There is a child in the classroom.
c) In London, the bus are red.
d) There are 100 people in the church.
e) There is an old men in the shop.
f) There are 5,733,000 boy in Britain.
g) This is my houses.

**4. Read these sentences and correct the spelling mistakes you find (there is *one* in *every* sentence)**

> ***Example***
> a) Are the childs happy ✗ children

b) The sandwichs are fresh.
c) Why are the buss late?
d) The teacheres are tired.
e) There are five churchs in the town.
f) There are 160,400 factorys in Britain.
g) There are 10 boies and 12 girls in the class.

**Practise with a friend:**
**A turn to page 127, B turn to page 135.**
You have two pictures of a street. They are similar but not identical. Find the differences.

> ***Example***
> A: 'In my picture there is a church'.
> B: 'In my picture there are *two* churches'.

# Unit 5: Present simple tense

**go/goes, eat/eats**

Talking about **general present time**

## Meaning

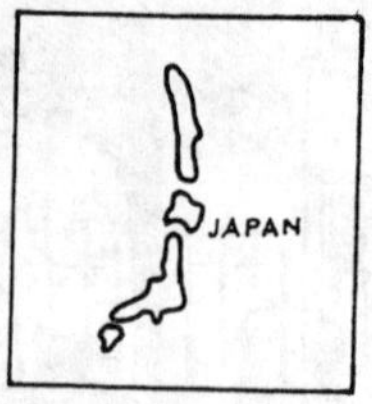


Japan is in the Pacific Ocean. It has four main islands. The capital is Tokyo – six million people live there.

The Japanese make good televisions, cars and computers. They work very hard and get up early – on average at 6.30 am. The working day finishes at about 7pm.

Mr Koshura gets up at 6.00 and has breakfast – rice and fish. At 7.00 he goes to work on the underground train. He works for Toyota. He likes his job and usually stays late at the office in the evenings. At the weekends he plays baseball.

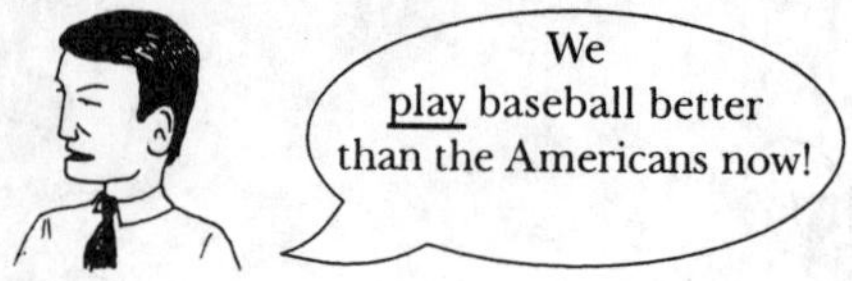

We play baseball better than the Americans now!


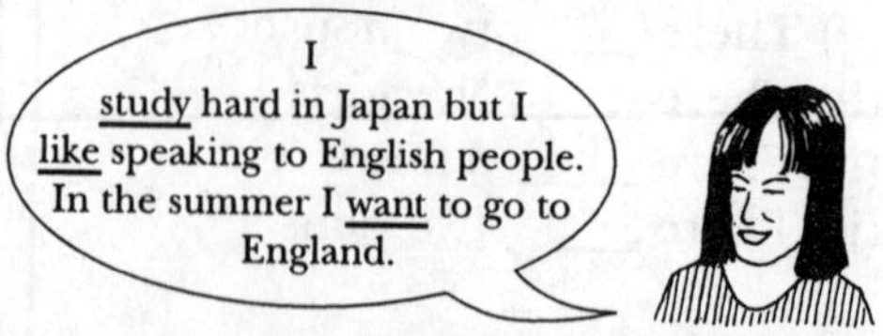

I study hard in Japan but I like speaking to English people. In the summer I want to go to England.


Yuko is a student. She studies English at Hiroshima Shudo University. She works hard but at the weekend she likes going shopping and, in the winter, she goes skiing.

**Look at the underlined verbs – this is the present simple tense. Do we use the present simple tense to talk about *now, at this moment* or about things that are *generally true*?** ____________________

## Form

**Can you complete the table?**

| | be | make | work | go | finish | have | play | study |
|---|---|---|---|---|---|---|---|---|
| I | | make | | | | | | |
| you | are | make | | | finish | | | |
| he/she/it | | makes | | | | | | studies |
| we | | make | | | | have | | |
| they | | make | | | | | | study |

What do you notice about the **form** of the verb after **he/she/it?** = We usually add ______.

There are some *irregular* verbs too [goes/has/am,is,are] and sometimes the *spelling* changes.

***Spelling***

**Complete the table with the *infinitive* or the *he/she/it* form.**

| | Infinitive | He/She/It | Infinitive | He/She/It |
|---|---|---|---|---|
| (a) | work | works | get up | ____________ |
| | make | makes | ____________ | lives |

**Rule:** Most verbs add ______ after he/she/it.

(b) ____________ finishes

watch ____________

**Rule:** When the last SOUND of the verb is /s/ /S/ /tS/ /dz/ we add ______ after he/she/it.

(c) study ____________

**Rule:** When the verb ends *consonant* + y the 'y' changes to ______.

(d) ____________ plays

**Rule:** When the verb ends *vowel* + y the 'y' does NOT change to -ies , we add ______ (like Rule (a)).

(e) go ____________

____________ has

be ____________

**Rule:** Some verbs (not many) are *irregular.*



**Answers and Explanations ➤page 149➤**

# Unit 5: Practice

**1. Complete using the verbs in brackets. ( )**

I (love)
____ Devon. We
(have)______ lots of
tourists because the sun
(shine)______ all
summer.

DEVON
Torquay

Devon(be) is in the southwest of Britain. The countryside (be)___ very beautiful and many tourists (go)___ there in the summer. They (swim)______ in the sea, (lie)______ on the beach and (walk)______ in the hills.

Mr Swinnon (live)_____ in Torquay. He (work)______ in a hotel. In the morning he (get)____ up early, (go)____ for a walk on the beach and then he (cook)______ breakfast for the visitors.

**2. Complete using these verbs: have(×2)/live/rain/like/be/eat/come/make/study/watch/play/think/go/enjoy/**

Portugal ___ in the southwest of Europe. It ____ many kilometres of beaches so the Portuguese ___ a lot of fish. They _____ very good wine too.

Jorge _____ from Angola but he ______ in Lisbon, the capital of Portugal. He ______ medicine at the university. At the weekend he ______ to the beach and ______ volleyball. When it _____ he _______ football on television.

PORTUGAL
Lisbon

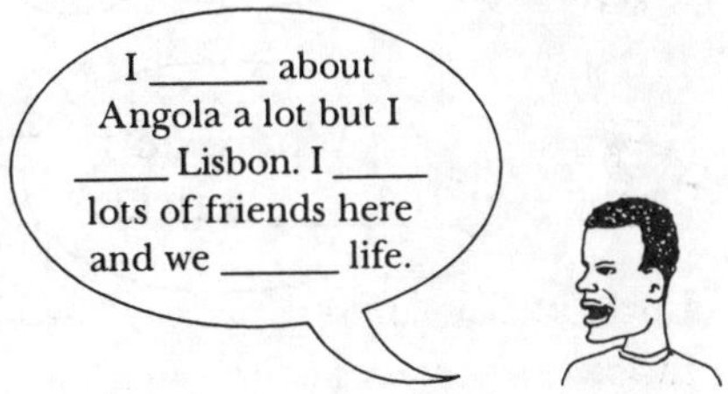
I ______ about
Angola a lot but I
_____ Lisbon. I _____
lots of friends here
and we _____ life.

**3. Correct the mistakes you find.**

I finishes work at
6.00pm and I always
feel very tired, so in the
evenings I read a book
or listens to music.

FINLAND
Saint Petersburg
RUSSIA

St Petersburg is in Russia, near the Baltic Sea. It is a beautiful old city, on forty-four small islands. It snow a lot in the winter and night comes very early, but in the summer the sun never go down.

Irena works as a tourist guide. She take visitors to the *Hermitage* Museum of Art. She gets up early and have breakfast – tea and bread and jam. Then she goes to work and meets the first group of tourists at 9.30am. She works hard and she walk a lot – the *Hermitage* is very big – 20 kilometres to see everything!

**4. Correct the spelling mistakes in *every* sentence**

a) Irena finishs work at 6.00.
b) Jorge plaies volleyball.
c) Yuko studys hard.
d) Mr Koshura workes for Toyota.
e) Irena gos to work at 9.00.
f) Jorge haves a lot of friends in Lisbon.
g) Jorge watchs football on television.

**5. Practise with a friend**
**Use these verbs (and others you know) to talk to your friend about *your* life and where you live. Then listen to your friend carefully.**

go live work study play stay finish make
watch have be get up like walk

> ***Example***
> 'I live in HongKong. It is a very exciting city. I work...'

**Now talk to a different friend and tell him/her about your first friend**

> ***Example***
> 'Joyce lives in HongKong. She works in a school...'

# Unit 6: Present simple auxiliaries: do/does *Do* we stop at Munich?

**Asking questions** and **making negatives** and **short answers** using the present simple

## Meaning

**Complete the gap with the right *INFINITIVE: leave/know/go/stop/go/arrive/buy***

What time **does** the train leave?
Sorry, I **don't**____
Where **do** I ____ a ticket?
TICKETS
When **do** we ____ in Paris?
**Does** this train ____ to Berlin?
This train **doesn't** ____ to Paris
**Do** we ____ at Munich?
Yes, we **do**


**Now write the sentences above in the right column**

| Questions | Negatives | Short Answers |
|---|---|---|
| What time does the train leave? | Sorry, I don't know | Yes, we do |
| ____? | ____ | |
| ____? | | |
| ____? | | |
| ____? | | |

## Form

**Look at *your examples* and complete the rules:**

- To make a **question** in the present simple tense with most verbs (go, arrive etc) we use:

  [QUESTION WORD] + ______ OR ______ + SUBJECT + INFINITIVE

- To make a **negative** in the present simple tense with most verbs we use:

  SUBJECT + ______ OR ______ + INFINITIVE

- To make a **short answer** in the present simple tense with most verbs we use:

  YES/NO + SUBJECT + ______ OR ______ (positive)/ ______ OR ______ (negative)

- When the subject is **I**, **you**, **we**, **they**, we use ______ (positive) or ______ (negative)
- When the subject is **he**, **she**, **it**, we use ______ (positive) or ______ (negative)



Answers and Explanations ➤page 149➤

# Unit 6: Practice

**1.** ***The train from Berlin to St Petersburg.*** **Put the words in the right order to make questions.**

> ***Example:***
> (a) The train to St Petersburg leaves Berlin in the evening
> [the/when/train/St Petersburg/to/leave/does?] When does the train to St Petersburg leave?

(b) It costs about US$150 [it/cost/does/how much?] ______________________

(c) It arrives thirty-three hours later [it/when/arrive/does?] ______________________

(d) It goes through Poland, Belarus, Lithuania, Latvia and Estonia
[countries/how many/it/go through/does?] ______________________

(e) You need to buy a visa in Belarus
[do/where/buy/need to/visa/a/you?] ______________________

(f) They sell the visas at Grodno station
[sell/they/where/the/do/visas?] ______________________

(g) The visa costs about US$45 [the/how much/does/cost/visa?] ______________________

**2. Write *short answers* about the train from Berlin to St Petersburg**

> ***Example:***
> (a) Does the train to St Petersburg leave in the evening? Yes, it does

(b) Does it arrive thirty-three hours later? ____________

(c) Does it go through Hungary? ____________

(d) Do you need to buy a visa in Poland? ____________

(e) Do you need to buy a visa in Belarus? ____________

(f) Do they sell the visas at Grodno station? ____________

(g) Does the *visa* cost US$150? ____________

**3.** ***Conversations on the train.*** **Complete the questions using *do/does/don't/doesn't* and these INFINITIVES: *check/stop/like/go/know/cost/arrive***

> ***Example:***
> 'When do we arrive in Vilnius?' 'Six o'clock'

'_______ you often _______ to Russia?' 'Yes, I _______'

'_______ you _______ travelling?' 'I love it!'

'_______ the train _______ in Krakow?' 'No, it _______'

'How much _______ it _______ to travel 1st class?' 'I _______ _______.'

'Oh no! I _______ _______ a reservation.' 'Thirty-three hours is a long time to stand up!'

'Where _______ they _______ your passport?' 'At the border.'

**4. Correct any mistakes you find.**

'Do you have a ticket?' 'Yes, I does.'

'Where does the train stops?' 'In Poland, Belarus, Lithuania, Latvia and Estonia.'

'When we arrive in Grodno?' 'I not know'

'Does the ticket inspector check the tickets?' 'Yes, he do!'

'I don't speak Russian.' 'I do.'

'We don't stop in Krakow.' 'Yes, I knows.'

**5. Practise with a friend**

*Asking for Information*

Student A turn to page 128
Student B turn to page 135

# Unit 7: Adverbs I: frequency

How often?

**always/never/sometimes**

**He *never* drives a car**

## Meaning

Mr Jones is very rich. He goes out every night to a bar or a club. He is very fat because he doesn't like exercise much. He eats caviar and drinks champagne every day. He likes travelling and goes on holiday every month. Once or twice a month he likes to smoke a cigar – but his wife doesn't like it!

Mr Smith isn't very rich. He stays at home every night and watches the television because it's cheap. He likes exercise though – he runs in the park three times a week. He doesn't have a car and he can't drive so he goes to work by bus every day. Holidays are expensive – he goes on holiday every five or six years. He enjoys going to football matches – he doesn't go every week but he goes when he has the money.

**Complete with *always/often/sometimes/rarely/never*.**

> ***Example:***
> Mr Jones is __never__ at home in the evenings.

He ______ eats caviar and drinks champagne.
He ______ goes on holiday.
He ______ takes exercise.
He ______ smokes a cigar.

Mr Smith is ______ at home in the evenings.
He ______ runs in the park.
He ______ drives a car.
He ______ goes on holiday.
He ______ goes to watch a football match.

**Now put the adverbs *in order* on the line:**

ALWAYS (100%) ______ ______ ______ NEVER (0%)

## Form

**Look at these examples:**

(a) Mr Jones *never stays* at home in the evenings.
(b) Mr Jones *is never* at home in the evenings.

**Now answer these questions to find the rule for word order**

What is the **verb** in sentence (a)? ______
What is the **verb** in sentence (b)? ______

With a verb like stay/go/drink etc does the **frequency adverb** (never, always etc) *usually** go **before** or **after** the verb? ______

With the verb 'to be' (is/are etc) does the **frequency adverb** *usually** go **before** or **after** the verb? ______
[*'*Usually*' because sometimes a different word order is possible but this one is *always* correct]



Answers and Explanations ➤page 150➤

# Unit 7: Practice

## 1. Put the words in the correct order to make sentences

> ***Example:***
> (a) Sarah/gets up/at/7.30/always    Sarah always gets up at 7.30

(b) eats/she/breakfast/never ____________________
(c) she/often/a cup of/has/coffee ____________________
(d) work/always/she/to/drives ____________________
(e) late/is/she/sometimes ____________________
(f) the traffic/bad/always/is ____________________

(g) often/in the evenings/watches/James/old films/on the television ____________________
(h) he/gets up/always/late ____________________
(i) he/never/to bed/goes/before 2.00am ____________________

## 2. Rewrite the sentences using adverbs of frequency.

> ***Example:***
> (a) Peter goes running every morning    Peter always goes running

(b) He goes swimming *nearly every week.*    He ____________ swimming
(c) He is vegetarian *so he doesn't eat meat.*    He ____________ meat
(d) He is very healthy *all the time.*    He ____________ very healthy
(e) He drinks beer *three or four times a year.*    He ____________ beer

(f) Simon gets up at 5.00 *every day.*    Simon ____________ at 5.00
(g) He is tired *all the time.*    He ____________ tired

## 3. Correct the *word order* mistakes you find.

*Julia is a nurse and works during the night at the hospital.*

*Interviewer*: 'What time do you finish work, Julia?'

*Julia*: 'Well, I finish often (✗ often finish) about 6.00am, but it is sometimes later. I don't get often home until 8.00am – then always I go straight to bed!'

*Interviewer*: 'What time do you get up?"

*Julia*: 'I get up usually at about 3.00pm to do some shopping and cooking. I get up rarely later than 4.00pm because the children always come home from school then. I always am busy in the evening but my husband often helps me to cook the dinner and he puts sometimes the children to bed.'

## 5. Practise with a friend

### A: Interview your friend using these questions

What time do you get up?
What do you have for breakfast?
What time do you start work/school?
What time do you finish work/school?
What do you do at the weekends?
Where do you go on holiday?

### B. Answer the questions using *always/sometimes/often/rarely/never.* *(Try to make your answers long – like Julia's)*

> ***Example:*** 'I *often* have toast for breakfast but I *sometimes* have cereal.'

# Unit 8: Subject and object pronouns: I/me, he/him  Please marry *me*

Referring to people and objects **without naming them**

## Meaning

John: 'Barbara, **I(*a*)** love **you.** (***b***) Please marry **me.(*c*)**'
Barbara: 'Maybe **you(*d*)** love **me(*e*)**, but **you(f)** don't love my family.'
John: '**They(*g*)** don't want **us(*h*)** to get married.'
Barbara: 'But **we(*i*)** never visit **them.** (***j***)'
John: 'Your parents are strange. **She(*k*)** never speaks to **him(*l*)** and **he(*m*)** never speaks to **her.(*n*)**'
Barbara: 'Well, **you and your family** never stop talking! **You(*o*)** talk all the time!'
John: 'Here's the ring. Please, Barbara.'
Barbara: '**It's(*p*)** beautiful... but **I(*q*)** don't want **it!(*r*)**'

**Match the pronouns with who (or what) they *refer to***
**Choose from these answers:** the ring/Barbara/John and Barbara/Barbara's parents/Barbara's mother/Barbara's father/John and his family/John

*Examples:*
(*a*) I = John
(*b*) you = Barbara
(*c*) me = John

(*d*) you =
(*e*) me =
(*f*) you =
(*g*) they =
(*h*) us =
(*i*) we =
(*j*) them =
(*k*) she =
(*l*) him =
(*m*) he =
(*n*) her =
(*o*) you =
(*p*) it =
(*q*) I =
(*r*) it =

## Form

| subject | verb | object |
|---|---|---|
| *I* | love | *you* |
| *You* | love | *me* |

**I** is the **subject** pronoun, **you** is the **object** pronoun
**You** is the **subject** pronoun, **me** is the **object** pronoun

**Write if the pronoun is *subject* or *object***

*Examples:*
(*a*) I = subject
(*b*) you = object
(*c*) me = object

(*d*) you =
(*e*) me =
(*f*) you =
(*g*) they =
(*h*) us =
(*i*) we =
(*j*) them =
(*k*) she =
(*l*) him =
(*m*) he =
(*n*) her =
(*o*) you =
(*p*) it =
(*q*) I =
(*r*) it =

**Complete the table of subject and object pronouns**

| Subject pronouns | | Object pronouns |
|---|---|---|
| I | ←------→ | me |
| ______ | ←------→ | you |
| he | ←------→ | ______ |
| ______ | ←------→ | her |
| it | ←------→ | ______ |
| ______ | ←------→ | us |
| you | ←------→ | ______ |
| ______ | ←------→ | them |



Answers and Explanations ➤page 150➤

# Unit 8: Practice

**1. Complete the sentence with the correct *object* pronoun**

> ***Example***:
> (a) John loves Barbara but John's friend doesn't like __her__ at all

(b) The ring is beautiful but Barbara doesn't want _______
(c) John thinks Barbara's family don't like _______
(d) 'We are Barbara's family – why doesn't John visit _______?'
(e) 'Barbara's family are strange. I don't like _______ much.'
(f) 'I love _______. Why don't you want to marry _______?'

**2. Choose *subject* or *object* pronoun**

Barbara: 'John wants **I/me** to marry **he/him**. What do you think?'
Barbara's father: 'Do you love **he/him**?'
Barbara: '**I/me** don't know. I *like* **he/him**. Do you like him?'
Barbara's father: 'Well, **he/him** never visits **we/us**...and his family is very strange – **they/them** talk all the time!'

John: 'Barbara doesn't want to marry **I/me.**'
Terry: 'Good! I don't like **she/her**. **She/her** is boring.'
John: 'But, Terry, **she/her** is very beautiful and **I/me** love **she/her**!'
Terry: 'Maybe, but there are lots of beautiful girls...look at **they/them**!'

**3.** This text is very strange because it says 'John' and 'Barbara' etc *too many times*. **Write it again but *replace* the underlined words with a *subject* or *object* pronoun**

> ***Example***: John loves Barbara but __she__ doesn't love __him__ ...

John loves Barbara but Barbara doesn't love John, Barbara *likes* John. John wants Barbara to marry him but Barbara doesn't want to marry John because John doesn't like her family. John thinks Barbara's family are strange. John never visits Barbara's family and he thinks Barbara's family don't like him. Maybe John's right!

**4. Correct any mistakes you find in these sentences.**
(a) Terry thinks Barbara is boring. He doesn't like she.
(b) Terry likes the girls in the pub. He thinks them are beautiful and he wants to speak to they.
(c) Barbara likes John but she doesn't want to marry him.
(d) John loves Barbara and him thinks she is beautiful.
(e) 'I love you, do you love I?'
(f) John is unhappy because Barbara doesn't love he.

**5. Practise with a friend.**
Look at these famous singers and groups. Add any others you know.

| The Spice Girls | Oasis | Michael Jackson | The Kelly Family | Sting | Madonna |
|---|---|---|---|---|---|
| ________ | ________ | ________ | ________ | ________ | ________ |

With your friend point and talk about who you *like* and *don't like*. Use him/her/them

> ***Example:*** 'I like him. He's a good singer.'
> ' Really? I hate him!'

# Unit 9: Possessive adjectives and 's     it's *my.../your.../his.../Harry's...*

Talking about **possession of**, or **relation to**, people and objects

## Meaning

Mary: 'This is **my(a)** grandfather – **your(b)** great-grandfather.'
Debbie: 'Who's this?'
Mary: 'That's **his(c)** oldest son – Uncle Harry. And this is Harry's wife. They live in Australia now.'
Debbie: 'What's **her(d)** name?'
Mary: 'Edith.'
Debbie: 'Are these Harry and Edith's children?*'
Mary: 'Yes, and this is **their(e)** dog. **Its(f)** name's Spot!'
Debbie: '**Our(g)** dog's name's Spot too!

(*Notice that we **don't** usually say Harry's and Edith's)

**Complete the gaps with the *noun(s) it refers to***

Possessive adjective ...'s

***Examples:***

(a) my = Mary's
(b) your = Debbie's
(c) his = Great-Grandfather's

(d) her = ______
(e) their = ______
(f) its = the ______
(g) our = ______

'Who**'s** this' ***means*** 'Who **is** this'
'And this is Harry**'s** wife' ***means*** **possession.** It does NOT ***mean*** **'is'**

**Look at the dialogue again and decide if *'s* means *is* or *possession***

Mary: 'This is my grandfather – your great-grandfather.'
Debbie: 'Who**'s (a)** this?'
Mary: 'That**'s (b)** his oldest son – Uncle Harry. And this is Harry**'s (c)** wife. They live in Australia now.'
Debbie: 'What**'s (d)** her name?'
Mary: 'Edith.'
Debbie: 'Are these Harry and Edith**'s (e)** children?'
Mary: 'Yes, and this is their dog. Its name**'s (f)** Spot.'
Debbie: 'Our dog**'s (g)** name**'s (h)** Spot too!'

***Examples:***

(a) is
(b) is
(c) possession

(d) ______
(e) ______
(f) ______
(g) ______
(h) ______

## Form

**Complete the table of possessive adjectives**

I my
you ______
he ______
she ______
it ______
we ______
they ______



**Answers and Explanations ➤page 151➤**

# Unit 9: Practice

**1. Complete the sentences about the family tree**

John = Muriel

Ann = Jonathan — Rose — Ruth = Brian

(Ann = Jonathan): Hannah, Vicky

(Ruth = Brian): Katy, Daniel, Georgina

> ***Example:***
> a) Rose's John and Muriel's daughter

(b) Hannah __ ______ sister
(c) Daniel __ ______ and ______ cousin
(d) Jonathan __ ______ and ______ brother
(e) Brian __ ______ husband
(f) Hannah and Vicky __ ______ and ______ daughters
(g) Muriel __ ______ wife
(h) Rose __ ______ and ______ sister

**2. Does *'s* mean *is* or *possession?***

(a) Vicky's ( is ) Hannah's ( possession ) sister
(b) Ruth's (________) Brian's (________) wife
(c) Jonathan's (________) a journalist
(d) Ann's (________) Vicky and Hannah's (________) mother
(e) Katy's (________) sister's (________) name's (________) Georgina
(f) John's (________) son's (________) a journalist

**3. These texts sound strange because there are *too many repetitions*. Change the *underlined* words for a *possessive adjective***

Ann and Ann's ( her ) husband live near London. They have two children. The children's (______) names are Hannah and Vicky. They have a cat. The cat's (______) name is Ruby.
Brian has three children. Brian's (______) son's name's Daniel and Brian's (______) daughters' names are Katy and Georgina. Daniel and Katy and Georgina's (______) cousins' names are Hannah and Vicky.
John and Muriel live near Oxford. John and Muriel's (______) house is very old.

**4.** Vicky is writing to her penfriend about her family but she has forgotten to put in any apostrophes ('). **Correct her letter.**

> Dear Mauricio,
> Let me tell you about my family. My fathers names Jonathan and my mothers names Ann. My fathers a journalist. I have one sister, her names Hannah. Shes OK but I like our cat better. Its names Ruby...

**5. Read these sentences and correct the mistakes you find.**

> ***Examples:***
> (a) Whos Hannah's sister? ✗ Who's
> (b) Vicky likes his sister Hannah ✗ her

(c) Ruby's Vicky and Hannah cat.
(d) Hannah and Vicky are sister's.
(e) My mother's name's Ruth.
(f) Brian lives with her wife, Ruth.
(g) Georgina's sister's name's Katy.
(h) Where's John and Muriels house?
(i) My name's Georgina. What's you name?

**6. Practise with a friend**

Draw your family tree. *Don't* show it to your friend.
Work in pairs and ask questions to find out your friend's family tree. Try to draw it using your answers

> ***Example:*** 'What's your mother's name?' 'Maria'

# Unit 10: Possessive pronouns: mine/yours

Talking about things which **belong to someone** or which **they are connected with**

## Meaning

'Whose is this?'
'I think it's her bag' (hers)

'Is this his suitcase?'

'These are our suitcases'

'Richard?
Is this your trolley?'

'I think these are their bags!'

'Look! Jane's bag is here now.'

'This isn't my suitcase'

'Where are your bags?'

**Replace the *underlined words* using the words in the box:**

| | | | | | | | |
|---|---|---|---|---|---|---|---|
| Jane's | his | hers | yours | theirs | mine | yours | ours |

## Form

**Complete the table**

| **Possessive adjective + noun** | | **Possessive pronoun** |
|---|---|---|
| my suitcase(s) | ←-------→ | mine |
| your bag(s) | ←-------→ | ______ |
| ______ suitcase(s) | ←-------→ | his |
| her bag(s) | ←-------→ | ______ |
| ______ bag(s) | ←-------→ | ours |
| their suitcase(s) | ←-------→ | ______ |
| | | |
| **'s + noun** | | **'s** |
| Jane's bag(s) | ←-------→ | ______ |

*Note: Do you remember **'it's'** from Unit 9? It's (the cat's) name is Ruby*
*There is **no** possessive pronoun for 'it's' (you **have** to use the noun)*

> ***Example:***
> It's name is Ruby (**not** It's is Ruby)

mistake



**Answers and Explanations ➤page 151➤**

# Unit 10: Practice

**1. Replace the possessive adjective and noun *(your suitcase)* with the possessive pronoun *(yours)***

> *Example:*
> (a) 'Is this **your suitcase**?' (yours)

(b) 'No, I think it's **his suitcase**' (_______ )
(c) 'Isn't it **her suitcase?**' (_______ )
(d) 'This isn't **my bag**' (_______ )
(e) 'Is it **your bag**?' (_______ )
(f) 'No, it isn't **my bag**' (_______ )
(g) 'Perhaps it's **their bag**' (_______ )
(h) 'Have you got **our bags**?' (_______ )
(i) 'No, I've got **my bag** (_______ ) but I don't know where (j) **our bags** (_______ ) are.'
(k) 'This isn't **my suitcase** (_______ )'
(l) 'No, it's **their suitcase** (_______ )'

**2. Choose the correct word**

(a) 'This isn't (*mine/my*) bag. (*My/Mine*) is bigger'
(b) 'Are these (*your/yours*) glasses?'
(c) 'Have you got (*our/ours*) bags?'
(d) 'It's (*my/mine*!)'
(e) 'I think (*my/mine*) bag is lost!'
(f) 'Can you help me carry (*my/mine*) bags?'
(g) 'Is that (*her/hers*?)'
(h) '(*Their/Theirs*) bags are heavy.'

**3. Rewrite the sentences *without the names***

(a) Give me **Jane's** bag  Give me her bag
(b) Is that **John's**? _______________?
(c) **John and Sheila's** bag is red _______________
(d) Are those **Jack and Tom's**? _______________?
(e) **Sarah's** is over there _______________
(f) Are those **Peter's** gloves? _______________?
(g) **Ann's** umbrella is green _______________
(h) **Simon's** is blue _______________

**4. Correct any mistakes you find.**

> *Example:*
> (a) 'This isn't my! ✗ mine

(b) 'Is that your newspaper?
(c) 'Mine parents are retired.'
(d) 'Their children are eight and ten.'
(e) 'There's a party at his house tonight.'
(f) 'They know our family but we don't know their.'
(g) 'Can you take a photo with my camera?'
(h) 'Your camera is better than my.'
(i) 'Is that hers coat?'

**5. Practise with a friend**

Who do these things belong to?

**Talk with your friend. Make guesses using *his/hers/theirs*.**

> *Example:* A: 'I think the gloves are *his*.'
> B: 'I think they're *hers*. They're quite small.'

# Unit 11: Articles



**Which one** do you use?

## Meaning

**Complete the text with *'a', 'an', 'the' or 'nothing [o]'***

> *Example:*
> Peter lives in ___o___ London. It's ___a___

big city. It's ________ capital of ________ Britain. It's ________ expensive city but Peter has ________ good job. He's ________ lawyer. He has ________ big house near ________ Thames. ________ house was very expensive but it's beautiful.

**Now *look at the comments* and *answer the questions* to discover the *rules*:**
***RULES***

1. London and Britain are places. **So, generally do we use *'a', 'the'* or *'nothing'* with *places*?** ________
2. The Thames is a river. **So, do we use *'a', 'the'* or *'nothing'* with *the names of rivers*?** ________
3. Lawyer is a job. **So, do we use *'a', 'the'* or *'nothing'* with *jobs*?** ________
4. Is there more than one capital of Britain? ________
   **So, do we use *'a', 'the'* or *'nothing'* when there is *only one*?** ________
5. Are there ***many*** big cities in Britain, or only ***one***? ________
   Are there ***many*** expensive cities, or only ***one***? ________
   Are there ***many*** good jobs, or only ***one***? ________
   Are there ***many*** big houses, or only ***one***? ________
   **So, do we use *'a', 'the'* or *'nothing'* when we talk about *one of many*?** ________
6. The first time the text talked about Peter's house it was one of many [*He has **a** big house*], but the second time [***The** house was very expensive*] did you know *which* house? ________
   **So, when we know *which* thing we mean do we use *'a', 'the'* or *'nothing'*?** ________

## Form and Pronunciation

**'A' or 'An'?**
**Look at these examples:**

***an*** expensive house   ***an*** apple   ***a*** lawyer   ***a*** policeman   ***an*** icecream
***a*** university   ***an*** umbrella   ***a*** big house   ***an*** orange   ***a*** hospital   ***an*** hour

**Complete the rules:**
We use ______ when the first **sound** of the next word is a *vowel* sound. [ae/e/i/i:/au etc]
We use ______ when the first **sound** of next word is a *consonant*. [b/d/f/t/g/h etc]
Sometimes the letter '__' is pronounced /ju:/ so we **don't** use 'an' [Example: a university]
Sometimes the letter '__' is silent so we **do** use 'an' [Example: an hour]



Answers and Explanations ➤page 152➤

# Unit 11: Practice

1. Peter is a **lawyer**. Here are some more jobs. **Write '*a*' or '*an*' next to the job**

| *Example:* |
|---|
| an artist a doctor |

___ electrician ___ politician ___ teacher ___ university professor
___ dentist ___ secretary ___ manager ___ housewife ___ shop assistant

2. **Complete the gaps in the text with '*a*', '*an*', '*the*' or *nothing* [*O*]**

| *Example:* |
|---|
| (a) O London is (b) a big city. (c) The centre is very busy. |

(d)___ Oxford Street is (e) ___ good place for shopping. You can also go to (f) ___ department store, like 'Harrods', (g) ___ very famous shop.

If (h) ___ weather is nice, you can go in (i) ___ boat on (j) ___ Thames, or walk in (k) ___ park.

It is difficult to find (l) ___ cheap hotel in (m) ___ London but, if you are rich you can stay in (n) ___ expensive hotel like the Park Lane Hilton – with (o) ___ restaurant on (p) ___ top floor of (q) ___ hotel.

3. **Now match the letters above with the numbers of the rules on page 22**

| *Examples:* | | |
|---|---|---|
| | (a) = | Rule 1 [We generally use *nothing* with the names of places] |
| | (b) = | Rule 5 |
| | (c) = | Rule 4 |

| | | | |
|---|---|---|---|
| (d) = Rule ___ | (h) = Rule ___ | (l) = Rule ___ | (p) = Rule ___ |
| (e) = Rule ___ | (i) = Rule ___ | (m) = Rule ___ | (q) = Rule ___ |
| (f) = Rule ___ | (j) = Rule ___ | (n) = Rule ___ | |
| (g) = Rule ___ | (k) = Rule ___ | (o) = Rule ___ | |

4. This is part of a letter from Peter's friend, Beata. She is Polish, and in Polish there is no '*a*' or '*the*', so she has some problems!
**Correct any mistakes with '*a*', '*an*', '*the*' or *nothing* that you find.**

> Dear Peter,
> How are you? I'm fine. I'm living in the Warsaw now. I have small flat in centre. It is very nice. I also have a new job. I'm secretary now in a big company. A company sells computers. I am a expert now about computers!
> Weather is very nice now in the Poland. It's sunny and warm...

5. **Practise with a friend**
Talk to your friend for **one minute** about where you live, your town or city. Listen carefully to your friend and try to write down any mistakes they make with **'a'**, **'an'**, **'the'** or **'nothing'**.

# Unit 12: Relative pronouns: who/which/that

## an animal *which* eats grass

**Defining** people and things

**Meaning**

**Match the words and the definitions**

| | |
|---|---|
| *Example:* A person who has children ... | a dictionary |
| An animal **that** has a very long nose ... | a husband |
| A house **which** only has one floor ... | a cow |
| A man **who** is married ... | a parent |
| An animal **which** eats grass ... | a bungalow |
| A book **that** students use ... | a pianist |
| A person **that** can play the piano ... | an elephant |

**Bungalow**

**Look at the examples above and complete with (a) (b) or (c)**

- We can use **who** to define **(a)** people **(b)** things **(c)** people and things (a) people
- We can use **which** to define **(a)** people **(b)** things **(c)** people and things ________
- We can use **that*** to define **(a)** people **(b)** things **(c)** people and things ________

(*It is possible to use 'that' for people but we usually prefer 'who'.)

So, to say more about **what sort of** *person* it is we use ________ (or sometimes ________)
To say more about **what sort of** *thing* it is we use ________ or ________

**Form**

We can use relative pronouns to do two things:

- to say more about *what sort of thing or person* it is (to *define*)
- to *join* two ideas together

**Look at the examples:**

1. A parent is a person. (*What sort of person?*) – *He/She* has children
**A parent is a person *who* has children**
What happens to 'he/she'? We *replace* 'he/she' with ________
2. A dictionary is a book (*What sort of book?*) – Students use *it*
**A dictionary is a book *that* students use**
What happens to 'it'? We *replace* 'it' with ________

**Make the sentences in the same way**

*Example:*
A wife is a woman. She has a husband
A wife is a woman who has a husband

A mechanic is a person. He/She repairs cars

________________________________

A Reliant Robin is a car. It only has three wheels

________________________________

Concorde is a plane. It goes very fast

________________________________



Answers and Explanations ➤page 152➤

# Unit 12: Practice

## 1. Choose the *correct* relative pronoun

*Example:*
(a) I don't like people (**which/who**) are unfriendly. I don't like people who are unfriendly

(b) An express is a train (**that/who**) goes fast. ____________
(c) I know someone (**that/which**) can play the violin really well. ____________
(d) I like children (**who/which**) don't make too much noise! ____________
(e) Do you know the woman (**which/that**) lives upstairs? ____________
(f) I like films (**which/who**) have a happy ending. ____________
(g) This book is about a man (**who/which**) falls in love. ____________
(h) He has a bicycle (**that/who**) cost £500! ____________

## 2. Complete the sentences with *who/that/which*

*Examples:*
(a) A giraffe is an animal that (or which) has a very long neck.
(b) The man who works in that office isn't very friendly.

(c) Is this the train ____________ is always late?
(d) Can you write a sentence ____________ uses a relative pronoun?
(e) Do you know the children ____________ live in that house?
(f) A suitcase is a big bag ____________ you take on holiday.
(g) Perfume is something ____________ makes you smell nice.
(h) A briefcase is a bag ____________ business people use.

## 3. Join the two sentences. Use *which/who/that*

*Example:*
(a) Chips are potatoes. *They* are cut and fried.
Chips are potatoes that (or which) are cut and fried

(b) Football is a game. *It* has eleven players.
____________

(c) A typewriter is a machine. *It* writes.
____________

(d) A waiter is a person. *He/She* works in a cafe.
____________

(e) Tea is a drink. People drink *it* in England.
____________

(f) A watch is a thing. *It* tells the time.
____________

(g) A husband is a man. *He* is married.
____________

## 4. Practise with a friend

**A: Write definitions of these *jobs***
(and any others you know)

*Example:*
teacher – a person who works in a school

baker – ____________
artist – ____________
musician – ____________
teacher – ____________
______ – ____________
______ – ____________
______ – ____________

**Now read your definitions to your friend.**
Can they guess the job?

**B: Write definitions of these *animals and birds***
(and any others you know)

*Example:*
elephant – an animal which (or that) has a long nose

cat – ____________
parrot – ____________
donkey – ____________
owl – ____________
______ – ____________
______ – ____________
______ – ____________

**Now read your definitions to your friend.**
Can they guess the animal or bird?

# Unit 13: Have got: I've got/he's got

Talking about **possessions**

## He's *got* more than a million

### Meaning

Many people collect things – stamps, dolls, coins. John Walton is a cigarette card collector. *He's got* more than 500,000 cigarette cards.

'John, exactly how many cigarette cards **have you got?'**
**'I've got** 652,000. This is a big collection but my friend, Mr Peters, **has got** even more!'
'How many **has he got?'**
Oh, **he's got** more than a million.'
'And do you have all the cards you want?'
'No, **I haven't. I haven't got** a complete set of Wills' *Birds and Flowers*. Mr Peters **hasn't got** it either. They're very rare cards...'

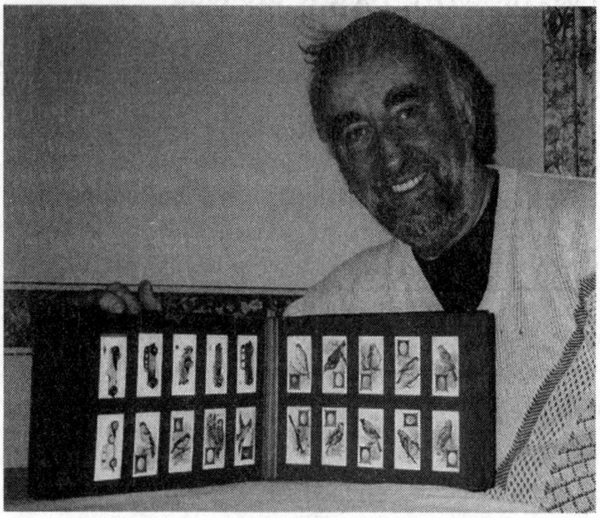

'These are cigarette cards. In the past there was a cigarette card in every packet of cigarettes.'

### Form

**Look at the examples above and complete the form. [Don't forget to *contract* when possible]**

| Positive sentences | Negative sentences | Questions | Short answers |
|---|---|---|---|
| *Example:* I've got | *Example:* I haven't got | *Example:* Have I got..? | *Example:* Yes, I have/No I haven't |
| You ___ _____ | You _____ _____ | _____ you _____ ..? | Yes, you _____/No, you ___ |
| He/She/It _____ _____ | He/She/It _____ _____ | _____he/she/it _____..? | Yes, he/she/it _____/ No, he/she/it _____. |
| We ___ _____ | We _____ _____ | _____ we _____..? | Yes, we _____/No, we _____ |
| They ___ _____ | They _____ _____ | _____ they _____..? | Yes, they ____/No, they ___ |

We can use **'have'** with **'got'**, or as a **normal present simple verb (see Unit 5)**

**'And *do you have* all the cards you want?'** has the same meaning as **'And *have you got* all the cards you want?**

**Change the sentences from *have got* to *have*.**

*Examples:*
He's got more than a million = He has more than a million
How many have you got? = How many do you have?
I haven't got a complete set = I don't have a complete set

How many has he got? = ____________________
He hasn't got it = ____________________
I've got 625,000 = ____________________

**Choose the correct *short answer***

*Example:*
Have you got a big collection? (✓) Yes, I have/(✗) Yes, I do

Does he have all the cards he wants? No, he hasn't/No, he doesn't
Has he got more than 100,000 cards? Yes, he has/Yes, he does
Do you have a complete set? No, I haven't/No, I don't



Answers and Explanations ➤page 153➤

# Unit 13: Practice

## 1. Change these sentences from *have* to *have got*

> ***Example:***
> (a) How many sisters do you have? How many sisters have you got?
> (b) I don't have any I haven't got any

(c) Does he have a car? ____________________
(d) No, he doesn't ____________________

(e) I have a big house in the country ____________________
(f) How many bedrooms does it have? ____________________

(g) Do you have any pets? ____________________
(h) Yes, I have a dog ____________________

(i) They have three children ____________________
(j) Do they have any grandchildren? ____________________
(k) Yes, they do ____________________

## 2. Look at the table and complete the sentences with *have(n't) got* or *has(n't) got*

| | *a car* | *a flat* | *a house* | *children* | *a television* | *a dog* |
|---|---|---|---|---|---|---|
| *John and Susan* | ✓ | ✗ | ✓ | ✓ | ✗ | ✓ |
| *Peter* | ✗ | ✓ | ✗ | ✓ | ✗ | ✗ |
| *Emma* | ✗ | ✗ | ✓ | ✓ | ✗ | ✗ |
| *Vicky and Tony* | ✗ | ✓ | ✗ | ✗ | ✗ | ✓ |

> ***Example:***
> (a) John and Susan have got a car

(b) Emma __________ children
(c) Vicky and Tony __________ a television
(d) Peter __________ a house
(e) John and Susan __________ a dog
(f) Emma __________ a flat
(g) Vicky and Tony __________ a car
(h) Emma __________ a car
(i) Peter __________ a dog
(j) John and Susan __________ a house

## 3. Complete the questions and write short answers *using the table above*

> ***Example:***
> (a) Has Emma got a house? Yes, she has

(b) _____ Peter _____ a dog? __________
(c) _____ Tony and Vicky _____ children? __________
(d) _____ Emma _____ a car? __________
(e) _____ John and Susan _____ a television? __________
(f) _____ Tony and Vicky _____ a flat? __________
(g) _____ Peter _____ children? __________

## 4. Practise with a friend

A turn to page 128
B turn to page 135

You both have a table like the one above – but you both have **different information**. Ask your friend questions to complete your table.

What can you count?

## Meaning

**Look at the advertisement.**

What can you **count**?
**Write the noun and the letter**

Eggs[b] ________ ________
________ ________

THESE ARE **COUNTABLE** NOUNS

What **can't** you **count**?

Milk[a] ________ ________
________ ________ ________

THESE ARE **UNCOUNTABLE** NOUNS

What can you **sometimes count** and **sometimes not count** – with a ***different meaning***?

Chocolate[f] Chocolates[g] ________ ________

SOME NOUNS CAN BE COUNTABLE **AND** UNCOUNTABLE – *WITH A DIFFERENT MEANING*

## Form

**Look at the examples and complete the rules:**

'I'd like a banana'
'Bananas are yellow'
'He ate six bananas'

Is 'banana' *countable* or *uncountable*? ____________
Can we use *a/an* with *countable nouns*? Yes/No
Can we use *a number* with *countable nouns*? Yes/No
Can we make *countable nouns plural*? Yes/No

'Milk is good for you'
'I'd like some milk'

Is 'milk' *countable* or *uncountable*? ____________
Can we use *a/an* with *uncountable* nouns? Yes/No
Can we use *a number* with *uncountable* nouns? Yes/No
Can we make *uncountable nouns plural*? Yes/No



Answers and Explanations ➤page 153➤

# Unit 14: Practice

**1. Look at the picture. What can you count? Write the names of the food in the *correct* columns:**

| COUNTABLE | UNCOUNTABLE |
|---|---|
| Eggs | Chocolate |
| | |
| | |
| | |
| | |
| | |

**2. Write *a/an* or *nothing (O)* before the nouns**

> ***Example:***
> an apple

| | | |
|---|---|---|
| ________ mineral water | ________ potato | ________ wine |
| ________ orange | ________ sugar | ________ egg |
| ________ bread | ________ orange juice | |

**3. Write the plural form next to these words – *if possible***

| | | |
|---|---|---|
| (a) rice not possible | (g) potato ________ | (m) flour ________ |
| (b) egg eggs | (h) apple ________ | (n) spaghetti ________ |
| (c) banana ________ | (i) money ________ | (o) salt ________ |
| (d) bread ________ | (j) pound (£) ________ | (p) sugar ________ |
| (e) milk ________ | (k) orange ________ | |
| (f) wine ________ | (l) orange juice ________ | |

**4. Practise with a friend**

Do you know this game?

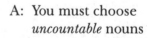

A: You must choose *uncountable* nouns

B: You must choose *countable* nouns

# Unit 15: 'Some' and 'any'

Talking about an **indefinite** quantity

**there are *some* bananas/ is there *any* milk**

## Meaning

**Read the dialogue and decide *which recipe* Bob and Marcia can make for dinner.**

Bob: 'There isn't much food in the house, Marcia. What can we have for dinner?'
Marcia: 'What have we got?'
Bob: 'Well, there are **some** potatoes'
Marcia: 'Is there **any** rice?'
Bob: 'Yes, there is, and there's **some** pasta, but there isn't **any** cheese.'
Marcia: 'Are there **any** onions?'
Bob: 'Yes, we've got **some** onions but we haven't got **any** peppers. There are **some** tomatoes though.'
Marcia: 'And is there **any** beef? If there is we can make................................'

**Spaghetti in tomato sauce**
Ingredients:
onions/pasta/tomatoes/cheese

**Shepherds' pie**
Ingredients:
onions/potatoes/beef

**Paella**
Ingredients:
rice/tomatoes/peppers/onions

**Look at the examples above and answer the questions:**

When we say **'some'** or **'any'** do we know *exactly* how many potatoes, peppers and onions there are? _____
Are **potatoes, peppers** and **onions** *countable* or *uncountable*? _____
Do we use **is**, or **are**, with plural countable nouns? _____
When we say **'some'** and **'any'** do we know exactly how much rice, pasta and beef there is? _____
Are **rice**, **pasta and beef** *countable* or *uncountable*? _____
Do we use **is** or **are** with uncountable nouns? _____
Do we usually* use **some**, or **any**, with positive sentences? _____
Do we usually* use **some**, or **any**, with negative sentences? _____
Do we usually* use **some**, or **any**, with questions? _____
[*'usually' because, **with a different meaning**, we can use 'some' in questions and 'any' in positive sentences]

## Form

**Complete the table with *is/are* *some/any/a***

| | **countable nouns** | **uncountable nouns** |
|---|---|---|
| ***positive*** | ***Singular***<br>There is a pepper<br>***Plural***<br>There __ _____ peppers | There is some rice |
| ***negative*** | ***Singular***<br>There __n't __ pepper<br>***Plural***<br>There __n't __ peppers | There __n't __ rice |
| ***questions*** | ***Singular***<br>___ there __ pepper?<br>***Plural***<br>___ there ___ peppers? | __ there ___ rice? |



**Answers and Explanations ➤page 154➤**

# Unit 15: Practice

## 1. Change these sentences from *singular* to *plural*

| |
|---|
| ***Example:*** |
| (a) There's a grapefruit There are some grapefruits |

(b) Is there an egg? ____________________

(c) Do you have a lemon? ____________________

(d) There isn't a pepper in the fridge ____________________

(e) Give me an apple ____________________

(f) Isn't there an orange on the table? ____________________

(g) We need an onion ____________________

## 2. Look at the picture and complete the sentences about it

| |
|---|
| ***Example:*** |
| (a) There are some onions but there aren't any potatoes. |

(b) There ____ ______ milk and ______ water

(c) There ____n't ______ peppers

(d) There ___ ______ egg

(e) There ______ ________ apples

(f) There _____n't _____ grapefruit

(g) There _____ _____ rice but there ___n't ____ pasta

(h) There _____n't _____ cheese or _____ bread

## 3. Complete the questions and short answers *about the picture above*

| |
|---|
| ***Example:*** |
| (a) Is there a banana? |
| No, there isn't |

(b) _____ there _____ peppers?
____________

(c) _____ there _____ apples?
____________

(d) _____ there _____ milk?
____________

(e) _____ there _____ pasta?
____________

(f) _____ there _____ potatoes?
____________

(g) _____ there _____ grapefruit?
____________

(h) _____ there _____ cheese?
____________

(i) _____ there _____ onions?
____________

(j) _____ there _____ egg?
____________

## 5. Practise with a friend

A turn to page 128. B turn to page 136

You each have a picture of a fridge. **Don't show your picture to your friend.**

There are **twelve** differences. **Tell your friend about your picture and ask questions to find the differences.**

| |
|---|
| ***Example:*** 'In my fridge there are six eggs. Are there *any* eggs in your fridge?' |

# Unit 16: Much/many/a lot



Talking about quantity

## Meaning

Customs Officer: 'Excuse me, madam. Have you got anything to declare?'
Passenger: 'No, I haven't.'
Customs Officer: 'Have you got any cigarettes?'
Passenger: 'Er ... yes.'
Customs Officer: **'How many?'**
Passenger: **'Not many** – about 600, I think.'
Customs Officer: '600?!! That's **a lot!** Please open your bags. **How many** cigars have you got here?'
Passenger: **'Not a lot**, really. Only 10.'
Customs Officer: 'That's OK. **How much** wine have you got?'
Passenger: **'Not much** – only one bottle. Look.'
Customs Officer: 'I see. **How much** perfume have you got?'
Passenger: **'Not a lot** – only a litre. Is that OK?'
Customs Officer: 'No it isn't! That's a lot. Please come with me ...'

Are cigarettes countable? ________
Are cigars countable? ________
**What question do we use with *countable* nouns? *How much ..? or How many ..?*** ________

Is wine countable? ________
Is perfume countable? ________
**What question do we use with *uncountable* nouns? *How much ..? or How many ..?*** ________

## Form

**Write the sentences under the *correct* picture**

a lot of ... not a lot of ... a lot of ... not much ... not a lot of ... not many ...

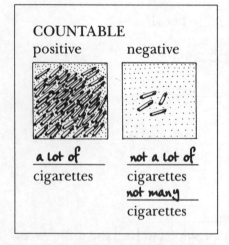

COUNTABLE

positive

a lot of
cigarettes

negative

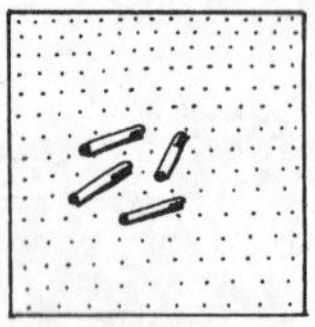

not a lot of
cigarettes
not many
cigarettes

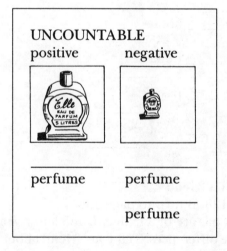

UNCOUNTABLE

positive

________
perfume

negative

________
perfume
________
perfume

Compare: *That's a lot! That isn't a lot!* [**Without** a noun]
*That's a lot of perfume! That isn't a lot of* perfume! [**With** a noun]



Answers and Explanations ➤page 154➔

# Unit 16: Practice

**1. Complete the questions about the picture using *How much/How many***

(a) How much shampoo have you got?
(b) __________ t-shirts have you got?
(c) __________ books have you got?
(d) __________ vodka have you got?
(e) __________ money have you got?
(f) __________ cassettes have you got?
(g) __________ cigars have you got?
(h) __________ wine have you got?

**2. Look at the picture again and *answer* the questions above**

(a) shampoo? A lot
(b) t-shirts? Not a lot or not many (2)
(c) books? __________ or __________ (2)
(d) vodka __________ or __________ (2)
(e) money? __________
(f) cassettes? __________ or __________ (2)
(g) cigars? __________
(h) wine? __________ or __________ (2)

**3. Complete the sentences about the picture using *is(n't)/are(n't)* and *much*, *many* or *a lot of***

(a) There is a lot of shampoo
(b) There __________ cassettes
(c) There __________ vodka
(d) There __________ cigars
(e) There __________ money
(f) There __________ books
(g) There __________ t-shirts
(h) There __________ wine

**4. Correct the mistakes you find.**

(a) There's a lot of cigars
X There are a lot of cigars
(b) There aren't much books
__________
(c) He hasn't got a lot of t-shirts
__________
(d) How much money have you got?
__________
(e) There isn't many vodka
__________
(f) There's a lot of money
__________
(g) How many vodka have you got?
__________
(h) There aren't a lot of cassettes
__________
(i) How many books is there?
__________
(j) Is there many wine?
__________

**5. Practise with a friend.**

A: Turn to page 128
B: Turn to page 136
You both have a picture of a suitcase.
They are similar but *not the same.*
**Ask questions to find the differences.**

> ***Example:***
> A: 'How much shampoo have you got?'
> B: 'A lot. Three bottles.'
> A: 'I haven't got much – 1 bottle.'

# Unit 17: 'Too' and 'not enough' — it's *too* big/it isn't small *enough*

Talking about an **unsatisfactory** amount

## Meaning

This is the 'Splendido' Language School in London. It's a terrible language school!
**What problems can you see?**

Is the size of the *class* (number of students) OK? No
Is it *more* than is good or *less* than is good? more
So, the class is **too** big

Is the size of the *room* OK? No
Is it *more* than is good or *less* than is good? less
So, the room **isn't** big **enough**

Is the number of students OK? Yes/No
Is it *more* than is good or *less* than is good? ______
So, there are **too many** students

Is the amount of noise OK? Yes/No
Is it *more* than is good or *less* than is good? ______
So, there is **too much** noise

Is the number of chairs OK? Yes/No
Is it *more* than is good or *less* than is good? ______
So, there are**n't enough** chairs

Is the amount of light OK? Yes/No
Is it *more* than is good or *less* than is good? ______
So, there is**n't** enough light

When there is **more** than is good do we use *too* or *not enough*? ______
When there is **less** than is good do we use *too* or *not enough*? ______

## Form

***With adjectives:***
**Look at the examples and answer the questions**
The class is **too** big
The room is**n't** big **enough**

TOO
Does 'too' come **before**, or **after** the adjective? ______

ENOUGH
Does 'enough' come **before**, or **after** the adjective? ______
Does 'not' come **before**, or **after** the adjective? ______

***With nouns:***
There's **too much** noise
There **isn't enough** light
There are **too many** students
There **aren't enough** chairs

When do we use *'much'* and *'many'**
– with *'too'* or with *'enough'*? ______

* For more information about 'much' and 'many' see Unit 16



**Answers and Explanations ➤page 155➤**

# Unit 17: Practice

**1.** Here are some student complaints about the 'Splendido' Language School.
**Rewrite the sentences *so they have the same meaning* using the adjective in brackets ( )**

***Examples:***
(a) The class (number of students) is too *big* (small) — The class isn't small enough
(b) The room isn't *light* enough (dark) — The room is too dark

(c) The teacher is too *inexperienced* (experienced) ____________
(d) The lessons are too *easy* (difficult) ____________
(e) The course isn't *cheap* enough (expensive) ____________
(f) My hotel isn't *near* enough (far) ____________
(g) The school is too *dirty* (clean) ____________
(h) The lessons aren't *long* enough (short) ____________

**2. Look at some more problems and complete the sentences about them using *too much, too many* or *not ... enough.***

***Examples:***
(a) 'The teacher never gives us homework!' There isn't enough homework
(b) 'The teacher gives us five hours of homework every day!' There is too much homework

(c) 'We only have one book for five students!' There are ____________ books
(d) 'We have a break every fifteen minutes! There are ____________ breaks
(e) 'We never have a break!' There are ____________ breaks
(f) 'There are only two desks for twenty students!' There are ____________ desks
(g) 'We never have listening practice!' There is ____________ listening practice
(h) 'We do writing practice all the time!' There is ____________ writing practice

**3.** Some people are *never* happy. Sarah lives in London but she hates it. **Read the conversation between Sarah and her friend Jack. Complete it with *too/enough/too much/too many.***

***Example:***
Sarah: 'I don't like London. It's too dirty. There's too much pollution.'

Jack: 'But it's very exciting – there are lots of shops.'
Sarah: 'Well, yes, but the shops are ________ expensive for me. I don't have ________ money and there are ________ people. Oxford Street is so crowded!'
Jack: 'What about transport? Don't you like the double-decker buses?'
Sarah: 'They look nice, but they're not cheap ________. It costs me £30 a week to go to work! My house is ________ far from the centre.'
Jack: 'Do you have a nice house?'
Sarah: 'No, it isn't big ________. I live with four students and they have parties every weekend. It's ________ noisy for me.'
Jack: 'So why don't you go out at the weekend? There's so much to do in London! There are lots of theatres and cinemas.'
Sarah: 'Yes, but there are ________ theatres and cinemas – I can't decide where to go!'

**4. Practise with a friend**
See page 129.

# Unit 18: Present continuous tense

talking about **now**

## she's *speaking* Chinese

**Meaning**

**She's speaking** Chinese. She also speaks French and Polish.

| | |
|---|---|
| Does she speak French? | Yes/No |
| Is she speaking French ? | Yes/No |
| Does she speak Polish? | Yes/No |
| Is she speaking Polish ? | Yes/No |
| Does she speak Chinese? | Yes/No |
| Is she speaking Chinese ? | Yes/No |

***Match* the sentence and the definition.**

1. She speaks French (=(a) or (b)?)
2. She's speaking Chinese (=(a) or (b)?)

(a) Now, at this moment. PAST NOW FUTURE

(b) Generally, but maybe not at this moment. PAST NOW FUTURE

**Form**

**Complete the following using the present continuous tense.**

| *Examples* | |
|---|---|
| I /eat/dinner | I'm eating dinner |
| You/look/well | You're looking well |
| She/speak/Chinese | She's speaking Chinese |

He/drink/coffee ______________

It/rain ______________

We/sit/down ______________

They/feel/ill ______________

**How is the present continuous *formed*?** ***Subject*** + ______ + ______

I am eating dinner

### *Question and Negative*

| *Examples* | |
|---|---|
| Is she speaking Polish? No, she isn't.<br>Is it raining? Yes, it is. | (see Units 1 and 2 – Questions and negatives using the present tense of the verb to be) |

### *Spelling*

Generally we add **-ing** to the infinitive of the verb. But sometimes the spelling changes:

A. bite – biting
smoke – smoking **(What happens to the *-e*?)**
write – writing

B. lie – lying
die – dying **(What happens to the *-ie*?)**

C. run – running
hit – hitting **(What happens to the last letter?)**
swim – swimming

# Unit 18: Practice

**1. Write sentences describing what is happening in the picture.**

> *Example*
> a) The dog/run   The dog is running.

b) The children/swim
c) Grandmother/sleep
d) Dad/lie down
e) The birds/sing
f) Mum and Dad/talk
g) Grandfather/eat
h) Sun/shine
i) The baby/cry
j) The tree/die

**2. Write questions and short answers about the same picture, using 'What' and 'Who'.**

> *Example*
> a) Who/smoke?   Q: Who's smoking?   A: Dad is.

b) Who/sleep?   Q:   A:
c) Who/cry?   Q:   A:
d) Who/eat?   Q:   A:
e) Who/swim?*   Q:   A:
f) What/die?   Q:   A:
g) Who/wear shorts?   Q:   A:
h) What/sing?   Q:   A:

*(*careful: In this case 'Who' is followed by 'is' even if the answer is plural)*

**3. Make questions about the picture and write true answers.**

> *Example*
> a) Grandmother/talk?   Q: Is Grandmother talking?   A: No, she isn't.
> b) Where/the children/swim? (lake)   Q: Where are the children swimming?   A: In the lake.

c) The birds/sing
d) What/Grandfather/eat?
e) The sun/shine?
f) The dog/sleep?
g) Who/Mum/talk/to?
h) Dad/write/a letter?

**4. Some of these sentences contain spelling mistakes. Correct any you find.**

> *Example*
> a) 'Help! The dog is bitting me!'   ✗   The dog is biting me.

b) 'John's eating an icecream. I want one!'
c) 'You're runing too fast for me.'
d) 'Mary's swiming really well.'
e) 'Why is Dad lying down?'
f) ' Mum's talkking to Dad.'
g) 'I love slepping in the afternoon.'

**5. Practise with a friend. A turn to page 129, B turn to page 137. You have two pictures that are similar but not identical. Ask questions using the present continuous tense to find the differences.**

> *Example*
> 'In your picture, **is** the dog **sleeping**?' 'No, **he's running**.'

# Unit 19: Present *simple* and present *continuous* — *I live* in England/ *I'm visiting* France

Choosing **which tense** to use

## Meaning

**Write the sentences under the correct pictures**

*Example*:
(i) Paul's a nurse
(a) He works in a hospital
(d) He's giving an injection

______________
______________
______________

______________
______________
______________

**(a)** He works in a hospital
**(b)** He's thinking about going home
**(c)** John's a journalist
**(d)** He's giving an injection
**(e)** He teaches small children
**(f)** He's interviewing someone
**(g)** Tom's a teacher
**(h)** He writes for a national newspaper
**(i)** Paul's a nurse

All these sentences are about the **present** but which sentences **emphasize NOW?** (b) _____ _____
Are these sentences ***present simple*** or ***present continuous***? ____________

Which sentences are about the present *in general*? (a) _____ _____ _____ _____ _____
Are these sentences ***present simple*** or ***present continuous***? ____________

## Form

For present simple see Unit 5
For present continuous see Unit 18

## Practice

**Write similar sentences about these pictures:**

Tim/mechanic ______________
He/mend/cars ______________
He/have/lunch ______________

Jo/secretary ______________
She/type/letters ______________
She/answer/the phone ______________



**Answers and Explanations ➤page 156➤**

Stuart/postman ______________________
He/deliver/letters ______________________
He/run/away from a dog ______________________

Sally/pilot ______________________
She/fly/planes ______________________
She/go/home ______________________

William/writer ______________________
He/write/books ______________________
He/read/a book ______________________

John/painter ______________________
He/paint/houses ______________________
He/have/a cup of tea ______________________

**2. Choose the correct sentence**

> ***Example:***
> (a) *Japan is* in the Pacific Ocean Correct
> *Japan is being* in the Pacific Ocean Wrong

(b) *John has* ten cups of tea every day _______
*John is having* ten cups of tea every day _______
(c) We can't go out – *it rains* _______
We can't go out – *it's raining* _______
(d) I can't hear you because *I listen* to music _______
I can't hear you because *I'm listening* to music _______
(e) Where's Julia? *She reads* a book _______
Where's Julia? *She's reading* a book _______
(f) *I* usually *get up* early _______
*I'm* usually *getting up* early _______
(g) *I* never *eat* chocolate – it makes you fat! _______
*I'm* never *eating* chocolate - it makes you fat! _______

**3. Make questions with the *present simple* or the *present continuous*.**

> ***Example:***
> (a) What/Sally/do? What does Sally do?
> She's a policewoman.
> (b) What/you/do? What are you doing?
> I'm reading a book.

(c) 'What languages/you/speak?' ________________
'French, Portuguese and Polish.'

(d) 'Where/you/usually/go/on holiday?' ________________
'Greece – but not this year.'
(e) 'How many sisters/you/have?' ________________
'Two.'
(f) 'Where/you/go/now?' ________________
'To the shops – do you want anything?'
(g) 'What/you/eat?' ________________
'Cake. It's delicious. Would you like some?'

**4. Practise with a friend**

Think about someone in the class. Tell your friend some things that are **generally true** about them and some things that they **are doing now**. Can your friend guess who it is?

> ***Example:*** **She's got** long hair. **She works** in a shop. **She's looking** out of the window...

# Unit 20: Prepositions of place: in/on/next to

***in* the box/*on* the table/*next to* the door**

Where?

## Meaning

**Complete the gaps using these *prepositions of place:* on/next to/in front of/opposite/behind/in/under**

***Where's the cat?***

***Example:***
It's in front of the fire

It's ________ the table

It's ________ my feet

It's ________ the television

It's ________ a box

It's ________ the dog

It's ________ the chair

It's ________ the bowl

It's ________ a cushion

It's ________ my feet

It's ________ the television

It's ________ a box

## Form

**Things to remember about prepositions of place**

Which preposition is this? ________ **to**
Which preposition is this? **in** ________ **of**
Can we say opposite **to**? ________



**Answers and Explanations ➤page 156➤**

# Unit 20: Practice

**1. Look at the pictures and *choose the correct preposition*.**

(a) The box is (*in front of/ next to*) the plant.

(b) The chair is (*opposite/ in front of*) the table.

(c) The saucer is (*on/ under*) the cup.

(d) The book is (*on/ in*) the table.

(e) The plant is (*near/ behind*) the television.

(f) The cup is (*on/ near*) the saucer.

(g) The picture is (*next to/ on*) the mirror.

(h) The cushion is (*behind/ on*) the sofa.

(i) The glass is (*near/ next to*) the apples.

**2. Look at the picture of the room and decide if these statements are TRUE or FALSE. If they are *false* – correct the statement.**

***Example:***

(a) The lamp is next to the television
False - the lamp is on the television

(b) The chocolates are on the table True

(c) The newspaper is on the sofa

____________________

(d) The videos are on the television

____________________

(e) The curtains are in front of the television

____________________

(f) The apples are behind the calendar

____________________

(g) The cat is near the shoes

____________________

(h) The cat is on the table

____________________

(i) The plant is next to the table

____________________

**3. Complete these sentences about the same room**

(a) The glasses are next to the bottle
(b) The apples are ________ the bowl
(c) The radio is ________ the table
(d) The photograph is ________ the lamp
(e) The shoes are ________ the floor
(f) The calendar is ________ the apples
(g) The table is ________ the sofa
(h) The remote control is ________ the sofa

**4. Practise with a friend**
A: Turn to page 130
B: Turn to page 137

You each have a picture of a different room.
A: Describe your room to B (*don't* show it)
B: Draw what A describes. Now look at the picture. Does it look the same?
Now change roles.

# Unit 21: Prepositions of time: in/at/on

***At* 6 o'clock/*on* Friday/ *in* the evening**

Talking about **when**

**Meaning and form**

*at* 6.00 *in* 1966 *in* the evening *on* Christmas Day *on* Saturday
*at* Easter *on* Friday evening *in* (the) summer* *at* midnight
*on* my birthday *at* night *in* the afternoon *in* the 1980s *at* the weekend
*on* 14th May *in* April *in* the future *next* week *in* the past
*last* night *at* the moment *at* teatime *at* noon *in* the 20th century
*at* Christmas

*You can say in summer/winter/autumn/spring, or in ***the*** summer/winter/autumn/spring

**Put the examples above next to the correct *rule* below:**

***At***

We use **at** for:
the time of day at 6.00 ______ ______
festivals of more than one day ______ ______
mealtimes ______
and three more you need to remember ______ ______ ______

***In***

We use **in** for:
years in 1966 ______ ______
periods of the day ______ ______
seasons ______
months ______
and two more you need to remember ______ ______

***On***

We use **on** for:
days on Saturday ______
special days ______ ______
dates ______

***No preposition***

When there is an *adjective* (this/next etc) we *don't* use preposition ______ ______

**'*The*' or '*nothing*?'**
**Write 'the' when necessary before these time expressions**

| AT | IN | ON |
|---|---|---|
| at _____ Christmas | in the future | on _____ Friday |
| at _____ moment | in _____ April | on _____ Tuesday morning |
| at _____ 11.00 | in _____ 15th Century | on _____ 25th December |
| at _____ midnight | in _____ morning | on _____ Valentine's Day |
| at _____ weekend | in _____ winter | on _____ Saturdays |



Answers and Explanations ➤page 157➤

# Unit 21: Practice

**1. Complete the sentences about holidays and festivals in Britain with *in, at, on* or *no preposition***

(a) St Valentine's day is ____ 14th February
(b) St Patrick's day is ____ March
(c) The British open their presents ____ Christmas Day
(d) The Queen has two birthdays – one ____ 21st April and the other ____ 14th June
(e) The British don't have a holiday ____ The Queen's Birthdays
(f) Some people go to church ____ midnight ____ Christmas Eve
(g) There is usually a three or four day holiday ____ Easter
(h) Most people don't work ____ the weekends.

**2. Look at Jane's diary and complete the sentences about her week with *in, at, on* or *no preposition***

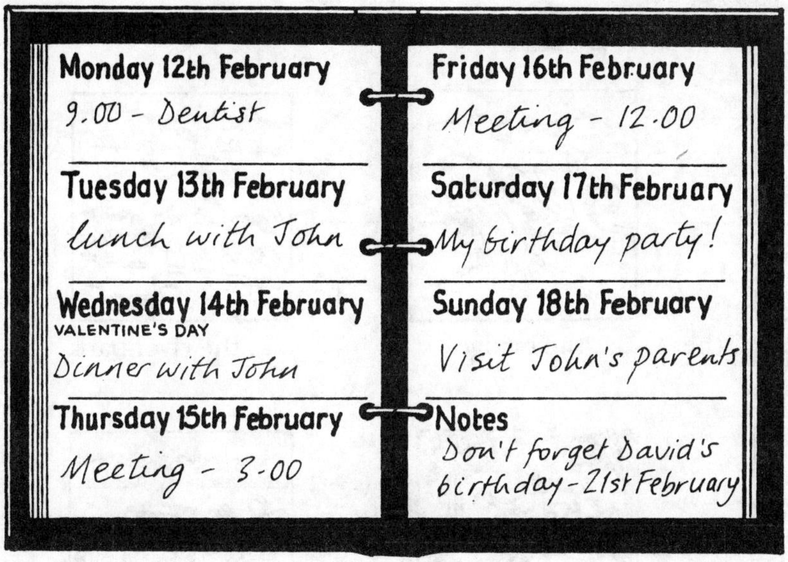

Monday 12th February
9.00 - Dentist
Tuesday 13th February
lunch with John
Wednesday 14th February
VALENTINE'S DAY
Dinner with John
Thursday 15th February
Meeting - 3.00
Friday 16th February
Meeting - 12.00
Saturday 17th February
My birthday party!
Sunday 18th February
Visit John's parents
Notes
Don't forget David's birthday - 21st February


(a) _____ Monday morning _____ 9.00 Jane's going to the Dentist
(b) She's meeting John _____ lunchtime _____ Tuesday
(c) _____ the evening _____ Valentine's Day she's going out to dinner
(d) She has a meeting _____ 3.00 _____ the afternoon _____ Thursday
(e) _____ 16th February she has a meeting _____ noon
(f) She's having a party _____ her birthday
(g) She isn't working _____ the weekend
(h) _____ Sunday she's visiting John's parents
(i) David's birthday is _____ next week _____ 21st February
(j) Jane is very busy _____ the moment

**3. Correct any mistakes you find in these sentences**

(a) I was born on the 1970s
(b) Are you very busy this week?
(c) I can't sleep in the night
(d) Are you going on holiday on Christmas?
(e) We got married in 1975
(f) Do you think life will be very different on the future?
(g) Life was different in past
(h) My birthday is on 29th November
(i) Is it cold in Poland at winter?
(j) I'm learning Spanish in moment
(k) The telephone rang on midnight
(l) I'm going on holiday in next week

**4. Practise with a friend**

**Ask your friend** **'When do you..........................?'** **Answer using 'in.../at.../on...'**

go to bed — eat ice-cream — get up — have a special meal — watch television
study English — visit friends or family — go on holiday — get presents
have your main meal — give presents — send cards — drink coffee
clean the house — go for a walk — go shopping — listen to the radio

> ***Example:***
> A: 'When do you go to bed?'
> B: 'Usually **at** midnight'
> A: 'When do you get presents?'
> B: '**On** my birthday'

# Unit 22: Prepositions of movement

Where to?

## Meaning

**Complete with the correct preposition of movement. Choose from this list:**

to from out of into on off up down over
under through round along across past

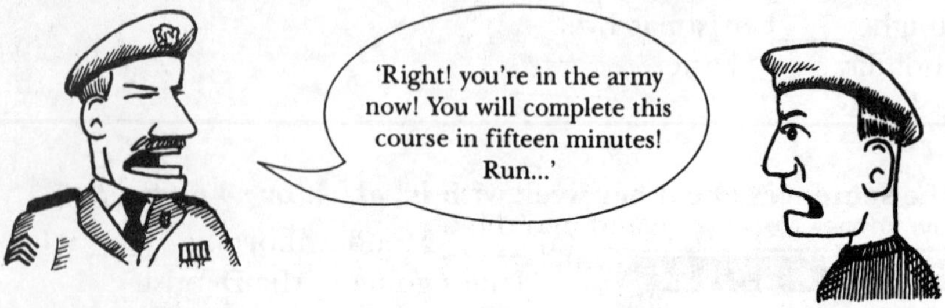

'Right! you're in the army now! You will complete this course in fifteen minutes! Run...'

...... the barracks

...... the barracks...... the river

...... the bridge

...... the river-bank

...... the hill

...... the hill

...... the park

...... the statue

...... the post-office

...... the road

...... the railway bridge

Then jump...... this box

and jump...... the box – 20 times!

Then you can go...... the barracks and rest.



Answers and Explanations ➤page 157➤

# Unit 22: Practice

**1. Match the *descriptions* with the *correct* map**
(four small maps, showing same area but different routes)

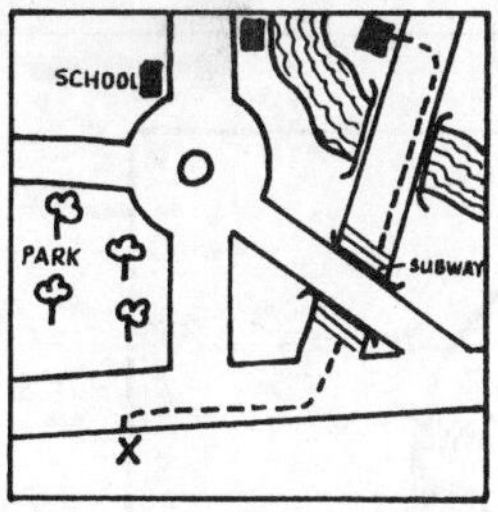

A

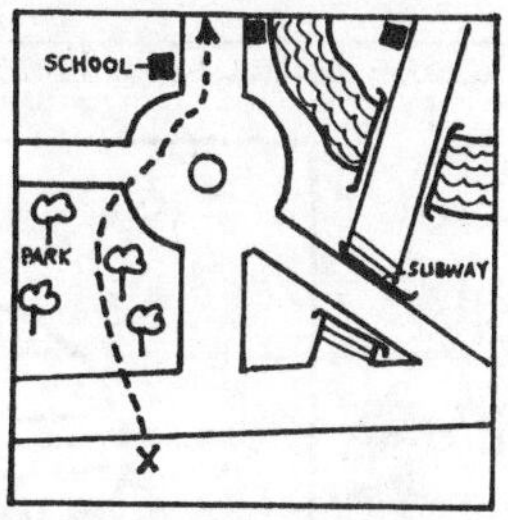

B

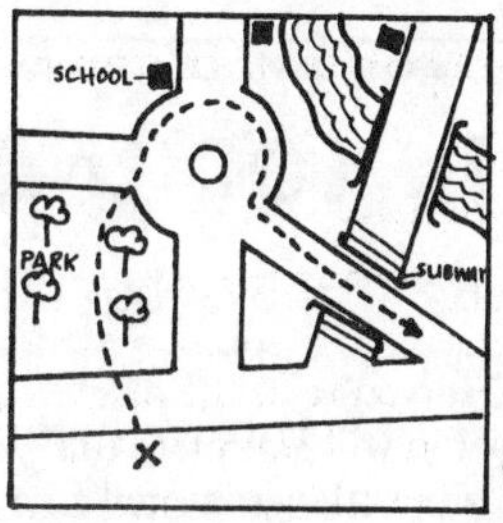

C

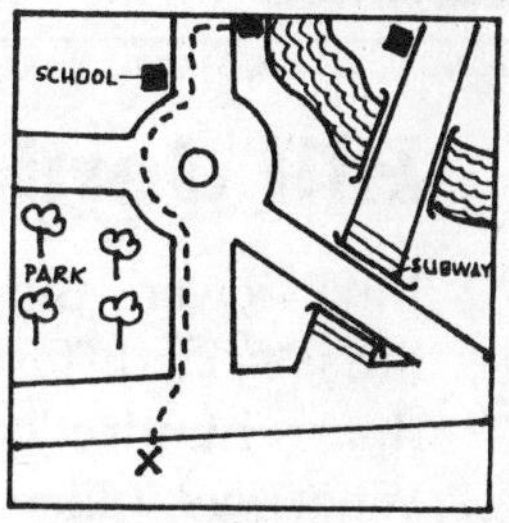

D

(a) Go across the road, then through the park, round the roundabout and past the school. __B__
(b) Go along the road, under the subway, across the bridge and into the building on your left. _____
(c) Go over the road, through the park, round the roundabout then over the bridge. _____
(d) Go across the road, round the roundabout, past the school and into the building on your right. _____

**2. Choose the correct preposition**

(a) Go (across/ round) the road

(b) How do I get (from/to) the post-office (from/to) the bank?

(c) Go (into/under) the hotel

(d) Get (on/over) the bus

(e) Go (through/ down) the hill

(f) Go (along/past) the road

(g) Go (through/ round) the shopping centre

(h) Go (over/ past) the supermarket)

(i) Go (out of/under) the subway

**3. Complete the dialogue with the correct preposition**
Use these prepositions: off/out of/to/from/round/over/on/along

A: 'How do I get ________ the school ________ the post office?'
B: 'Go ________ the school, ________ the road, ________ the roundabout, then turn left. Go ________ the bridge and it's the building on your left.'
A: 'Is it a long way?'
B: 'About half an hour. You could get ________ a number 9 bus outside the school and get ________ next to the bridge.'

**4. Practise with a friend**
See page 130.

# Unit 23: Past simple tense of verb 'to be' **was/were**

Talking about **the past** using the verb **'to be'**

## Meaning

### Bill Jenkins is 100 today.

Interviewer: 'Bill, I expect life is very different today than a hundred years ago. What **was** it like?'

Bill: 'Yes, it is very different. Life **was** much quieter then. There are so many cars now. There **weren't** any cars when I was a boy.'

Interviewer: '**Were** you happy as a child?'

Bill: 'Oh yes, I **was** very happy – but I'm still happy now!'

Interviewer: 'Tell me about your family.'

Bill: 'Well, my father **was** a postman and my mother **was** a cook. We **weren't** rich – but we **weren't** poor either. There **were** five children. My brothers and sisters **were** all younger than me but I'm the only one still here.'

## Form

**Look at the examples above and complete the table of the verb *'to be'* in the simple past**

| SIMPLE PRESENT | | | SIMPLE PAST | | |
|---|---|---|---|---|---|
| **Positive** | **Negative** | **Question** | **Positive** | **Negative** | **Question** |
| I am | I'm not | Am I..? | I was | I wasn't | Was I..? |
| You are | You aren't | Are you..? | You _____ | You _____ | _____ you..? |
| He is | He isn't | Is he..? | He _____ | He _____ | _____ he..? |
| She is | She isn't | Is she..? | She _____ | She _____ | _____ she..? |
| It is | It isn't | Is it..? | It _____ | It _____ | _____ it..? |
| We are | We aren't | Are we..? | We _____ | We _____ | _____ we..? |
| They are | They aren't | Are they..? | They _____ | They _____ | _____ they.. |

[any problems with the verb 'to be' in the ***simple present tense*** – see Units 1 & 2]



**Answers and Explanations ➤page 158➤**

# Unit 23: Practice

**1. Choose *was* or *were***

(a) He (**was/were**) a policeman. He was a policeman

(b) We (**was/were**) very happy. ______________

(c) (**Was/Were**) you busy? ______________

(d) They (**wasn't/weren't**) interested in it. ______________

(e) I (**was/were**) at school. ______________

(f) It (**wasn't/weren't**) expensive. ______________

(g) (**Was/Were**) she your teacher? ______________

**2. Complete the text with *was* or *were***

Interviewer: 'What __was__ it like during the First World War, Bill?

Bill: 'It _____ a terrible time. I _____ a young man, so I _____ in the army. We _____ in France.'

Interviewer: 'Where _____ your wife and children?'

Bill: 'They _____ in London. That _____ dangerous too. There _____ bombs and there _____n't a lot of food. The children _____ very young and they _____ very frightened.'

**3. Are these statements *true* or *false*? Correct the *false* statements using *wasn't* or *weren't*.**

> ***Example:***
> (a) Bill was an old man during the First World War False - Bill wasn't an old man during the First World War
> (b) Bill was in the army. True

(c) Bill was in Poland ______________________________

(d) Bill's wife and children were in France ______________________________

(e) It was dangerous in London ______________________________

(f) There was a lot of food in London ______________________________

(g) The children were quite old ______________________________

(h) The children were frightened ______________________________

**4. Make questions about the text using *was* or *were***

> ***Example:***
> (a) How old/Bill/during the First World War? How old was Bill during the First World War?

(b) /Bill/in the army? ______________________________?

(c) Where/Bill? ______________________________?

(d) Where/Bill's wife and children? ______________________________?

(e) /It dangerous in London? ______________________________?

(f) /there bombs? ______________________________?

(g) /there a lot of food? ______________________________?

(h) How old/the children? ______________________________?

(i) /the children frightened? ______________________________?

**5. Practise with a friend**
**Write down some dates in the past you can remember.**
**Ask and answer these questions about *you and your family* at those times.**
How old/you, your mother, your sisters, etc...?
Where/you, your husband, your children, etc...?

> ***Example:***
> A: 'March 1992. How old **were** you?' B: 'I **was** 17.'
> A: 'Where **were** you?' B: 'I **was** on holiday in Switzerland.'

# Unit 24: Past simple tense

Talking about the **past**

## They *built* a small aeroplane

## Meaning

**The story of flight**

The first flight in the history of man **was** in a hot air balloon. Two brothers called Montgolfier **made** a balloon from linen and paper. They **decorated** it in bright colours. Two passengers **got** in. Then they **lit** a fire underneath the balloon and it **rose** up into the air.
The first men to fly an aeroplane **were** Americans. They were brothers called Wilbur and Orville Wright. They **built** a very small aeroplane. It only **stayed** up in the air for a few seconds. Later, a Frenchman, Louis Bleriot, **flew** an aeroplane across the Channel.

This story is about the **past** so the verbs are in the **past tense**. Write their **infinitive** form.

***Example:***
was – be

| | | |
|---|---|---|
| made – | lit – | built – |
| decorated – | rose – | stayed – |
| got – | were – | flew – |

## Form

- 'Decorate' and 'stay' are **regular** verbs. So, to form the past tense of regular verbs what do we add to the infinitive? ____________
- The other verbs are **irregular**. They are formed in different ways, which are sometimes difficult to guess. Do you know the past tense forms of these useful verbs?

| Infinitive | Past Simple | Infinitve | Past Simple |
|---|---|---|---|
| ***Example:*** begin ◄-----► | began | | |
| break ◄-----► | ________ | buy ◄-----► | ________ |
| can ◄-----► | ________ | do ◄-----► | ________ |
| drink ◄-----► | ________ | go ◄-----► | ________ |
| have ◄-----► | ________ | say ◄-----► | ________ |
| see ◄-----► | ________ | take ◄-----► | ________ |
| write ◄-----► | ________ | | |

(A list for you to learn and/or use for reference is in Appendix 1)

***Spelling of regular verbs***

**Look at the examples and complete the rules**

(a) carry – carried
study – studied
**When the verb ends consonant (b, c, d, etc) + y the 'y' changes to** ________

(b) play – played
enjoy – enjoyed
**When the verb ends vowel (aeiou) + y, the 'y' does not change to 'i', we add** ________

(c) travel – travelled
stop – stopped
**When the verb ends consonant + vowel + consonant we double the final** ________

BUT: say – said/pay – paid (these are *irregular* verbs)



**Answers and Explanations ➤page 158➤**

# Unit 24: Practice

**1. Complete this crossword with the past tense forms of the verbs (Appendix 1 will help)**

| Down | Across |
|---|---|
| 1. Bring | 3. Take |
| 2. Rise | 5. Sing |
| 4. Drink | 6. Begin |
| 6. Blow | 7. Know |
| 8. Write | 9. Steal |
| 9. Stand | 10. Be |
| 11. Swim | 13. See |
| 12. Hate | 14. Think |
| 15. Give | 16. Make |
| 17. Eat | 18. Ride |

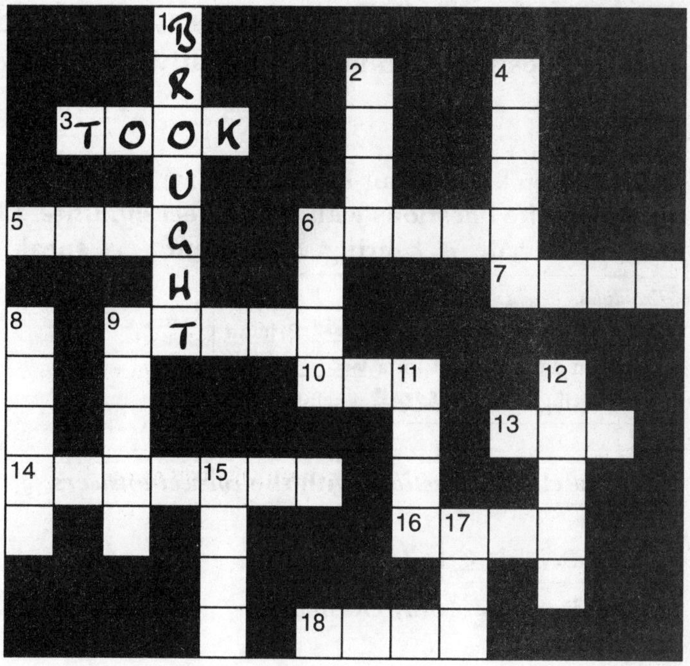


**2. Complete this story with the past tense forms of the verbs in brackets.**

**THE STORY OF MOTOR CARS**

> *Example:*
> Carl Benz (invent) invented the petrol engine.

Another German, Daimler, (design) ______________ a car with an engine. This (be) ______________ the start of the modern car. At first, there (be/not) ______________ many cars. In England, a man (have) ______________ to walk in front of every car with a red flag. Then, in America, Henry Ford (build) ______________ a cheaper car, (call) ______________ the Model T. Ford, which ordinary people (can) ______________ buy.

**3. Complete this story with appropriate past tense forms, choosing from the verbs in the box.**

**THE STORY OF THE RAILWAY**

> *Example:*
> George Stephenson invented

the first steam train, ______________ "Locomotion". Steam engines ______________ coal and ______________ water. The hot water ______________ steam and the steam ______________ the wheels go round. Railways ______________ very popular. Trains ______________ faster. They ______________ passengers, parcels, letters and food.

| | | | | | | |
|---|---|---|---|---|---|---|
| *carry* | *become* | *travel* | *invent* | *heat* | *produce* | *make* |
| *call* | *burn* | | | | | |

**4. Practise with a friend. Look at these holiday photos. Talk with a friend or write sentences about what Sarah did on holiday.**

> *Example:*
> 'She **ate** spaghetti.'

# Unit 25: Past simple auxiliary: did/didn't *Did* you go?/I *didn't* eat it

**Asking questions** and **making negatives** using the past simple

## Meaning

What do you know about British History?

**Complete the questions with the correct *infinitive.* Choose from:**

**die invade bring invent speak kill give up have**

*Examples:*
1 When **did** the Normans invade Britain?
2 When **did** Queen Victoria die?
3 **Did** King George I speak English?

4 What **did** John Logie Baird _______?
5 **Did** Queen Victoria _______ nine children?
6 Why **did** Edward VIII _______ the throne?
7 **Did** the English ever _______ their king?

**Now match the *questions* with the *correct answers***

*Example:*
(a) The television 4

(b) No, **he didn't** (only German) ___
(c) In 1066 ___
(d) Yes, **she did** ___
(e) Because he wanted to marry a divorced woman ___
(f) In 1901 ___
(g) **Yes, they did** (Charles the First) ___

**True or false?**

*Example*
Henry the Eighth **didn't have** six wives FALSE

Queen Elizabeth the First **didn't get married** _______
The Duke of Wellington **didn't win** the Battle of Waterloo _______
Cromwell **didn't win** the Civil War _______
The English people **didn't like** Queen Victoria _______

## Form

**Write the examples from above in the tables below:**

QUESTIONS

| | [Question word] | + did | + subject | + infinitive | + (other) |
|---|---|---|---|---|---|
| *Examples:* | | | | | |
| 1 | When | did | The Normans | invade | Britain? |
| 2 | When | did | Queen Victoria | die? | |
| 3 | | Did | King George I | speak | English? |
| 4 | | | | | |
| 5 | | | | | |
| 6 | | | | | |
| 7 | | | | | |

NEGATIVES

| Subject | + didn't | + infinitive (+) |
|---|---|---|
| Example: | | |
| Henry VIII | didn't | have six wives |
| | | |
| | | |
| | | |
| | | |

SHORT ANSWERS

| Yes/No | + subject | + did/didn't |
|---|---|---|
| Example: | | |
| No | he | didn't |
| | | |
| | | |



Answers and Explanations ➤page 159➤

# Unit 25: Practice

Queen Victoria was born in 1819. She didn't have any brothers or sisters so she was probably quite a lonely child. She studied with a private teacher, Fraulein Lehzen, at home. She had lessons every day from 9.30 until 5.00. From 5.00–6.00 she learned poetry in English, French and German. She had an interesting hobby - she collected dolls and made clothes for them. She had 132 dolls.

When she was only eighteen her uncle, William IV, died and Victoria became Queen. She married her cousin, Prince Albert, in 1840 and they had nine children (five girls and four boys). She loved Albert very much and when he died in 1861 she was very unhappy and wanted to die. However, she was Queen for another forty years until she died in 1901.

**1. Make *Yes/No* questions about the text. Answer the questions with *short answers***

***Example:***
(a) Victoria/have/any brothers or sisters? Did Victoria have any brothers or sisters? No, she didn't

(b) she/go/to school? ____________? ________
(c) she/speak/French and German? ____________? ________
(d) William IV/die/in 1837? ____________? ________
(e) Victoria and Albert/get married/in 1840? ____________? ________
(f) she/love/her husband? ____________? ________
(g) they/have/ten children? ____________? ________
(h) she/die/in 1861? ____________? ________

**2. *Complete* the questions *to match* the answers**

***Examples:***
(a) Where did Victoria study? — At home
(b) When did she have lessons? — Every day from 9.30–5.00

| | |
|---|---|
| (c) What ________ collect? | Dolls |
| (d) How many dolls ____________? | 132 |
| (e) When ________ William IV ________? | When Victoria was 18 |
| (f) When ________ Victoria ________ Queen? | In 1837 |
| (g) When ____________ Albert? | In 1840 |
| (h) How many children ________ they ________? | Nine |
| (i) When ________ Albert ________? | In 1861 |

**3. Correct the sentences that are NOT TRUE with a full sentence using *'didn't'***

***Example:***
(a) Victoria studied at home True
(b) Victoria went to school Victoria didn't go to school

(c) Victoria spoke French and German
____________

(d) Victoria spoke Chinese
____________

(e) Victoria had 200 dolls
____________

(f) Victoria became Queen when she was twelve
____________

(g) Victoria and Albert got married in 1845
____________

(h) Victoria and Albert had 9 children
____________

(i) Victoria and Albert had five sons
____________

(j) Albert died in 1861 ____________
(k) Victoria died in 1861 ____________

**4. Practise with a friend**

You are going to read two texts about William Shakespeare - but with different information. Ask your friend questions to find out more information. A: Turn to page 130. B: Turn to page 138

# Would you like a cup of tea?/ I'd like some chocolate, please

Offering something **to** someone; requesting something **from** someone

## Meaning

**Read the dialogues and answer the questions**

Ann: **(a)** '**Do you like** chocolate?'
Bob: 'Oh yes! I like chocolate more than anything!'
Ann: **(b)** '**Would you like** some* chocolate?'
Bob: 'No thanks. I'm on a diet. **I'd like** an apple, please.'

Does Bob like chocolate? _______
Does Bob like apples? _______
Does Bob want chocolate **now**? _______
Does Bob want an apple **now**? _______

When Ann asks '**Do you like** chocolate?' is she talking about *now* or *in general*? _______________
When Ann asks '**Would you like** some chocolate?' is she talking about *now* or *in general*? _______________
Which question **means the same** as 'Do you want...? – **(a)** or **(b)**? _______
**Notice that we use 'some' with 'would you like......?*

Paul: **(c)** '**Do you like** going to the theatre?'
Susan: 'Yes, I do.'
Paul: **(d)** '**Would you like** to go to the theatre with me next Friday?'
Susan: 'Oh! Er... sorry, I can't, I'm busy.'

Does Susan like going to the theatre? _______
Does she want to go with Paul on Friday? _______
Which question **means the same** as 'Do you want...? – **(c)** or **(d)**? _______

## Form

**Write the *contractions***

I would like ____________

> ***Example:***
> You would like *You'd like*

He would like ____________
She would like ____________
We would like ____________
They would like ____________

**Make *questions***

> ***Example:***
> You would like *Would you like?*

He would like ____________
She would like ____________
We would like ____________
They would like ____________

**Complete with *-ing* or *to+infinitive***

> ***Example:***
> I like (cook) *cooking*
> I'd like (cook) *to cook* dinner tonight

He likes (watch) _________ television
He'd like (watch) _________ the football this afternoon

She likes (go) _________ to the cinema
She'd like (go) _________ and see a film tonight

We like (play) _________ tennis
We'd like (play) _________ tennis this afternoon



**Answers and Explanations ➤page 159➤**

# Unit 26: Practice

**1. Match the questions to the answers.**

*Example:*
(a) Do you like tea? — 4. Yes, I do/No, I don't

(b) Would you like a cup of tea?
(c) Do you like going to the cinema?
(d) Would you like to go to the cinema?

1. Yes, I do/No, I don't
2. Yes, please/No, thanks
3. Yes, I'd love to/Sorry, I can't
4. Yes, I do/No, I don't

**2. Choose *like* or *would like*.**

*Example:*
(a) **Do you/would you** like a coffee? Yes, please. Would you

(b) **I** like/**I'd** like to go and see the new film at the Roxy Cinema this weekend
(c) What **do you/would you** like to do tonight?
(d) **Do you/Would you** like getting up early? No, I hate it!
(e) **I'd** like/**I** like getting up late on Saturdays
(f) **Do you/Would you** like London? It's OK, but it rains all the time!
(g) When he's older, **he'd** like/**he** like to be a doctor
(h) Why are you a teacher? Because **I like/I'd** like teaching!
(i) **Would you/Do you** like to go out to dinner? Yes, I'd love to

**3. Complete with *-ing* (cooking) or to + *infinitive* (to cook)**

*Example:*
(a) Would you like (go) to go to the beach?

(b) Do you like (play) __________ tennis?
(c) What do you like (do) __________ on holiday?
(d) I really like (lie) __________ on the beach and (do) __________ nothing! My wife likes (sightsee) __________
(e) I like (cook) __________ but I don't like (do) __________ the washing up
(f) I'd like (see) __________ Macbeth tonight. I really like (go) __________ to the theatre
(g) Would you like (dance) __________? No, sorry, I don't like (dance) __________

**4. Complete the dialogues using *would like (to + infinitve)* or *like (-ing)***

*Example:*
A: 'What would you like to do (do) today?'

B: 'Well, I think I ____________________ (go swimming) in the sea. It's a lovely day. So, what ____________________ (do) today, then?'
A: 'I ____________________ (visit) the Castle.'
B: 'But it's so hot! Why don't we go to the castle later?'

A: 'Do you ____________________ (play) tennis?'
B: 'No, not much.'
A: 'What sports do you __________?'
B: 'I __________ (run).'
A: 'Oh, good! Would you __________ (go) running with me this evening?'
B: 'Sorry, I can't. I'm going to the cinema.'

**5. Practise with a friend**
See page 131

# Unit 27: Requests and permission: can/could/may

## *could* you help me?/*can* I go?

Making **requests** and asking **permission**

### Meaning

(a) '**Can** you give me a lift?'
(b) '**Can** I have some more dessert, please?'

Both these sentences use '**can**'.
Which sentence is *asking someone to do something*? (a) or (b) ______
Which sentence is *asking permission*? (a) or (b) ______

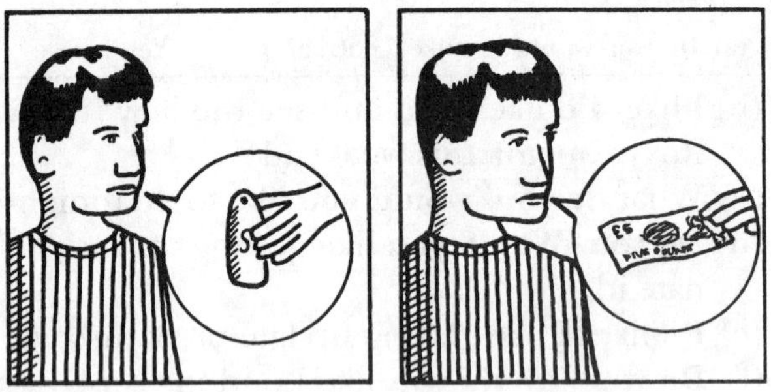

**Look at these dialogues and answer the questions**

John: 'Can you pass me the salt, please?'
Emma: 'Here you are.'

John: 'Could you lend me £5 please?'
Emma: 'Yes, OK. Don't forget to give me it back!'

What **two** words can you see for *asking someone to do something*? ________ ________
Which is more formal/polite? ________
**Why** is John more polite in the second dialogue? ________

Child: 'Mum, can I watch tv?'
Mother: 'Yes, of course.'

Child: 'Mum, may I go to a party on Saturday?'
Mother: 'Well...'

What **two** words can you see for *asking permission*? ________ ________
Which is more formal/polite?* ________
**Why** is the child more polite in the second dialogue? ________

(*some people think that 'may' is more correct than 'can', but most people now think 'can' is OK)

### Form

*Requests (asking for something)*
**Which sentence is correct? (only one)**
Can/Could you *to help* me? _______ (✗ ✓)
Can/Could you *helping* me? _______ (✗ ✓)
Can/Could you *help* me? _______ (✗ ✓)

*Permission*
**Which sentence is correct? (only one)**
Can/May I *smoking*? _______ (✗ ✓)
Can/May I *smoke*? _______ (✗ ✓)
Can/May I to *smoke*? _______ (✗ ✓)



Answers and Explanations ➤page 160➤

# Unit 27: Practice

**1. Put the words in the correct order to make sentences.**

*Example:*
(a) tell/the time/can/me/you/please? Can you tell me the time, please?

(b) you/that/spell/please/could? ______________?
(c) I/here/sit/can? ______________?
(d) smoke/I/may? ______________?
(e) your/can/pen/borrow/please/I? ______________?
(f) a lift/you/could/give/please/me? ______________?
(g) you/can/me/pass/the salt? ______________?
(h) I/may/to/go/Mum/the disco? ______________?

**2. Divide** *the sentences from exercise one* **into two columns.**

| REQUESTS | ASKING FOR PERMISSION |
| --- | --- |
| Can you tell me the time, please? | Can I sit here? |
| ______________ | ______________ |
| ______________ | ______________ |
| ______________ | ______________ |

**3. What do you say?**

*Example:*
(a) You want someone to *open the window*.
Could you open the window, please?

(b) You are in a train and you want to *sit* down
______________ here, ______?
(c) You are in class and you want someone to *say* something again
______________ that again, ______?
(d) You are in class and you want someone to *spell* something
______________ that, ______?
(e) You are in class and you want to *leave early*
______________?
(f) You want someone to *help* you?
______________ me ______?

4. Manuel is a Spanish student staying with an English family. **Complete the conversation with his English host, Mr Jackson.**

Manuel: '______ use the kitchen?'
Mr Jackson: 'Yes, you can.'
Manuel: '______ invite my friends round?'
Mr Jackson: 'Yes, of course, but ______ ask us first?'
Manuel: '______ give me a key to the house?'
Mr Jackson: 'Yes, but ______ be quiet if you come in late?'
Manuel: '______ smoke in my room?'
Mr Jackson: 'No, I'm sorry. This is a non-smoking house.'

**5. Practise with a friend**

You and your friend are going to have a party.
There is a lot to do!
Here are some of the things you have to do:

do the washing up ______ ______
clean the bathroom ______ ______
make the sandwiches ______ ______
open the wine ______ ______

**Think of some more ideas together. Then ask each other to do the things.**

*Example:* A: '**Could** you do the washing up?'
B: 'OK. **Can** you make the sandwiches?'

# Unit 28: Ability (can/could)

Talking about **being able** to do something

## I *can* swim/I *could* swim when I was seven

**Meaning**

Match the jobs with what they *can* do

| | | |
|---|---|---|
| *Example:* a secretary | can | type |
| a waiter | can | make a cake |
| a cook | can | write |
| a translator | can | add up a bill |
| a journalist | can | speak two or more languages |

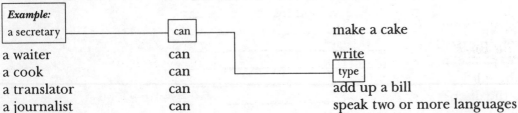

Ben is a translator

Interviewer: 'Do you like your job?'
Ben: 'It's hard work but very interesting.'
Interviewer: 'How many languages **can** you speak?'
Ben: 'Three. **I can** speak French, German and Italian. My parents are Italian, so **I could** speak Italian when I was a child.'
Interviewer: '**Could** you speak Italian well then?'
Ben: 'Yes, **I could**. We always spoke Italian at home.'
Interviewer: '**Could** you speak French and German then too?'
Ben: 'No, **I couldn't**. I learnt French at University and **I couldn't** speak German until I went to live in Germany after University.'
Interviewer: '**Can** you speak any Japanese?'
Ben: 'No, **I can't**. **I can't** speak any other languages.'

Do we use **can/can't** to talk about the *past*, or the *present*? ____________
Do we use **could/couldn't** to talk about the *past*, or the *present*? ____________

**Form**

**Write the underlined sentences from the dialogue in the table.**

| | PRESENT | PAST |
|---|---|---|
| **Question** | How many languages can you speak? | ____________? |
| **Positive** | | I could speak Italian when I was a child |
| **Positive Short answer** | Yes, I can | |
| **Negative** | I can't speak any other languages | |
| **Negative Short answer** | | |

What is the *present* tense form of **can** for I/you/he/she/it/we/they (all persons)? ____________
What is the *past tense* form of **can** for I/you/he/she/it/we/they (all persons)? ____________



Answers and Explanations ➤page 160➤

# Unit 28: Practice

**1. Match the verbs to the jobs. Then write sentences using *can*.**

type fast take orders take dictation explain grammar make a speech
serve food answer the phone help students understand politics
write on the board add up a bill

*a teacher* *a politician* *a waiter* *a secretary*

***Example:***
(a) A teacher can write on the board

(b) A teacher ______________
(c) A teacher ______________
(d) A politician ______________
(e) A politician ______________
(f) A waiter ______________
(g) A waiter ______________
(h) A waiter ______________
(i) A secretary ______________
(j) A secretary ______________
(k) A secretary ______________

2. Two people are applying for a job as a secretary. **Look at the table of what they *can* and *can't* do and complete the questions and answers**

***Example:***
(a) Can Sarah take dictation? Yes, she can

| | Sarah Smith | John Andrews |
|---|---|---|
| type 100 words a minute | ✗ | ✓ |
| take dictation | ✓ | ✓ |
| write shorthand | ✗ | ✓ |
| answer the phone | ✓ | ✓ |
| use a computer | ✓ | ✗ |

(b) ________ John answer the phone? ________
(c) ________ Sarah use a computer? ________
(d) ________ John type 100 words a minute? ________
(e) ________ Sarah answer the phone? ________
(f) ________ John write shorthand? ________
(g) ________ Sarah type 100 words a minute? ________
(h) ________ John take dictation? ________
(i) ________ Sarah take dictation? ________
(j) ________ John use a computer? ________

**Who do you think should get the job?** ____________

**3. Which of these things can *you* do? Write true sentences using *can/can't***

read play the piano speak English play chess ride a bicycle cook
ski run swim speak your (my) own language write drive a car

***Example:***
I can read

**4. Which of these things in exercise 3 could you do when you were ten years old?
Write true sentences using *could/couldn't***

***Example:***
I could read

**5. Practise with a friend.**

Talk with your friend. Ask and answer questions to find:

- three things A *can do* and B *can't*
- three things A *could do when they were ten* that B *couldn't*

*three things B *can do* and A *can't*
*three things B *could do when they were ten* that A *couldn't*

***Example:***
A: '**Can** you play the piano?'
B: 'Yes, I can. **Can** *you* play the piano?'
A: 'No, I can't. **Could** you play the piano when you were 10?'
B: 'No, I couldn't.'
A: '**Could** you play any musical instrument?'
B: 'Well, I could play the recorder!'

# Unit 29: Obligation (have to)

**I *have to* go home**

Talking about something **necessary**

## Meaning

Tom: 'I hate my school! We **have to** wear a uniform and I always **have to** do lots of homework.'

Tom's father: 'You're lucky! When I was at school **I had to** wear a hat! And we **had to** do a lot more homework.'

Tom: 'But you **didn't have to** eat school dinners. Yeuch! You went home to eat.'

Tom's father: 'O.K., but you **don't have to** study Latin! French is much easier.'

***Answer* the questions and *complete* with: had to/has to/ doesn't have to/didn't have to**

Is it necessary/obligatory for Tom to wear a uniform? ***Yes/No***

So, Tom ________ wear a uniform.

Is it necessary/obligatory for Tom to study Latin? ***Yes/No***

So, Tom ________________ study Latin.

Is it necessary/obligatory for Tom's father to wear a hat *now*? ***Yes/No***

**Was** it necessary/obligatory for Tom's father to wear a hat when he was at school? ***Yes/No***

So, Tom's father ________ wear a hat when he was at school

Is it necessary/obligatory for Tom's father to eat school dinners *now*? ***Yes/No***

**Was** it necessary/obligatory for Tom's father to eat school dinners when he was at school? ***Yes/No***

So, Tom's father ______________ eat school dinners when he was at school

## Form

**Use the examples *above* to complete the table**

| PRESENT | PAST |
|---|---|
| NECESSARY | NECESSARY |
| *Example:* I have to study French | *Example:* I had to study Latin |
| You ____________ study French | You ____________ study Latin |
| He/She ____________ study French | He/She ____________ study Latin |
| We ____________ wear a uniform | We ____________ wear a hat |
| They ____________ wear a uniform | They ____________ wear a hat |
| *NOT* NECESSARY | *NOT* NECESSARY |
| *Example:* I don't have to study Latin | *Example:* I didn't have to study French |
| You ____________ study Latin | You ____________ study French |
| He/She ____________ study Latin | He/She ____________ study French |
| We ____________ wear a hat | We ____________ eat school dinners |
| They ____________ wear a hat | They ____________ eat school dinners |

**Make questions and short answers**

He has to study French — Does he have to study French? — Yes, he does/No, he doesn't

They have to wear a uniform ________________________? ________________________

He *had* to wear a hat ________________________? ________________________

They *had* to study latin ________________________? ________________________



Answers and Explanations ➤page 161➤

# Unit 29: Practice

**1. Look at the 'contract' which a teacher made with her students.**

| The Teacher | The students |
|---|---|
| I promise to ...<br>- be friendly<br>- give some homework<br>- help the students<br>- speak clearly | We promise to ...<br>- work hard<br>- do the homework<br>- be on time<br>- speak English in class |

**Write sentences about the contract using *have to/has to*.**

*Example:*
(a) The teacher has to be friendly

(b) The students ____________
(c) ____________
(d) ____________
(e) ____________
(f) ____________
(g) ____________
(h) ____________

**2.** *Last year* Jane was a secretary. *Now* she has a new job – she's a travelling salesperson.
**Write sentences about her old job and her new job using *has to/had to* (+) and *doesn't have to/didn't have to*(-)**

When Jane was a *secretary:*

*Example:*
(a) She had to type letters (+)

(c) She ____________ travel a lot (-)
(e) She ____________ work at the weekend (-)
(f) She ____________ work from 9.00–5.00 (+)
(h) She ____________ work hard (+)

Now Jane is a *salesperson:*

(b) She doesn't have to type letters (-)

(d) She ____________ travel a lot (+)
(e) She ____________ work at the weekend (+)
(g) She ____________ work from 9.00–5.00 (-)
(i) She still ____________ work hard (+)

**3. Complete the text with *have to/don't have to/have to/had to/didn't have to***

I am a teacher. I work in the centre of London but I live in the Southeast, quite a long way from the school. So every morning I ________ get up at 7.00. There are no buses so I ________ walk to the train station. I get a train to Victoria Station and then I usually go on the Underground. The school is quite near so I ________ go on the Underground – if the weather is good, I sometimes walk. I ________ be at work at 8.45 because classes start at 9.00.

Yesterday was terrible because there was a train strike, so there were no trains to Victoria. I ________ get up at 6.00 and walk a long way to catch a bus. When I got to the bus stop the buses were all full so I ________ wait a long time. Luckily a friend gave me a lift home at the end of the day so I ________ walk or wait for a bus again.

**4. Write questions (using *have to/had to*) and answers about the text.**

*Example:*
(a) What time/she/get up? What time does she have to get up? 7.00

(b) Why/she/walk to the train station? ____________? ________
(c) She/go on the underground? Does ____________? ________
(d) What time/she/be at work? ____________? ________
(e) What time/she/get up *yesterday*? ____________? ________
(f) Why/she/wait a long time? ____________? ________
(g) She/walk at the end of the day? Did ____________? ________

**5. Practise with a friend.**
Turn to page 131.

# Unit 30: Advising (should/shouldn't)

Giving advice

**you *should* relax/ you *shouldn't* work so hard**

## Meaning

Are these good or bad things to do if you want to be healthy? ***Tick*(✓) if you think they are good. *Cross* (✗) if you think they are bad things to do**

*Example:*
- smoke ✗
- eat less fat ✓

- eat fruit
- exercise three times a week
- eat a big meal before you go to bed
- walk up the stairs and not take the lift
- drive everywhere
- stay awake all night

Is it a good idea to smoke if you want to be healthy? ______
So, if you want to be healthy you **shouldn't** (**should not**) smoke.

Is it a good idea to eat less fat if you want to be healthy? ______
So, if you want to be healthy you **should** eat less fat.

**Write sentences about the other things using *You should...* or *You shouldn't...***

*Example:*
- You should eat fruit

- ________ exercise three times a week
- ________ eat a big meal before you go to bed
- ________ walk up the stairs
- ________ drive everywhere
- ________ stay awake all night

## Form

What is the *present tense form* for **should/shouldn't** with I/you/he/she/it/we/they (all persons)? ________

**Which is correct?** (only one)
- I shouldn't **to smoke** ______ (✗ ✓)
- I shouldn't **smoking** ______ (✗ ✓)
- I shouldn't **smoke** ______ (✗ ✓)



**Answers and Explanations ➤page 161➤**

# Unit 30: Practice

Here is some advice about learning English. **Rewrite the sentences using *should/shouldn't***

> ***Example:***
> (a) It's a good idea to read in English
> You should read in English

(a) 

(b) 

(c) 

(b) It's a good idea to write vocabulary in a notebook
________________________________

(c) It *isn't* a good idea to try and translate every word you read
________________________________________

(d) 

(e) 

(d) It's a good idea to listen to the radio in English
________________________________

(e) It *isn't* a good idea to speak your own language in your English class
______________________________________________

(f) It *isn't* a good idea to forget to do your homework ________________________

(g) It's a good idea to watch English films
____________________________

(h) It's a good idea to study hard!
________________________

(f) 

(g) 

(h) 

**2.** Jonny is studying for an important exam. **Complete the advice his friend, Jackie, gives him.**

> ***Example:***
> Jonny: 'I'm really worried about my exam, Jackie.'
> Jackie: (not/worry) 'You shouldn't worry. You'll be OK.'

Jonny: 'Yes, but I've got too much work to do!'
Jackie: '(plan your time) __________________.'
Jonny: 'I know, but I don't have much time. I'm going to a party on Saturday.'
Jackie: 'Well, (not/go to the party) __________________!'
Jonny: 'But I need to relax sometimes.'
Jackie: 'Yes, well, (not/work all the time) __________________. You can work on Sunday.'
Jonny: 'I'm going skiing on Sunday.'
Jackie: 'I think (work harder) __________________!'

**3. Write advice for these people, using *he/she/they***

(give up smoking)

(not drink so much)

(exercise more)

(not eat so much chocolate)

(speak English in class)

(buy a new car)

(spend less money)

(be careful!)

**4. Practise with a friend**
See page 131.

# Unit 31: Possibility (may/might)

Talking about **possibility**

## Meaning

King: 'Right, then, daughter. Which Prince are you going to marry? You have to make a decision!'
Princess: 'Well... I **might** marry Prince Humphrey, he's quite goodlooking.
King: 'What about Prince Alfred, he's quite intelligent.'
Princess: 'Well, I **may**. On the other hand, I **mightn't** marry either of them. In fact, I **may not** marry anyone!'

***Positive***

Is the Princess *definitely* going to marry **Prince Humphrey**? _____
Is she definitely **not** going to marry him? _____
What *word* does she use to show she is *not sure*? _______________

Is the Princess *definitely* going to marry **Prince Alfred**? _____
Is she definitely **not** going to marry him? _____
What *word* does she use to show she is *not sure*? _____
Do *may*, and *might* have the same meaning when talking about *possibility*? _____

***Negative***

Is the Princess definitely **not** going to marry either of the princes? _____
What *word* does she use to show she is *not sure*? _____
Is the Princess definitely **not** going to marry anyone? _____
What *word(s)* does she use to show she is *not sure*? _____
Do *may not* and *mightn't* have the same meaning when talking about *negative possibility*? _____

## Form

What is the form of **might/mightn't** for I/you/he/she/it/we/they (all persons)? ________
What is the form of **may/may not** for I/you/he/she/it/we/they (all persons)? ________
Is it possible to write **mayn't**? ________



**Answers and Explanations ➤page 162➤**

# Unit 31: Practice

**1. Make these sentences *negative***

> ***Example:***
> (a) The Princess may make a decision. The Princess may not make a decision

(b) The Princess may want to be rich. ____________________
(c) The Princess might like Prince Humphrey better. ____________________
(d) Her father may like Prince Alfred better. ____________________
(e) Prince Alfred may love someone else. ____________________
(f) Prince Humphrey might love someone else. ____________________

**2.** The Princess has a lot of important decisions to make about her life – but she isn't sure what to do. **Write the answers to her father's questions using *might***

> ***Example:***
> (a) 'Who are you going to marry?'
> (Prince Humphrey/Prince Alfred.) I might marry Prince Humphrey or I might marry Prince Alfred

(b) 'When are you going to decide?' (this week/next year) ____________________
(c) 'What will you do if you don't marry either of them?' (travel the world/write a book) ____________________
(d) 'Where are you going to live?' (Here/abroad?) ____________________

**3.** Prince Humphrey is thinking about the Princess. He wants to marry her, but he isn't sure if it will happen. **Rewrite his sentences using: *may* or *may not***

> ***Example:***
> (a) Perhaps the Princess will **marry me** The Princess may marry me

(b) Perhaps we will **live in my castle.** We ____________________
(c) Perhaps she wo**n't like that.** She ____________________
(d) Perhaps we will **live with her father.** We ____________________
(e) Perhaps her father does**n't like me.** Her father ____________________
(f) Perhaps I will **build a new castle in her country.** I ____________________
(g) Perhaps my people will **not like that.** They ____________________
(h) It's all very complicated! Perhaps she wo**n't marry me.** She ____________________

**4.** Tonight there will be a big party at the Princess' castle. Prince Humphrey and Prince Alfred will be there. **Rewrite the sentences using *might/mightn't***

> ***Example:***
> (a) Perhaps the Princess will dance with Prince Humphrey The Princess might dance with Prince Humphrey

(b) Perhaps Prince Humphrey will ask the Princess to marry him. ____________________
(c) Perhaps the Princess will say 'No'. ____________________
(d) Perhaps Prince Humphrey will be sad. ____________________
(e) Perhaps Prince Alfred will be successful. ____________________
(f) Then perhaps Prince Humphrey will be angry. ____________________
(g) Perhaps Prince Humphrey will hit Prince Alfred. ____________________
(h) Perhaps the Princess will be very angry. ____________________
(i) Perhaps she won't marry either of them. ____________________
(j) Perhaps she won't get married at all. ____________________

**5. Practise with a friend.**
See page 131.

# Unit 32: Past continuous



Talking about something happening at a **specific time** in the past

## Meaning

A man is dead! Someone killed him **at 6.00 yesterday afternoon.**
There are three suspects: Bill Bother, Tom Trouble, Tina Trouble
The police ask them the question:
'What **were you doing** at 6.00 yesterday afternoon?'

**Bill Bother:**
'I **was playing** the piano for an Old People's Club dance'

**Tom and Tina Trouble:**
'We **were visiting** Tina's grandmother in hospital'

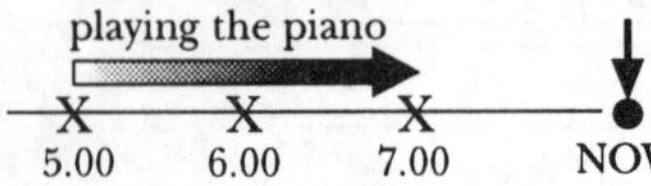


**Look at the time-line**
What time did Bill start playing the piano? _____
What time did he finish playing the piano? _____

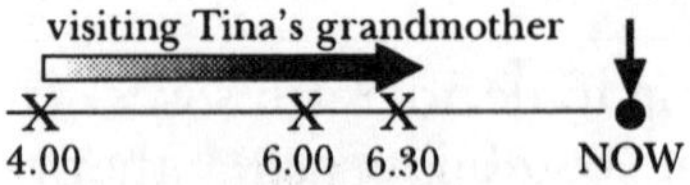


**Look at the time-line**
What time did Tom and Tina start visiting? _____
What time did they finish visiting? ______

**Look at the difference:**

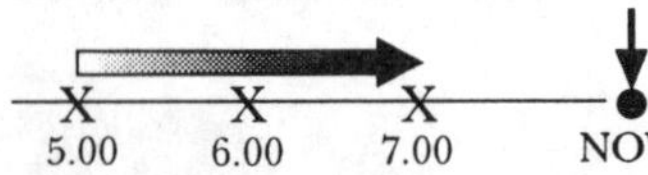


**(a)** I **was playing** the piano

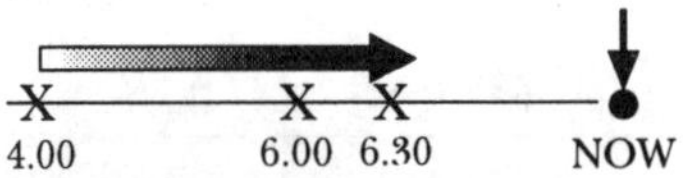


**(b)** We **were visiting** Tina's grandmother

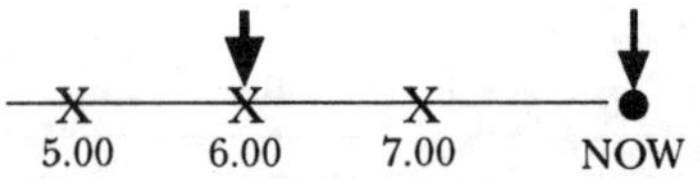


**(c)** Someone **killed** a man

What tense are sentences **(a)** and **(b)**? __________
What tense is sentence **(c)**? __________

## Form

**Complete the table**

| SUBJECT + | VERB TO BE (past) + | VERB+ing |
|---|---|---|
| ***Example:*** I | was | reading |
| You | ________ | speak_____ |
| He/She/It | ________ | eat_____ |
| We | ________ | play_____ |
| They | ________ | work_____ |

*Note:* for **spelling** rules with '-ing' see Unit 18

**Now make *questions***

| | |
|---|---|
| ***Example:*** I/read | Was I reading? |
| You/speak | ____________________ |
| He/eat | ____________________ |
| We/play | ____________________ |
| They/work | ____________________ |

**Now make *negative* sentences**

| | |
|---|---|
| ***Example:*** I/read | I wasn't reading |
| You/speak | ____________________ |
| He/eat | ____________________ |
| We/play | ____________________ |
| They/work | ____________________ |



Answers and Explanations ➤page 162➤

# Unit 32: Practice

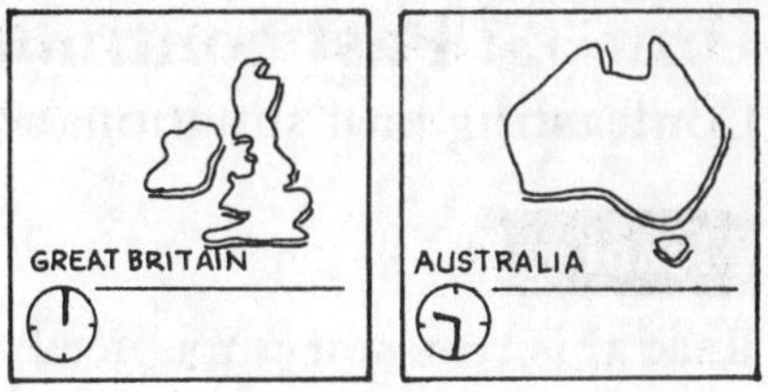


**1.** Joe and Susan are friends but Joe lives in Australia and Susan lives in Britain. It's difficult for them to telephone each other because the time is so different.
**Write sentences about what they were doing yesterday.**

*Example: have breakfast/leave work*
At 8.00 am in Britain
Susan was having breakfast
But, in Australia
Joe was leaving work

*have lunch/have a beer*
At 12.00 pm in Britain
________________
But in Australia
________________

*go to bed/get up*
At 10.00 pm in Britain
________________
But in Australia
________________

*read in bed/go to work*
At 11.00 pm in Britain
________________
But in Australia
________________

**2. Complete the telephone conversation between Joe and Susan**

Joe: 'Hi, Susan?'
Susan: 'Joe! I tried to telephone you yesterday but you were never at home. What were you doing?'
Joe: 'What time did you ring?'
Susan: 'Well, first I rang at 8.00 am – that's 5.30 pm in Australia.'
Joe: 'I _____ __________ work.'
Susan: 'Then I rang at 12.00 pm – that's 9.30 pm in Australia.'
Joe: 'Oh, I _____ __________ a beer with my friends.'
Susan: 'Then I rang at 5.00 pm – oh dear, that's 2.30 am in Australia!'
Joe: 'Yes, I _____ __________ – or I was *trying* to sleep!'

**3.** Joe went for a beer last night with his friends. **Look at the picture and complete the sentences about what was happening when he arrived.**

***Example:***
(a) Tim/talk to Lisa — Tim was talking to Lisa

(b) John and Stuart/have an argument ________________
(c) Jane/have a hamburger ________________
(d) Mary and Louisa/dance ________________
(e) Pete/drink a beer ________________
(f) Tim and Stuart/smoke ________________
(g) Tim and Lisa/sit on a bench ________________
(h) Joe's friends/have a good time! ________________

**4. Write questions and short answers about the picture**

***Example:***
(a) Tim/talk to Louisa? — Was Tim talking to Louisa? — No, he wasn't

(b) Jane/drink a beer? ________________? ____________
(c) Mary and Louisa/dance? ________________? ____________
(d) Tim and Lisa/eat? ________________? ____________
(e) Tim/smoke? ________________? ____________
(f) Lisa/stand up? ________________? ____________
(g) Joe's friends/have a good time? ________________? ____________

**5. Practise with a friend.**
See page 132.

# Unit 33: Past continuous and past simple — It *was raining* when I *left*

**Contrasting** past situations and events

## Meaning

**Read this true story.** You need to understand these words:

**clamp:** Look at the picture. If you park your car in the wrong place or leave it too long someone may put a **clamp** on your car, or **clamp** your car so that you cannot drive away.

**steering wheel lock:** Look at the picture. You can use a steering wheel lock to stop a thief driving your car away.

**strike:** If you want more money for doing your job you can **stop working** (or go on **strike**.)

**fine:** If you park your car in the wrong place or leave it too long you may have to **pay some money** (or a **fine**.)

I was feeling really tired and annoyed when I finally arrived home, at Gloucester Station. I was twenty four hours late because of a railway strike. I really needed to get home and sleep. I went to the railway car-park to get in my car but as I was walking across the car-park I saw a yellow clamp on my car! I couldn't believe it. The car park attendent was sleeping in his van when I woke him up. 'Take that clamp off my car!' I said. 'Sorry, sir. Your car has been here for more than twenty four hours. You have to pay a fine of £40,' he replied...

**Match the sentences from the story with the time-line**

**(a)** I was feeling really tired
= (1) or (2)? _______

**(b)** I finally arrived home
= (1) or (2)? _______

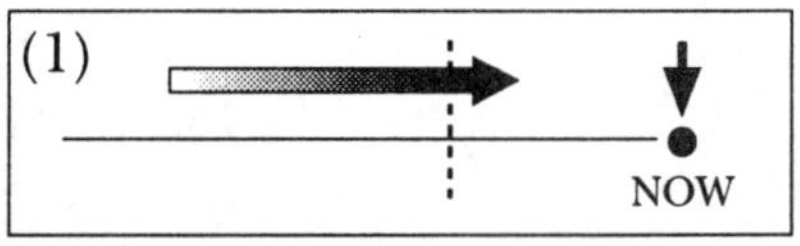


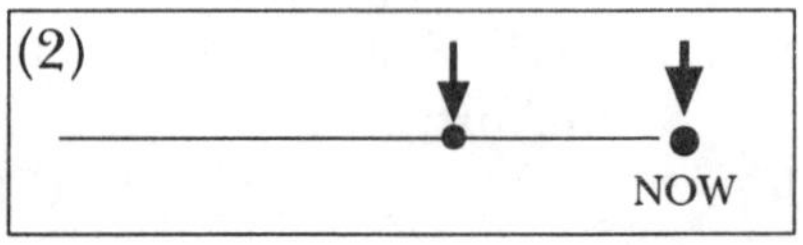


Was he feeling tired *before* the train arrived in Gloucester Yes/No ________________
Did he *continue* feeling tired after the train arrived in Gloucester? Yes/No ________________
Which sentence describes the *background situation?* **(a)** or **(b)** _______
What *tense* is this sentence? ________________
Which sentence describes an *action* that happened *during* the background situation? **(a)** or **(b)** _______
What *tense* is this sentence? ________________

**(c)** The car park attendent was sleeping
= (1) or (2)? _______

**(d)** I woke him up
= (1) or (2)? _______

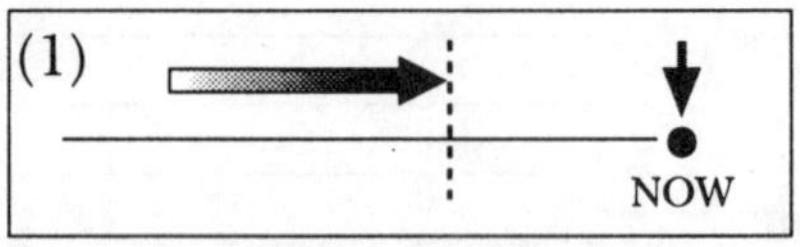


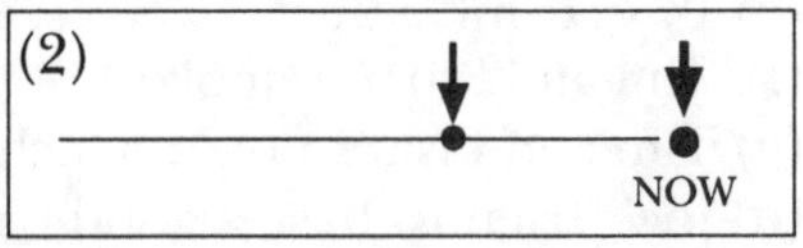


Was the car-park attendent sleeping *before* the man found him? Yes/No ________________
Did he *continue* sleeping after the man found him? Yes/No ________________
Which sentence describes the *background situation?* **(c)** or **(d)** _______
What *tense* is this sentence? ________________
Which sentence describes an *action* that happened *after* the background situation? **(c)** or **(d)** _______
What *tense* is this sentence? ________________

## Form

For the form of past continuous see Unit 32
For the form of past simple see Unit 24



**Answers and Explanations ➤page 163➔**

# Unit 33: Practice

**1. Choose *past simple* or *past continuous* to complete the story**

... I explained that I was twenty four hours late because there was a railway strike.
'Sorry, sir,' he said, ' Rules are rules – £40 please.'
I was so angry that while (**he was writing/he wrote**) the ticket for the fine (**I was going/I went**) to my car and (**taking out/took out**) my steering wheel lock and (**was locking/locked**) *his* steering wheel. 'Right,' I said. 'Now I can't move my car and you can't move your van!'
'I'll call the police!' he said. 'No, *I* will.' I replied and so we both called them.
But while we were waiting for the police to arrive (**he was saying/he said**), 'OK, you win.' and (**he was taking/he took**) the clamp off my car. So I took off the steering wheel lock. I got in my car but as I was leaving (**the police were arriving/the police arrived**) and I had to stop and explain the whole story. They couldn't stop laughing. I don't know what they thought was so funny!'

**2.** The next morning the car-park attendent went home and told his wife the story. **Complete his story using *past simple* or *past continuous*.**

Last night I (feel tired) was feeling tired. I (sleep) ______________ when this man (wake me up) ______________. He was really angry because his car had been clamped. While he (shout) ______________ at me I tried to tell him he had to pay a fine of £40. As I (write) ______________ the ticket he (go) ______________ to his car and came back with a steering wheel lock and he locked my steering wheel! I couldn't believe it! I called the police – and so did he. While we (wait) ______________ for the police he got angrier and angrier. I felt quite scared so I decided to let him go. He (drive) ______________ away when the police (arrive) ______________ but he stopped to talk to them. For some reason the policemen thought the story was really funny.

**3. Look at the examples and answer the questions**

**(a)** He drove away when the police arrived.
**(b)** He was driving away when the police arrived.
Which sentence means he *started* driving *before* the police arrived? ______________
Which sentence means he *started* driving *at the same time* as the police arrived? ______________

**(c)** I was feeling really tired and annoyed when I arrived home.
**(d)** I felt really tired and annoyed when I arrived home.
Which sentence means he *started* feeling tired and annoyed *before* he arrived home? ______________
Which sentence means he *started* feeling tired and annoyed *at the same time* as he arrived home? __________

**4. Write sentences using *when* and the past simple and the past continuous to describe these pictures**

***Example:***
(I/drive home/see an accident)
I was driving home when I saw an accident

(It/rain/I/arrive)
______________
______________

(I/read/the phone/ring)
______________
______________

We/dance/the electricity/go out)
______________
______________

(They/rob a bank/the police/arrive)
______________
______________

(She/shop/she/meet him)
______________
______________

**5. Practise with a friend.**
See page 132.

# Unit 34: Adjectives I

**a *black* cat/a *big* house**

**Describing** people, places and objects (nouns)

## Meaning

**Put the correct *adjective* under each picture**

A ________ cat  A ________ cat

(***white/black***)

A ________ man  A ________ man

(***fat/thin***)

An _______ house  A _______ house

(***new/old***)

A _______ woman  An _______ woman

(***young/old***)

He's _________  He's _________

(***sad/happy***)

We're_________  We're _________

(***tall/short***)

## Form

**Look at the examples above.**
**Does the adjective go *before* or *after* the noun?** _________
**So, which is correct? – '*a big house*' or '*a house big?*'** ________________

We can also make a sentence with the verb **to be** and an adjective:
**Make sentences:**

| | |
|---|---|
| ***Example:*** | |
| he/thin | he's thin |

they/rich __________
it/cold __________
I/hungry __________ *

*Careful! In English we **don't** say 'I have hunger' – we use an adjective

**Which is the correct plural?**
A big house – '***big houses***', or '***bigs houses***'? ________________
So, in English the adjective **does not change** for plural.



**Answers and Explanations ➤page 163➤**

# Unit 34: Practice

**1.  Write the *opposite* of the adjectives.** Choose from this list:

| young | sad | poor | hot | exciting | noisy | easy | bad | fast |
|---|---|---|---|---|---|---|---|---|
| cheap | tall | new | | | | | | |

(a) quiet    _noisy_          (e) cold    _____    (i) short    _____
(b) expensive _____    (f) good    _____    (j) happy    _____
(c) rich    _____      (g) difficult _____  (k) old (people) _____
(d) boring    _____    (h) slow    _____    (l) old (things) _____

**2.  Rewrite the sentences using the *opposite* adjectives.**
(a) The children are very quiet today.    _The children are very noisy today_
(b) He bought an old car. It was very cheap.    _____
(c) The weather was hot today.    _____
(d) I love cold weather!    _____
(e) This TV programme is really boring.    _____
(f) This is an easy exercise.    _____
(g) My aunt is really old.    _____
(h) He wrote a really bad essay.    _____
(i) The train is really slow.    _____
(j) My brother is quite tall.    _____
(k) He bought me a big present.    _____

**3.  Remember we can put the adjective before the noun (1) *or* use the verb 'to be' (2)**
**Write (1) or (2) next to the sentences from exercise 2.**
(a) The children are very quiet today.   _2_        (g) My aunt is really old.   ____
(b) He bought an old car. It was very cheap. _1 and 2_  (h) He wrote a really bad essay.   ____
(c) The weather was hot today.   ____       (i) The train is really slow.   ____
(d) I love cold weather!   ____             (j) My brother is quite tall.   ____
(e) This TV programme is really boring.   ____  (k) He bought me a big present.   ____
(f) This is an easy exercise.   ____

**4.  Put the words in brackets ( ) in the correct order to complete the postcard.**
The weather (beautiful/really/is)
_is really beautiful_

Brighton (is/an/town/exciting)

_____

but it (quite/is/expensive)

_____

Yesterday I went to see (play/great/a)
_____ at the theatre.
The actors (good/very/were)

_____

Today I'm going shopping. There are some
(shops/wonderful)  _____
I want to buy (dress/new/a)

_____

Then tomorrow we're going on a boat-trip
– if (calm/the sea/is)  _____

Greetings from Brighton!
The weather (beautiful/really/is)
Brighton (is/an/town/exciting)
but it (quite/is/expensive)
Yesterday I went to see (play/
great/a) at the theatre.
The actors (good/very/were)
Today I'm going shopping. There
are some (shops/wonderful)
I want to buy (dress/new/a)
Then tomorrow we're going on a
boat-trip - if (calm/the sea/is)
Wish you were here!
Love, Jackie
x    Brighton

BRIGHTON
SUSSEX
1220591

Mr. and Mrs. N. Jones
33 Fir Tree Road
Kings Vale
York
YO2 4NZ

PUBLISHED IN THE UK BY HAPPY HOLS POSTCARDS LTD, ROCKALL

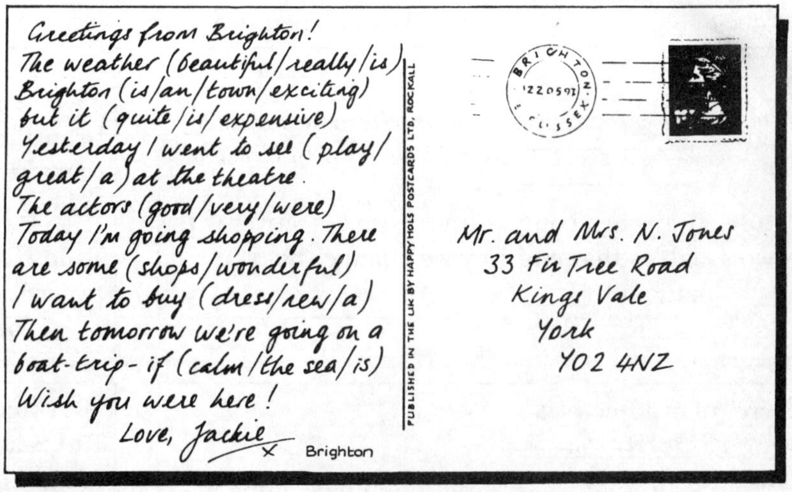

**5.  Practise with a friend.**
See page 132.

# Unit 35: Comparatives

## bigger/better/more beautiful

Making **comparisons** between two things

**Meaning**

Brasilia is the capital of Brazil but forty years ago the capital was Rio de Janeiro. Many Brazilians argue about which city is *better*.

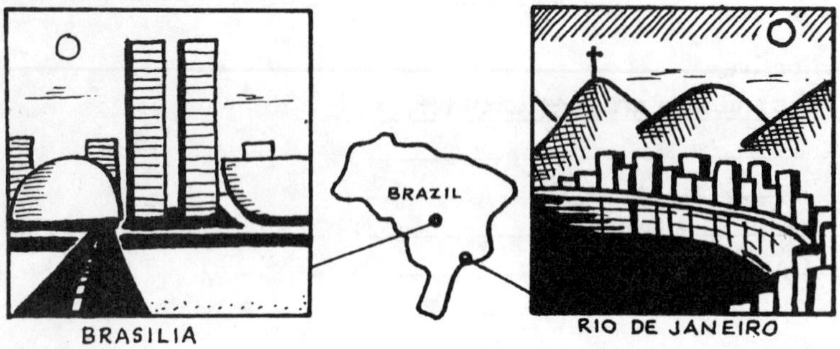


*Julia is from Rio*

Rio is a much better place to live than Brasilia. It's bigger and certainly more beautiful. The bars and restaurants are cheaper and it's hotter and nearer the sea. People say it's more dangerous than Brasilia - but I think Brasilia is worse.

*Cristina is from Brasilia*

It's not true that Brasilia is uglier or more boring than Rio. It's just different! It is smaller but it's safer too - and the air is cleaner. It's further from the sea but we have beautiful river beaches. The beaches in Rio are dirtier than ours.

**Form**

**Write the underlined words from the texts next to the matching adjectives.**
**Then use the examples to *complete the rule***

**One syllable adjectives**

clean cleaner
cheap ____
small ____
near ____

**Rule**: To make a comparative from adjectives with *one* syllable we add ____

*Spelling*

big ____ What happens to the last letter of the adjective? ____
hot ____ What happens to the last letter of the adjective? ____
safe ____ Do we need two 'e's? ____

**-y adjectives**

ugly ____
dirty ____

**Rule**: To make a comparative from adjectives with two syllables that **end in y** we change the 'y' to ____ and add ____

**Two or more syllable adjectives**

beautiful ____
dangerous ____
boring ____

**Rule**: To make a comparative from adjectives with two syllables that **DON'T end in y** we use the word ____ before the adjective.

**Irregular adjectives**

good better
bad ____
far ____

(there aren't many irregular adjectives but you need to learn them)

We often use **'than'** with comparatives:
Rio is a much better place to live **than** Brasilia.
It's not true that Brasilia is uglier or more boring **than** Rio.
The beaches in Rio are dirtier **than** ours.



Answers and Explanations ➤page 164➤

# Unit 35: Practice

**1. Divide these adjectives into *four* columns:**

*old* *easy* *important* *good*
nice exciting cheap sunny
noisy warm quiet far
expensive tall lucky fast
comfortable heavy bad

| – er | – ier | more... | irregular |
|---|---|---|---|
| old | easy | important | good |
| | | | |

**2. Correct any *spelling* mistakes you find.**

*Example:*
(a) Rio is hoter than Brasilia X hotter

(b) Brasilia is smallier than Rio
(c) Rio is nearer the sea than Brasilia
(d) Brasilia is sunnyer than Rio
(e) Rio is older than Brasilia
(f) Rio is poorer than Brasilia
(g) Rio is niceer than Brasilia
(h) Brasilia is dryer than Rio

**3. Look at the information about York and Manchester**

**Manchester**
Population 438,500
Distance from London 300km
Cost of train to London £32

**York**
Population 300,000
Distance from London 320km
Cost of train to London £34

**Complete the sentences about York and Manchester**
Use the **comparative form** of these adjectives: ***big/small/clean/dirty/cheap/expensive/far/near***

*Example:*
(a) Manchester is bigger than York

(b) Manchester is _________ London than York
(c) The train ticket from York to London is _________ than from Manchester to London
(d) Manchester is _________ than York (look at the picture!)
(e) York is _________ than Manchester
(f) York is _________ from London than Manchester
(g) The train ticket from Manchester to London is _________ than from York to London
(h) York is _________than Manchester

**4. Look at the information about Faro and Oporto**

| **Oporto** | |
|---|---|
| Population | 700,000 |
| Sunshine hours | 1600 per year |
| Average temperature | 58F |
| Rainfall | A lot |

| **Faro** | |
|---|---|
| Population | 500,000 |
| Sunshine hours | 3000 per year |
| Average temperature | 64F |
| Rainfall | Very little |

**Write sentences comparing Faro and Oporto**
Use the comparative form of the adjectives in brackets ( )

*Example:*
(a) (big) Oporto is bigger than Faro
(b) (small) Faro is smaller than Oporto

(c) (sunny) _______________
(d) (cloudy) _______________
(e) (hot) _______________
(f) (cool) _______________
(g) (rainy) _______________
(h) (dry) _______________

**5. Practise with a friend**
Talk together about two cities in your country (or countries). Compare them using some of the words in this unit.

# Unit 36: Superlatives

Comparing something with **two or more other things**

## Meaning

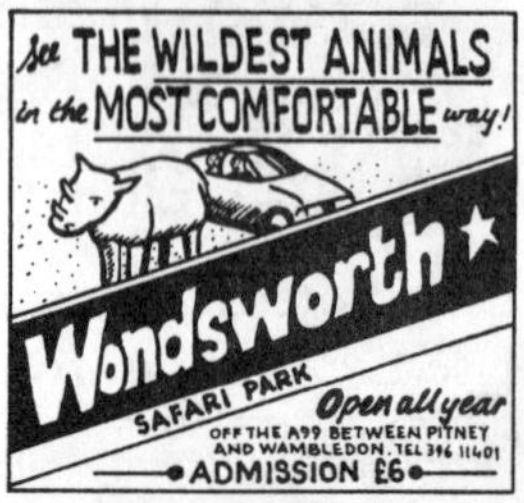


Dad: 'So, where do you want to go for a day out this weekend?'

Tim: 'Can we go to Bolton Towers? They've got a new rollercoaster and it's **the fastest** in the world! It's much **faster** than the one at Courtney Amusement park – and that's **fast**!

Dad: 'Hmmm, it's probably very **expensive**. Isn't Courtney Park **cheaper**? It's only £8 and Bolton Towers is £12!

Mum: 'Well, **the cheapest** is probably Wondsworth Safari Park, that's only £6 – and it's much **more educational**. It's also **the nearest** to where we live.'

Tim: 'Oh, Mum! Bolton Towers is much **more exciting** – all my friends are going there.'

Dad: 'Exactly – so it will have **the longest** queues.....'

**Look at the sentences and answer the questions**

(**a**) The Courtney Park rollercoaster is **fast**
(**b**) The Bolton Towers rollercoaster is **faster** (than the Courtney Park rollercoaster)
(**c**) The Bolton Towers rollercoaster is **the fastest** in the world

Which sentence (a), (b) or (c) compares *one* roller coaster to a *second* rollercoaster? b
Write the comparative adjective* in the sentence? faster

Which sentence compares *one* rollercoaster to *all* the other rollercoasters? ________
What is the superlative adjective in the sentence? ________

Which sentence just describes one rollercoaster? ________ *see Unit 35
What is the adjective** in the sentence? ________ **see Unit 34

| | | |
|---|---|---|
| (a) Bolton Towers is £12 | Which is **the most expensive**? ________ | |
| (b) Courtney Park is £8 | Which is **the cheapest**? ________ | |
| (c) Wondsworth Safari Park is £6 | Is Courtney Park **more expensive** than Wondsworth Safari Park? | (Yes/No) ______ |

## Form

**Complete the table using the examples from the advertisements and the dialogue.**

| ADJECTIVE | COMPARATIVE ADJECTIVE | SUPERLATIVE ADJECTIVE | |
|---|---|---|---|
| ***One syllable adjectives***<br>fast<br>cheap<br>big<br>near<br>long | <br>faster<br>________<br>bigger<br>nearer<br>longer | <br>the fastest<br>________<br>________<br>the nearest<br>________ | *To make a superlative adjective from an adjective with one syllable we add* ________ |
| ***Two syllables or more***<br>exciting<br>________<br>educational<br>comfortable | <br>________<br>more expensive<br>________<br>more comfortable | <br>________<br>the most expensive<br>the most educational<br>________ | *To make a superlative adjective from an adjective with two syllables or more we add* ________ |
| ***Irregular***<br>good<br>bad<br>far | <br>better<br>worse<br>further | <br>________<br>the worst<br>the furthest | |



Answers and Explanations ➤page 164➤

# Unit 36: Practice

**1. Write the *superlative* form of these adjectives**

(a) beautiful the most beautiful
(b) delicious ________
(c) cheap ________
(d) safe ________
(e) dangerous ________
(f) hot ________
(g) boring ________
(h) good ________
(i) large ________
(j) small ________
(k) relaxing ________
(l) expensive ________
(m)clean ________
(n) bad ________
(o) near ________

**2. Look at these holiday advertisements and make sentences.**

**Hotel Boa Viagem**
[5 minutes from the beach]
Recife, Brazil
14 nights £789

**Hotel Thai**
[20 minutes from the beach]
Phuket, Thailand
7 nights £632

**Palm Hotel**
[15 m from the beach]
Key West, Florida
10 nights £423

(a) Recife is (expensive) the most expensive holiday.
(b) Hotel Boa Viagem is (near) ________ to the beach.
(c) Recife is (long) ________ holiday.
(d) Hotel Thai is (far) ________ from the beach.
(e) Hotel Thai is (big) ________ hotel.
(f) Phuket is (short) ________ holiday.
(g) Key West is (cheap) ________ holiday.
(h) Palm Hotel is (small) ________ hotel.

3. Jon and Rebecca are deciding where to go on holiday: Brazil, Thailand or the United States. **Complete their conversation with the correct *superlative* form.**

Jon: 'Well, I think (a) (good) the best place to go is Thailand. It's certainly (b) (cheap) ________ country and it's got (c) (beautiful) ________ beaches. The weather is wonderful – Bangkok is (d) (hot) ________ city in the world.'
Rebecca: 'But Brazil has beautiful beaches too and I think it's (e) (relaxing) ________ place.'
Jon: 'Relaxing!! It's (f) (dangerous) ________! We'll probably get shot!'
Rebecca: 'Rubbish! The United States is (g) (bad) ________. Florida is really dangerous for tourists.'
Jon: 'So, let's go to Thailand. Its (h) (safe) ________. It's (i) (interesting) ________ place too – a completely different culture. And the food is (j) (delicious) ________ in the world.'
Rebecca: 'Well, yes, American food is probably (k) (boring) ________ – all hamburgers and steaks and it's (l) (expensive) ________ place to go too.'

**4. Correct the mistakes you find.**

(a) Brazil is the most far place. the furthest
(b) French food is the goodest is the world. ________
(c) Bangkok is the hottest city in the world. ________
(d) Madame Tussauds is the interestingest thing to see in London. ________
(e) Are you the most old in your family? ________
(f) I sat in the comfortablest chair. ________

**5. Correct the *spelling* mistakes you find**

(a) Tokyo is the bigest city in Japan. biggest
(b) Jonny is the noisyest student in the class! ________
(c) I answered the easiest question. ________
(d) The fasttest car won the race. ________
(e) Jane and Sue are both thin but Mary is the thinest. ________
(f) Who is the busyest person in the office? ________

**6. Practise with a friend.**

See page 133.

# Unit 37: Adverbs II: Manner

Describing **how** we do something

## Meaning

***A ghost story:*** It was a cold night. The wind blew noisily around the house. Sarah climbed up the stairs slowly. The house was dark and she was holding a long candle. At the top of the stairs she heard a strange voice. 'Welcome', it said, quietly. Sarah was really frightened. She started to run quickly down the stairs. Suddenly the candle went out. Sarah screamed loudly...

**Divide the underlined words from the story into verbs and nouns**

| | |
|---|---|
| *Example:* | |
| night | noun |
| blew | verb |

climbed ______
house ______
candle ______
voice ______
said ______
Sarah ______
run ______
went out ______
screamed ______

An **adjective** describes a *noun*
(Problems with adjectives? See Unit 33)
**What *adjectives* describe the nouns above?**

| | | |
|---|---|---|
| *Example:* | | |
| cold | night | (It was a *cold* night) |

______ house
______ candle
______ voice
______ Sarah

An **adverb** describes a *verb*. It says *how* something happens. **What *adverbs* describe the verbs above?**

| | | |
|---|---|---|
| *Example:* | | |
| blew | noisily | (The wind blew *noisily* around the house) |

climbed ______
said ______
run ______
went out ______
screamed ______

## Form

Is **'quick'** an adjective, or an adverb? __________
Is **'quickly'** an adjective, or an adverb? __________
What do we usually ***add*** to an ***adjective*** to make an ***adverb***? __________
**noisy – noisily: what happens to the *spelling* when the adjective ends in -y?** __________

**What are the *adverbs* from these *adjectives*?** Careful! They are all *irregular*.

| ADJECTIVE | ADVERB |
|---|---|
| *Example:* I am a **good** tennis player | I play tennis well |
| This is a **fast** car | He drives ______ |
| This unit is quite **hard** | You need to work ______ to learn English! |
| I am always **late** | He arrived ______ again. |

**Does an *adjective* usually go *before*, or *after*, the *noun*?** ______
**Does an *adverb* usually go *before*, or *after*, the *verb*?** ______



**Answers and Explanations ➤page 165➤**

# Unit 37: Practice

**1. Make these *adjectives* into *adverbs***

| | | |
|---|---|---|
| (a) bad badly | (e) angry ____________ | (i) silent ____________ |
| (b) good ____________ | (f) quiet ____________ | (j) violent ____________ |
| (c) easy ____________ | (g) noisy ____________ | |
| (d) careful ____________ | (h) slow ____________ | |

**2. Read the dialogue and write *how* they said the sentences.**

'I'm really looking forward to our holiday.' she said (happy) happily

'Er, do you think we have enough money to go on holiday, darling?' he asked (nervous) ____________

'Of course we do!' she said, (confident) ____________

'But, have you forgotten we've got to pay for the new car?' he asked, (quiet) ____________

'I thought you did that last month!' she shouted, (angry) ____________

'No, we had to pay for your new clothes last month – £500!' he replied, (cross) ____________

'Oh, well, no holiday, then' she said (sad) ____________

**3. Use an *adverb* to write another sentence about the situations**

| | |
|---|---|
| (a) It was an **accident.** | He did it accidently |
| (b) His laugh was **wicked.** | He laughed ____________ |
| (c) His English is **fluent.** | He speaks English ____________ |
| (d) She is very **polite.** | She behaves ____________ |
| (e) They wear **different** clothes. | They dress ____________ |
| (f) He is **good** at singing. | He sings ____________ |
| (g) It was **easy** for him to win. | He won ____________ |
| (h) She was **happy** when she laughed. | She laughed ____________ |

**4. Choose an *adjective* or *adverb***

Driving in London is not (a) (*easy/easily*). The traffic moves very (b) (*slow/slowly*) in central London – about 12 km per hour. You also need to drive (c) (*careful/carefully*) because some drivers are very (d) (*impatient/impatiently*) and drive (e) (*dangerous/dangerously.*) Another problem is finding a place to park. Car-parks are very (f) (*expensive/expensively.*) It is often better to leave your car outside the city centre and then you can (g) (*easy/easily*) travel into the centre on public transport. The buses and underground are very (h) (*good/well*).

There are lots of (i) (*excellent/excellently*) restaurants in London and – if you have the money – you can eat very (j) (*good/well*). Some people think that the British cook very (k) (*bad/badly*) but in London you can eat Indian, Thai, French, Chinese food....everything!

**5. Practise with a friend.**

Tell your friend *how* you do some of these things (and other things you can think of):

run talk play tennis speak English drive play music
eat spaghetti study

> ***Example:***
> A: 'I drive **fast**'
> B: 'I eat spaghetti **noisily**!'

# Unit 38: Present tenses for future use

## *I'm meeting* John tonight/ the train *leaves* at 6 o'clock

Talking about **arrangements**; talking about **programmes** and **timetables**

## Meaning

***Look* at the dialogues and *answer* the questions**

Tom: 'What time are we leaving **(a)** tomorrow?'
Beatrice: 'Well, the plane leaves **(b)** at 10.00, so we should leave at 6.00.'
Tom: 'Are we meeting **(c)** John and Susie at the airport?'
Beatrice: 'No, they're coming **(d)** here first.'

Alison: 'What time are you doing **(e)** tonight?'
Cathy: 'I'm going **(f)** to the cinema with John.'
Alison: 'What time does the film start? **(g)**'
Cathy: '7.00.'

Daniel: 'When is James going **(h)** back to school?'
Jill: 'School starts **(i)** on the 6th January.'

What are the names of the two **tenses** underlined above? ________________ and ________________
***In these examples*** are they talking about ***present*** **time** or ***future*** **time**? ________________

Which sentences are talking about ***an arrangement between people***? (a) ____ ____ ____ ____ ____ ____
What *tense* are they? ________________

Which sentences are talking about ***an event happening at a specific time/on a specific date***?
(b) ____ ____
What *tense* are they? ________________

## Form

For the *form* of the present simple and present continuous see Units 5 and 18.



Answers and Explanations ➤page 165➔

# Unit 38: Practice

**1.** Mr Brown is going on a business trip to Jakarta. **Look at his desk.**

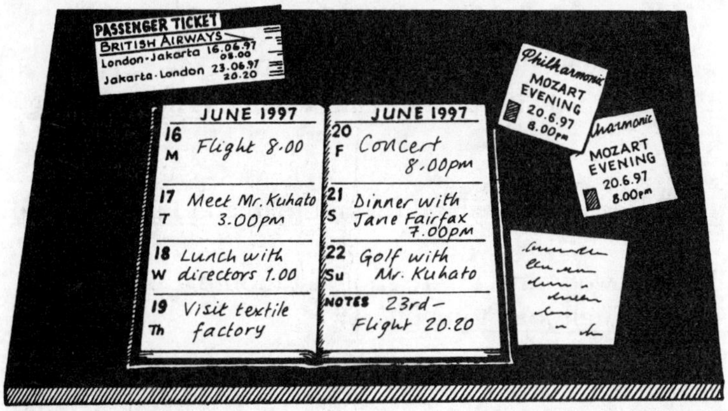


**Write sentences about his arrangements using *present simple* and *continuous*.**

(a) The plane (leave) ___leaves___ at 8.00 on 16th June.
(b) Mr Brown (meet) __________ Mr Kuhato at 3.00 pm on 17th June.
(c) He (have) __________ lunch with the Directors at 1.00 on 18th June.
(d) On 19th June he (visit) __________ a textile factory.
(e) On 20th June he (go) __________ to a concert.
(f) The concert (start) __________ at 8.00pm.
(g) On the 21st June he (have) __________ dinner with Jane Fairfax.
(h) On the 22nd June he (play) __________ golf with Mr Kuhato.
(i) The plane back to London (leave) __________ at 20.20 on the 23rd June.

**2. Complete the questions about Mr Brown's business trip.**

(a) What time/the plane/leave London? ___What time does the plane leave London?___
(b) Who/he/meet on 17th June? ______________________
(c) What/he/do on 18th June? ______________________
(d) Where/he/visit on 19th June? ______________________
(e) What time/the concert start? ______________________
(f) When/he/have dinner with Jane Fairfax? ______________________
(g) What/he/do on 22nd June? ______________________
(h) What time/the plane back to London/leave? ______________________

**3. Find the mistakes – *using the wrong tense* – and *correct* them.**

Susan: 'When are you leaving for Jakarta?'
Mr Brown: 'Well, the plane (a) <u>is leaving</u> at 8.00 am so I (b) <u>stay</u> with friends near the airport.'
Susan: 'What time (c) <u>does the plane</u> arrive in Jakarta?'
Mr Brown: 'About 2.00 pm, local time. I (d) <u>meet</u> Mr Kuhato at 3.00 pm.'
Susan: '(e) <u>Do you visit</u> the textile factory?'
Mr Brown: 'Yes, on the 19th. I've got lots of meetings but also time for some relaxation. (f) <u>I'm playing</u> golf with Mr Kuhato on the 22nd, for example.'
Susan: 'When (g) <u>are you coming back</u>?'
Mr Brown: 'On the 23rd. The plane (h) <u>is landing</u> at Heathrow at 3.00am on the 24th. Too early in the morning!'

(a) ___leaves___
(b) __________
(c) __________
(d) __________
(e) __________
(f) __________
(g) __________
(h) __________

**4. Practise with a friend.**

What arrangements do you have this week? Tell your friend about *your* arrangements and ask questions – What..? Where..? about *their* arrangements.

# Unit 39: Going to/Will – I

*I'm going to* **be a doctor/**
***I'll ring* you tonight**

Decisions taken **previously**, and **now**, about **the future**

## Meaning

Richard: 'Where are you going on holiday this year?'
Nick: '<u>We're going to Florida and Disneyland</u>. **(a)** *[1] The children are really excited. <u>They're going to meet Mickey Mouse</u>!' **(b)**
Richard: 'What are you and Joan going to do there?'
Nick: 'Well, <u>our cousins are going to take the children to Disneyland</u> **(c)** and <u>Joan and I are going to lie on the beach</u>.' **(d)**
Richard: 'It's quite dangerous at the beach, you know. Two tourists were shot last month.'
Nick: 'Really?! <u>We won't go to the beach then</u>! **(e)** <u>I'll tell Joan tonight</u>.' **(f)**

**Look at the underlined sentences.**
Which sentences show what Nick decided **about the future *before*** the conversation with Richard?
(a) ________ ________ ________
Does he use **going to** or **will**? ________
Which sentences show what Nick decided **about the future *during*** the conversation with Richard?
(e) ________
Does he use **going to** or **will**? ________

## Form

### GOING TO

**Complete the rule using these words:** VERB 'TO BE' (is/am/are)  GOING TO

To make the **going to** future we use
SUBJECT (I/you/he etc) + ______________ + ______________ + INFINITIVE (eat/drink etc)

**Make these sentences using 'going to' into *questions***

| | |
|---|---|
| ***Example:*** | |
| They're going to take the children | Are they going to take the children? |

He's going to lie on the beach ______________?
We're going to visit Disneyland ______________?

### WILL

What is the form of will for I/you/he/she/it/we/they (all persons)*[2]? ________
What is the **negative** form of will? ________

**Write the *contractions***

| Example: | | | | | |
|---|---|---|---|---|---|
| I will | I'll | You will | ______ | It will | ______ |
| | | He will | ______ | We will | ______ |
| | | She will | ______ | They will | ______ |

**Which sentence is correct? (only one)**
I think I'll **go** to the cinema ______ (✗ ✓)
I think I'll **to go** to the cinema ______ (✗ ✓)
I think I'll **going** to the cinema ______ (✗ ✓)

*[1] When the infinitive is *go* we **don't** usually say 'I am *going to go* to Florida' because it is too long! We say '*I am going*' to Florida.

*[2] Some people say '**I shall**' and '**We shall**' but we normally only use 'shall' in offers and suggestions.

| | |
|---|---|
| ***Examples:*** | Shall I open the window? |
| | Shall we go to the cinema? |



**Answers and Explanations ➤page 166➤**

# Unit 39: Practice

**1.** Fiona is an advertising manager. She works very hard but **next week** she is going on a really relaxing holiday to Sri Lanka. She wants to completely forget about work.
**Write sentences about what she *is going to do* or *not going to do*.**

(a) lie on the beach — She's going to lie on the beach
(b) take her mobile phone — She's not going to take her mobile phone
(c) sleep late every day ________
(d) take her lap-top computer ________
(e) telephone her office every day ________
(f) eat delicious healthy food ________
(g) go scuba diving ________
(h) have a really good time ________

**2.** These are some of the things Fiona is thinking as she lies on the beach. **Match each one with a verb and write what she *decides to do***

go in the shade     have something to drink     go for a swim
have something to eat     put on some suncream     read a book

(a) 'I feel hungry' — 'I'll have something to eat.'
(b) 'The sun's really hot.' ________
(c) 'I feel thirsty' ________
(d) 'I think I'm burning' ________
(e) 'The sea looks wonderful' ________
(f) 'I'm bored' ________

**3. Choose *going* to or *will* to complete the dialogue.**

Mary: 'What (are you going to do/will you do) next week Fiona?'
Fiona: 'Didn't I tell you? (I'm going [to go]/I'll go) on holiday.'
Mary: 'You lucky thing! Where (are you going [to go]/will you go?)'
Fiona: 'Sri Lanka. (Are you going [to go]/will you go) anywhere this year?'
Mary: 'I don't know yet. Maybe we (are going to visit/will visit) friends in Wales.'
Fiona: 'Well, (I'm going to send/I'll send) you a postcard!'
Mary: 'Thanks!'

**4. Complete Fiona's postcards with *'will'* or *'am going to'***

Dear Mary,

Having a lovely time in Sri Lanka. Tomorrow I'm going to visit an old palace in the jungle but today it's really hot so I think I ________ just lie on the beach. It's so relaxing! I ________ ring you when I get back, OK?

Love, Fiona

Dear Mum and Dad,

I'm really enjoying my holiday in Sri Lanka. I ________ stay here three weeks and really relax. Next week I ________ go on a trip into the jungle. – Don't worry! I ________ be very careful!

Love, Fiona

**5. Practise with a friend.**
**Talk together about your plans for next weekend.** You could use these verbs:

visit     go     play     cook     go shopping     relax     sleep     meet     study

***Remember*** – if you decided *before* use: going to/not going to
– if you decide *as you're speaking* use: will/won't

# Unit 40: Going to/Will – II   it's *going to* rain/you'll *(will)* be rich

Making **predictions**

## Meaning

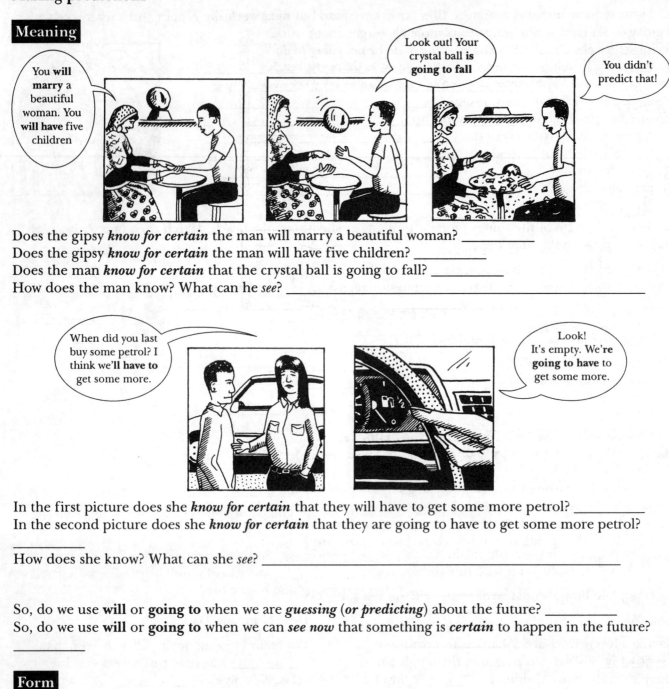

Does the gipsy ***know for certain*** the man will marry a beautiful woman? __________
Does the gipsy ***know for certain*** the man will have five children? __________
Does the man ***know for certain*** that the crystal ball is going to fall? __________
How does the man know? What can he *see*? __________

In the first picture does she ***know for certain*** that they will have to get some more petrol? __________
In the second picture does she ***know for certain*** that they are going to have to get some more petrol? __________

How does she know? What can she *see*? __________

So, do we use **will** or **going to** when we are *guessing* (*or predicting*) about the future? __________
So, do we use **will** or **going to** when we can ***see now*** that something is ***certain*** to happen in the future? __________

## Form

For the form of **going to** and **will** see Unit 39



**Answers and Explanations ➤page 166➔**

# Unit 40: Practice

**1. Look at these pictures from the film *'The Adventurer'*.** Complete the sentences about what you *can see* **is going to** happen and what probably **will** happen.

(a) the train/come
The train is going to come
the hero/rescue her
The hero will rescue her

(b) they/fight
______________________
one of them die
______________________

(c) they/fall in love
______________________
they get married
______________________

(d) he/fall
______________________
he/die
______________________

(e) he/ask her to marry him
______________________
she/say 'Yes'
______________________

(f) he/give her flowers
______________________
she/be happy
______________________

**2. Make *questions* from the sentences in exercise 1**

(a) Is the train going to come?
Will the hero rescue her?

(b) ______________________?
______________________?

(c) ______________________?
______________________?

(d) ______________________?
______________________?

(e) ______________________?
______________________?

(f) ______________________?
______________________?

**3.** The Director of the film is explaining to the actors what's going to happen in a scene. **Complete the dialogue using *'going to'***

Director: 'OK, in this scene the villain (kidnap) is going to kidnap the heroine and he (tie) ______________ her to the train tracks. She (scream) ______________ very loudly and, before the train comes, the hero (hear) ______________ her screaming and rescue her.'
Actor: 'they (fall in love) ______________?'
Director: 'Yes, but first the hero and villain (fight) ______________.'
Actor: 'the hero (win) ______________?'
Director: 'Of course!'

**4. What do you *think* will happen at the end of the film? Make sentences using *'will'***

(a) The hero (kill) the villain. The hero will kill the villain
(b) The villain (apologise) and the hero (not kill) him. ______________________
(c) The heroine (be) very happy. ______________________
(d) The hero and heroine (get married). ______________________
(e) They (live) happily ever after. ______________________
(f) They (have) two children. ______________________

**5. Practise with a friend.**
Look at page 133. Talk together about the picture. Make sentences about what you **can see *is* going to happen** and what you **think *will* happen.**

# Unit 41: Present perfect I: experience *Have* you ever *been* to China?

Talking about a **non-definite** time in the past

## Meaning

Jane is an English Teacher. She **has been** to lots of different countries.
Look at her photos. Where **has** she **been**? She's **been** to:

**Budapest**

**Prague**

**Paris**

**Berlin**

**Riga**

Do you know **when** she went to these places? ***Yes/No*** What **tense** is 'She's been'? ______________

'**Been**' is the past participle * of the verb '______________'

*The past participle is the third part of the verb- there is a list of irregular past participles in Appendix 1

Interviewer: 'Jane, **have** you ever **been** to Paris?'
Jane: 'Yes, I **have**. Actually, **I've been** there five or six times. I first went there in 1985 and fell in love with it!'
Interviewer: 'What other cities **have** you **visited**?'
Jane: 'Well, I'**ve been** to most of the big cities in Europe, but I'**ve** never **been** to Moscow. I went to St Petersburg last year though.'
Interviewer: 'Did you visit the Winter Palace when you were in St Petersburg?'
Jane: 'Yes, of course.'
Interviewer: '**Have** you **been** to Seoul?'
Jane: 'No, I **haven't**. I **haven't been** to South East Asia. Maybe next year!'

'**I've been** there five or six times.' – Do you know **when**? ***Yes/No***
What **tense** does she use? ***Present Perfect*** or ***Simple Past***? ______________
'I first went there in 1985' – Do you know **when**? ***Yes/No***
What **tense** does she use? ***Present Perfect*** or ***Simple Past***? ______________
'Did you visit the Winter Palace when you were in St Petersburg?'
Is the interviewer talking about **a definite time** in the past? ***Yes/No***
'**Have** you **been** to Seoul?'
Is the interviewer talking about **a definite time** in the past? ***Yes/No***

## Form

***Positive***
'She **has been** to lots of different countries'
'**I've been** there five or six times'
The positive form of Present Perfect is:
**Subject + has or ________ + past participle (been/visited/eaten etc)**

***Question***
'**Have** you **been** to Seoul?'
'Where **has** she **been**?'
The question form of Present Perfect is:
________ **or** ________ **+ subject +** ________

***Negative***
I **haven't been** to South East Asia
The negative form of Present Perfect is:
**subject +** ________ **or have + not +** ________

***Short answers***
Yes, I **have**.



**Answers and Explanations ➤page 167➤**

# Unit 41: Practice

**1. Write the past participle of the verbs** (Look in Appendix 1 if you are not sure)

*Example:*
(a) be – been (b) break – broken

(c) buy – ______
(d) come – ______
(e) cut – ______
(f) drink – ______
(g) drive – ______
(h) eat – ______
(i) fall – ______
(j) forget – ______
(k) get – ______
(l) give – ______
(m) go – ______ or ______
(n) have – ______
(o) know – ______
(p) make – ______
(q) meet – ______
(r) read – ______
(s) see – ______
(t) speak – ______
(u) steal – ______
(v) take – ______
(w) think – ______
(x) wear – ______
(y) write – ______

**2. Look at the table to complete the *questions* and *short answers***

| | *eat snails* | *read Shakespeare* | *meet the Queen* | *drive a lorry* | *go to Australia* |
|---|---|---|---|---|---|
| *George* | ✓ | ✓ | ✗ | ✓ | ✗ |
| *Jane* | ✓ | ✗ | ✓ | ✓ | ✓ |
| *Philip and Sue* | ✗ | ✓ | ✓ | ✗ | ✗ |

*Example:*
(a) Has George ever eaten snails?
Yes, he has

(b) ______ Jane ever ______ Shakespeare?
______

(c) ______ Philip and Sue ever ______ the Queen?
______

(d) ______ George ______ a lorry?
______

(e) ______ Jane ______ to Australia?
______

(f) ______ Philip and Sue ______ snails?
______

**3. Make questions to match the answers**

*Examples:*
(a) You/eat/snails? Have you (ever) eaten snails? Yes, I have
(b) Where/you/eat them? Where did you eat them? In France

(c) Philip and Sue/meet the Queen? ______? Yes, they have
(d) When/they/meet her? ______? Last year
(e) George/read/Shakespeare? ______? Yes, he has
(f) What/he/read? ______? Hamlet
(g) Jane/drive/a lorry? ______? Yes, she has
(h) When/she/drive it? ______? A few years ago
(i) You/meet the Queen? ______? Yes, I have
(j) Where/you/meet her? ______? At Buckingham Palace

**4. Choose the correct form of the verb**

*Example:*
(a) Have you *went/been* to China? Have you been to China?

(b) I have *been/went* there last year
(c) I have never *ate/eaten* sushi
(d) *Has/have* she been to France?
(e) They *has/have* travelled all over the world

**5. Practice with a friend**
See page 133

# Unit 42: Present perfect II: time up to now *I've worked* here since November

Talking about something that **started in the past** and **continues up to now**

## Meaning

Joe is British but he lives in Venezuela.

Interviewer: 'How long have you lived in Venezuela?'
Joe: 'Well, I came here in 1991, so I've been here for six years now.'
Interviewer: 'You must like it here. Are you going to stay?'
Joe: 'Yes. I've been married to a Venezuelan since 1993. It's a great country – I love the people, the weather...'

Joe *lives* in Venezuela. Is this talking about **now,** or the **past**? __________
Joe *came* to Venezuela **in 1991**. Is this talking about **now,** or the **past**? __________
Joe *has lived* in Venezuela **for six years**. Is this talking about **now, the past,** or **now *and* the past**? __________

Joe *is married*. Is this talking about **now,** or the **past**? __________
Joe *got married* **in 1993**. Is this talking about **now,** or the **past**? __________
Joe *has been married* **since 1993**. Is this talking about **now, the past,** or **now *and* the past**? __________

**Match sentences (a) and (b) with time-line (1) or (2).**

(a) I've been married **since 1993** (1 or 2?)

(1)
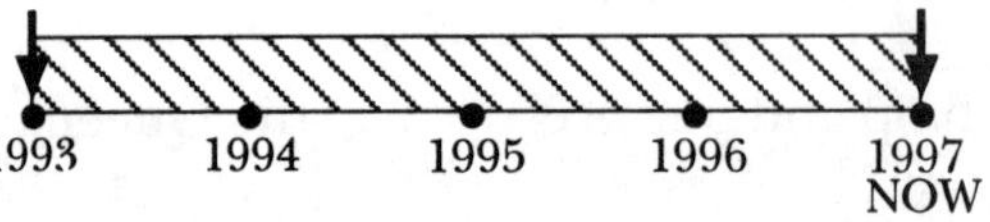


(b) I've been married **for four years** (1 or 2?)

(2)
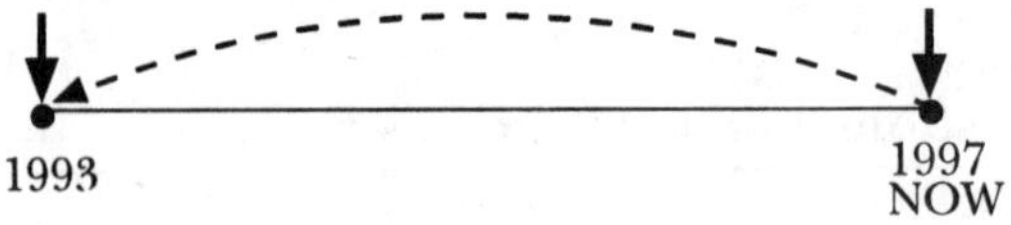


**Divide these time expressions into *since* and *for*:**

| | | | | | |
|---|---|---|---|---|---|
| last February | a long time | 1989 | two months | a week ago | I was born |
| yesterday | a couple of hours | 9.00 | three years | | |

| since | for |
|---|---|
| *Example:* last February | *Example:* a long time |
| __________ | __________ |
| __________ | __________ |
| __________ | __________ |
| __________ | |
| __________ | |

## Form

For the form of present perfect see Unit 41



Answers and Explanations ➤page 167➤

# Unit 42: Practice

**1. Complete the sentences using the underlined verb and *for* or *since***

> ***Examples:***
> (a) It is June. John is in England. He arrived in England in March
> John has been in England since March
> John has been in England for three months

(b) It is 1997. Jack and Mary know Peter. They met him in 1995.
Jack and Mary ________ Peter ________ 1995
Jack and Mary ________ Peter ________ two years

(c) It is 1997. I have a cat. I bought the cat in 1996.
I ________ a cat ________ a year
I ________ a cat ________ last year

(d) It is 1997. Sheila lives in Peru. She came to Peru in 1993.
She ________ in Peru ________ 1993
She ________ in Peru ________ four years

(e) It is November 30th. Terry is 21. His birthday was 16th November.
Terry ________ 21 ________ two weeks
Terry ________ 21 ________ 16th November

(f) It is April. We work in London. We started working in London in January.
We ________ in London ________ January
We ________ in London ________ three months

**2. Make questions about the situations in exercise 1**

> ***Example:***
> (a) How long/John/be/in England? How long has John been in England?

(b) How long/Jack and Mary/know/Peter? ________
(c) How long/you/have/cat? ________
(d) How long/Sheila/live/in Peru? ________
(e) How long/Terry/be/21? ________
(f) How long/you/work/in London? ________

**3. Make negative sentences using ....n't .......long**

> ***Example:***
> (a) He/be married He hasn't been married long

(b) We/live in England ________
(c) They/work here ________
(d) I/be a teacher ________
(e) She/have a car ________
(f) He/know her ________
(g) You/be married ________

**4. Complete the texts with the verb in the *correct form***

Jan (has been/is) a teacher for ten years. She (has become/became) a teacher when she left university in 1987. She likes travelling and (went/has been) all over the world. Last year she (went/has been) to China.

My wife and I (got married/have got married) in 1976, so we (have been married/are married) more than twenty years now. When we got married we (lived/have lived) with my wife's mother but we (have bought/bought) this house fifteen years ago and since then we (have lived/live) here.

**5. Practise with a friend**

***Ask*** and ***answer*** questions about your friend's possessions using **How long...?** and **for** and **since**

> ***Example:*** '**How long** have you had your watch?' '**Since** Christmas' — '**How long** have you had your car?' '**For** a year.'

# Unit 43: Present perfect III: present result — They'*ve lost* their keys

Talking about an action in the **past** with a result **now**

## Meaning

Johnny went skiing *last weekend* for the first time. It was terrible!

He fell off the ski-lift and cut his head.

He fell over and broke his leg.

Never again!

*Now* he is recovering at home.

**Look at the pictures and answer the questions**

**When** did he break his leg? __________
Is this talking about the **past** or the **present**? __________

Is his leg still broken **now**? __________
Is this talking about the **past** or the **present**? __________

He **has broken** his leg.
Is this talking about the **past**, the **present,** or a **past action with a present result**? __________

**When** did he cut his head? __________
Is this talking about the **past** or the **present**? __________

Is his head still cut **now**? __________
Is this talking about the **past** or the **present**? __________

'He **has cut** his head.'

Is this talking about the **past**, the **present,** or a **past action with a present result**? __________

## Form

For the form of the Present Perfect Simple see Unit 41



**Answers and Explanations ➤page 168➤**

# Unit 43: Practice

**1. Write the *past participle* of these verbs.** (Look up any new words in your dictionary)

(a) hurt hurt
(b) break ______
(c) burn ______
(d) drink ______
(e) sprain ______
(f) catch (measles) ______
(g) watch ______
(h) cut ______
(i) bump ______

**2.** Johnny is at the hospital, waiting to see the doctor. **Write sentences about what you can see *has happened* to the other people in the waiting room.** Use the verbs from exercise 1.

(a) He has bumped his head.
(b) ______ too much television!
(c) ______ poison by accident.
(d) ______ measles.
(e) ______ his ankle.
(f) ______ his arm.
(g) ______ his leg.
(h) ______ her finger.
(i) ______ her back.

**3. Choose *simple past* or *present perfect*.**

(a) I (lost/have lost) my keys – I can't get into my house! I've lost my keys
(b) I (broke/have broken) my leg, but it's OK again now. ______
(c) I (ate/have eaten) too much. I feel sick. ______
(d) He (fell/has fallen) over – help him to stand up! ______
(e) I (won/have won). Shall we play again? ______
(f) Duncan (arrived/has arrived) early but he's gone now. ______
(g) Why are you wet? (Did you go/have you been) swimming? ______

**4. Complete the sentences with *simple past* or *present perfect*.**

(a) '(you/eat) enough? Have you eaten enough?'
'Yes, thanks. It was delicious.'
(b) 'Why is the dog barking?'
'Because the post (arrive) ______'
(c) 'Oh no! It's raining and I (forgot) ______ my umbrella!'
(d) 'She (dye) ______ her hair purple but her mother didn't like it so she (dye) ______ it brown again now.'
(e) 'She (miss) ______ the train so she caught a bus instead.'
(f) 'Your shoes look new. (you/clean) them? ______'
(g) 'I (feel) ______ terrible this morning but now my headache (go) ______'

**5. Practise with a friend.**
See page 134.

# Unit 44: Present perfect IV: 'yet' and 'already'

Happen**ed**? or **going to** happen?

## I've *already* been to Germany

### Meaning

**Lisa is travelling around Central Europe.**

Interviewer: 'Why did you decide to come to Central Europe?

Lisa: 'Oh, I think it's fascinating. There are so many things to do and see.'

Interviewer: 'What have you done so far?'

Lisa: 'Well, I've **already** been to Germany. I've walked along Unter den Linden and visited Checkpoint Charlie.'

Interviewer: 'Have you been to Poland **yet**?'

Lisa: 'Yes, I've seen Krakow and been skiing in Zakopane. It was beautiful!'

Interviewer: 'What are you going to do next?'

Lisa: 'Well, I've **already** been to Czech but I have**n't** been to Slovakia or Hungary **yet**. I'm really looking forward to visiting the Thermal baths in Budapest and eating lots of goulash!

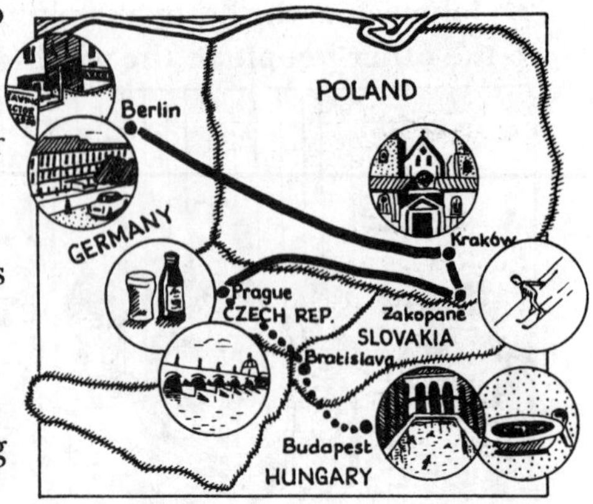


Look at the examples of *yet* and *already*.

Which means something *has happened* before now? 'Yet' or 'already?' ____________

Which means something has *not happened* before now, but it is *going to happen*? 'Yet' or 'already?' ____________

**Look at the map and the dialogue and complete the chart with the things Lisa *has done* or *wants to do*:**

| **ALREADY** DONE | NOT DONE **YET** |
|---|---|
| walked along Unter den Linden | visited Bratislava |
| | |
| | |
| | |
| | |
| | |

walked along Unter den Linden
visited Checkpoint Charlie
seen Krakow
been skiing in Zakopane
crossed the Charles Bridge in Prague
drunk Czech beer
visited Bratislava
eaten goulash
visited the Thermal Baths in Budapest.

### Form

Look at the examples and complete the form:

'I've already been to Czech' SUBJECT + _____/_____ + __________ + PAST PARTICIPLE

*We usually use* **already** *in **positive sentences.***

'Have you been to Poland yet? _____/_____ + SUBJECT + PAST PARTICIPLE + __________?

'I haven't been to Hungary yet.' __________ + HAVEN'T/HASN'T + __________ + __________.

*We usually use* **yet** *in **questions** and **negative sentences.***

**Make sentences about what Lisa *has done* or *wants to do***

| **ALREADY** DONE | NOT DONE **YET** |
|---|---|
| She's already walked along Unter den Linden | She hasn't visited Bratislava yet |
| | |
| | |
| | |
| | |
| | |



Answers and Explanations ➤page 168➤

# Unit 44: Practice

**A Weekend in Krakow**

**Saturday**
10.00 am: Tour of the Old Town
1.00 pm: Lunch at Ariel's in Kazimierz, the Jewish Quarter
3.00 pm: Free for shopping (Visit the Sukiennice Market)
6.00 pm: Chopin Concert
8.00 pm: Traditional evening meal at Staropolska Restaurant.

**Sunday**
10.00 am: Visit Wawel Castle
1.00 pm: Lunch at the Cafe Jama Michalika
2.30 pm: Trip to Wieliczka Salt Mines

**1.** Rob and Sarah are spending a weekend in Krakow, Poland. ***It's now 8.00 pm on Saturday.*** **Complete the sentences about their trip using *yet* and *already***

(a) see the Old Town — They've already seen the Old Town
(b) have lunch at Ariel's ____________
(c) go shopping ____________
(d) visit the Sukiennice ____________
(e) hear the Chopin Concert ____________
(f) eat at Staropolska Restaurant ____________
(g) visit Wawel Castle ____________
(h) have lunch at the Cafe Jama Michalika ____________
(i) go on a trip to Wieliczka Salt Mines ____________

**2. Make *questions* and write *short answers* about their trip so far using *yet*.**

(a) see the Old Town — Have they seen the Old Town yet? — Yes, they have
(b) go shopping ____________? ____________
(c) visit Wieliczka ____________? ____________
(d) see Wawel Castle ____________? ____________
(e) hear the Chopin Concert ____________? ____________
(f) have dinner at Staropolska Restaurant ____________? ____________

**3. Put the words in the *right order* to *make sentences***

(a) already/have/seen/I/the museum — I've already seen the museum
(b) you/yet/been/have/to Prague? ____________
(c) haven't/they/eaten/*pierogi*/yet ____________
(d) lots of photos/have/I/already/taken ____________
(e) spent/much money/I/haven't/yet ____________
(f) We/already/been/have/to the Castle ____________
(g) hasn't/she/the bridge/crossed yet ____________
(h) Lisa/visited/Bratislava/yet/has? ____________

**5. Practise with a friend**

A: You are on a Round the World Trip. Look at the map on page 134 and see where you've **already been** and where you **haven't been yet.** Your partner must try to find out where you are now. They can ask questions: 'Have you been to Bali yet?' and you can tell them some information 'I've already been to Bombay.' ***But don't tell them where you are now!***

B: You are on a Round the World Trip. Look at the map on page 138 and see where you've **already been** and where you **haven't been yet**. Your partner must try to find out where you are now. They can ask questions: 'Have you been to Bali yet?' and you can tell them some information 'I've already been to Buenos Aires.' ***But don't tell them where you are now!***

# Unit 45: Questions Revision 1: Asking questions by changing the word order

**is/are/was/can/were/will**

## Meaning

| | |
|---|---|
| (a) Can you play the piano? | (f) Can I borrow £1? |
| (b) What are you doing with that gun?! | (g) May I go now? |
| (c) Have you been to Paris? | (h) Where were you yesterday? |
| (d) What are you going to do next? | (i) Would you like a drink? |
| (e) Are you meeting John tomorrow? | (j) What were you doing? |

Find **two** questions asking about someone's plans or arrangements d _____ [Units 38 & 39]
Find **one** question making a request _____ [Unit 27]
Find **one** question asking for permission _____ [Unit 27]
Find **one** question asking politely if someone wants something _____ [Unit 26]
Find **one** question asking about a non-definite time in the past _____ [Unit 41]
Find **one** question asking about NOW, this moment. _____ [Unit 18]
Find **one** question asking about ability _____ [Unit 28]
Find **three** questions asking about the past _____ [Units 23, 32 & 41]

## Form

All these questions are formed in the same way. Write the questions into the table

| | [QUESTION WORD] + | AUXILIARY VERB + | SUBJECT + | MAIN VERB | |
|---|---|---|---|---|---|
| (a) | | Can | you | play | the piano? |
| (b) | What | are | you | doing | with that gun? |
| (c) | | | | | |
| (d) | | | | | |
| (e) | | | | | |
| (f) | | | | | |
| (g) | | | | | |
| (h) | | | | | |
| (i) | | | | | |
| (j) | | | | | |



Answers and Explanations ➤page 169➤

# Unit 45: Practice

**1. Make these sentences into *Yes/No questions***

(a) He's a Portuguese builder. Is he a Portuguese builder?
(b) They're dancing. ______
(c) You were late. ______
(d) Peter can dance really well. ______
(e) They're going to the seaside. ______
(f) Your computer was very expensive. ______
(g) You'd like to go. ______
(h) He's coming home by train. ______
(i) She could swim. ______
(j) You're feeling better. ______

**2. Put the words in the correct order *to make a question***

(a) you/have/here/lived/how long? How long have you lived here?
(b) pass/you/can/the salt? ______?
(c) he/happy/was? ______?
(d) you/will/do/what? ______?
(e) he/going/where/is? ______?
(f) help/you/can/I/ ______?
(g) Who/going to/you/are/marry? ______?
(h) the film/how long/was? ______?
(i) your bag/is/where? ______?
(j) going/they/where/were? ______?

**3. Complete the questions *to match the answers***

(a) Where are you from? Nigeria.
(b) _____ I use the phone? Yes, of course.
(c) Where _____ _____ _____ on holiday? We're going to Kenya.
(d) What _____ _____ like to eat? Pizza, please.
(e) How old _____ you in 1975? Three.
(f) _____ you ever _____ squid? Yes, it was delicious.
(g) Where _____ you going? To the station.
(h) _____ you finished yet? Nearly.

**4. Practise with a friend.**

How many correct questions can you make using the words in the box? [You can use other words to complete your questions]

| | | | | | | | | |
|---|---|---|---|---|---|---|---|---|
| am | What | are | How | is | How long | have | has | were |
| was | Where | you | I | Can | Could | they | she | he |

*Example:*
A: '**What are you** doing tomorrow?'
B: '**Where have you** been in Europe?'

# Unit 46: Questions Revision 2



Asking questions by using an extra auxiliary

## Meaning and Form

**Make these sentences into questions**

**A.**

1. Elephants eat leaves.
   Do elephants eat leaves?
2. He comes from Ecuador.
   Where ______________________?
3. I went to the office.
   Where ______________________?
4. She gave up smoking.
   ______________________?
5. They like strong coffee.
   ______________________?
6. I have three children.
   How many children ___________?

**B.**

1. Tigers can run very fast.
   Can tigers run very fast?
2. The Galapagos Islands are near Ecuador.
   Where ______________________?
3. I've forgotten my book.
   What ______________________?
4. She's going to give up smoking.
   ______________________?
5. They would like some tea.
   ______________________?
6. He's got three cars.
   ______________________?

What **three words** do we use to **make questions** in column **A**? ________ ________ ________

These three words are *auxiliaries*. Write the auxiliaries used in the questions in column **B**.

1. Can 2. _______ 3. _______ 4. _______ 5. _______ 6. _______

[Any problems? See Unit 45]

We use **do**, **does** and **did** to make a question when there is **no other auxiliary**, only a main verb.
Which one do we use to talk about the past? did
Which one do we use with *he, she, it* to talk about the *present*? _______
Which one do we use with *I, you, we, they* to talk about the *present*? _______

# Unit 46: Practice

**1. Read the story and *make questions* to match the answers**

Once upon a time there was a poor woman who lived in a little house in the wood with her two daughters – Snow White and Rose Red. Snow White had blond hair and Rose Red had dark hair but they were both very pretty. One cold winter's day someone knocked on the door and Rose Red answered it. There was a big brown Bear outside but he said he was hungry so they let him come in. They gave him some food and the Bear fell asleep by the fire. He came back every day through the winter.

The spring came and one day Snow White and Red Rose were out walking in the forest when they saw a Dwarf with a long white beard. His beard was caught in a tree. The girls tried to help him but they couldn't free him. So Snow White took out some scissors and cut off the beard. The Dwarf was not grateful. 'You stupid girl!' he said and picked up a big bag of gold that was in the tree. Then he walked off.



Answers and Explanations ➤page 169➔

The next day the girls saw the Dwarf again. He was fishing in the river but his beard was caught on the fishing-line and he couldn't free himself. They tried to help him but they couldn't free him. So Snow White took out some scissors and cut off the end of his beard. The Dwarf was free but very angry. 'You stupid girl! Look at my beard!' he said, and picked up a bag of jewels that was at the end of his fishing line. Then he walked off.

A few days later they saw the Dwarf again. This time he was counting a big pile of jewels and gold. 'What are you looking at?!' he shouted. Suddenly the Bear jumped out from behind a tree. 'Are you stealing my treasure?!' he shouted at the Dwarf. 'Oh! No, sir.' said the Dwarf. 'Don't eat me! Eat these nice young girls! 'But the Bear hit the Dwarf and killed him. Then the Bear turned into a Prince. He explained that the Dwarf had turned him into a bear and stolen his treasure. Snow White married the Prince and Rose Red married his brother. They all lived happily ever after.

(a) In a little house in the wood — Where/live *where did the poor woman and her children live?*
(b) blond — What colour hair/have ____________________?
(c) On a cold winter's day — When/knock on the door ____________________?
(d) That he was hungry — What/say ____________________?
(e) some food — What/give the bear ____________________?
(f) a Dwarf — Who/see in the forest ____________________?
(g) a bag of gold — What/find in the tree ____________________?

**2. Make the sentences about the story into questions**

(a) Snow White *took out* some scissors. — What *did Snow White take out?*
(b) She *cut off* the end of his beard. — What ____________________?
(c) He *picked up* a bag of gold. — What ____________________?
(d) The next day they *saw* him again. — When ____________________?
(e) 'You stupid girl!' he *said*. — What ____________________?
(f) He *explained* that the Dwarf had turned him into a bear. — What ____________________?
(g) Rose Red *married* the Prince's brother. — Who ____________________?

**3. Write 'Yes/No' questions about these sentences**

(a) The bear *killed* the Dwarf. — *Did the Bear kill the Dwarf?*
(b) The Bear *hit* the Dwarf. — ____________________?
(c) They *tried* to help him. — ____________________?
(d) The Bear *fell asleep* by the fire. — ____________________?
(e) He *came back* every day. — ____________________?
(f) He *walked off*. — ____________________?
(g) The Dwarf *stole* the treasure. — ____________________?

**4. Put these questions into the present tense.**

(a) Did Snow White have some scissors? — *Does Snow White have some scissors?*
(b) Where did the family live? — ____________________?
(c) Did the Bear eat people? — ____________________?
(d) Did the Dwarf steal the Prince's gold? — ____________________?
(e) Did the Dwarf like fishing? — ____________________?
(f) Did Snow White and Rose Red love their husbands? — ____________________?

# Test-yourself exercises

Identifying areas for study *or* revision

***Note: for answers and study/revision guide, see Appendix 3 (page 139)***

## Part one: (Units 1–4) Talking about people, places and objects

**Answers ➤page 139➤**

**1. Put the words in the *right order* to make QUESTIONS**

> *Example:*
> teacher is a he Is he a teacher?

(a) this is what ________________
(b) expensive are these ________________
(c) Post Office is the this ________________
(d) we are late ________________
(e) sister that is your ________________
(f) they German are ________________
(g) shoes these her are ________________

**2. Complete the conversation.**

> *Example:*
> Tim: Hello. What's your name?
> Susan: Susan.

Tim: **(a)** _____ you John's sister?
Susan: Yes, that's right.
Tim: Is **(b)** _____ your party?
Susan: No, it **(c)** _____. It's Tom's.
Tim: Is **(d)** _____ your boyfriend over there?
Susan: Yes, it **(e)** _____ and he's very jealous!
Tim: Oh.

**3. Make these sentences *plural*.**

> *Example:*
> This is a woman. These are women

(a) That child is very intelligent. ________________
(b) Is this your bag? ________________
(c) This is an English dictionary. ________________
(d) Is this a cheese sandwich? ________________
(e) The bus is red. ________________
(f) This is your key. ________________

**4. There are *mistakes* in some of the sentences below. Find them and correct them.**

> *Example:*
> Is these your children? Are these your children?

(a) What's your job? ________________
(b) I like childs ________________
(c) I are an artist ________________
(d) Are that your sisters? ________________
(e) No, he isn't. ________________
(f) Those are factories. ________________
(g) We aren't very happy? ________________
(h) That's very interesting. ________________
(i) He's is my boyfriend. ________________
(j) These are good photographs ________________
(k) These photographs are good ________________
(l) Is your this husband? ________________

**5. Choose the *right word* to complete the sentences.**

> *Example:*
> Italy *is/are* a very beautiful country is

(a) We *are/is* French. ________________
(b) *This/these* are my parents. ________________
(c) What *am/is* your name? ________________
(d) The people *is/are* happy. ________________
(e) Yes, it *isn't/is* ________________
(f) The men *is/are* in the pub. ________________
(g) Are you a student? No, *I/I'm* not. ________________
(h) What's *that/those*? ________________

## Part two: (Units 5–7) Talking about routines and habits

Answers ➤page 139➔

**1. Complete the following sentences using the correct form of the verb in brackets ( ).**

(a) Many tourists go to Spain (go)
(b) The Japanese ________ very good cars (make)
(c) I ________ in Devon (live)
(d) Yuko ________ to go to England (want)
(e) In the winter he ________ skiing (go)
(f) Suzanne and Jo ________ breakfast at 8am (have)
(g) Renata ________ work at 6pm (finish)
(h) She ________ French in the evening (study)
(i) Sarah ________ at 6am every day (get up)

**2. Make these sentences *negative***

(a) Alessandra comes from Lisbon . Alessandra doesn't come from Lisbon
(b) Tony and Vicky live in Italy. ________________
(c) We get up early on Sundays. ________________
(d) Jorge studies medicine at University. ________________
(e) I stay late at the office in the evenings. ________________
(f) Helen likes going shopping. ________________

**3. Make *questions* to match the answers**

(a) 'When/the train to London/leave?' When does the train to London leave ?
'At 8.30.'
(b) 'How much/a ticket/cost?' ________________ ?
'£3.75.'
(c) 'You/like/living in London?' ________________ ?
'Yes, I do.'
(d) 'She/work/for Toyota?' ________________ ?
'No, she doesn't.'
(e) 'Where/Kate and Ian/study?' ________________ ?
'At the University of London.'
(f) 'When/the plane/arrive in New York?' ________________ ?
'At 9.30am.'

**4. Rewrite these sentences using adverbs of frequency (always/often/sometimes/rarely/never)**

(a) I go swimming every morning.
I always go swimming
(b) Once or twice a week Sarah gets up early.
Sarah ________________
(c) Sheila can't drive and doesn't have a car.
Sheila ________________
(d) They are very happy all the time!
They ________________
(e) Emma smokes once or twice a year.
Emma ________________
(f) I go running four or five times a week.
I ________________

**5. Put the words in the *right order* to make sentences**

(a) often/Ann and Tony/on holiday/go Ann and Tony often go on holiday
(b) never/Jo/wine/drinks ________________
(c) to watch/Nick/sometimes/goes/a football match ________________
(d) often/swimming/go/I ________________
(e) to the disco/rarely/goes/Debbie ________________
(f) hungry/Jim/always/is ________________

**6. Correct any mistakes you find**

(a) Do you likes bananas? X- like
(b) Jean and Brian go always to Spain on holiday.
(c) The buses never are late.
(d) When the sun shine, I go swimming in the sea.
(e) The train doesn't stop in Cambridge.
(f) What time gets up Mr Koshura?
(g) Richard finishs work at 5.30.
(h) What do Steven do at the weekend?
(i) He plaies football.
(j) Alison never go to the cinema.

## Part three: (Units 8–12) Referring to people, places and objects

**Answers ➤page 140➔**

**1. Choose the correct pronoun (eg *he/him*) or possessive adjective (eg *his*)**

(a) Do you like *he/him/his?* him
(b) No, but I like *she/her/hers.* _____
(c) *We/us/our* don't live in *we/us/our* old house now. _____
(d) Is that car *you/your/yours?* _____
(e) No, it's *she/her/hers.* _____
(f) *They/their/theirs* daughter is a doctor. _____
(g) Where does *she/her/hers* live? _____
(h) Where is *she/her/hers* house? _____
(i) Please write to *I/me/my* soon. _____
(j) That book isn't *my/mine.* _____
(k) I don't think that house is *their/theirs.* _____

**2. Rewrite the sentences *without using the names.***

(a) Mary and Jackie's flat is in central London.
Their flat is in central London
(b) What floor is Duncan's flat on?
______________________?
(c) Rachel and Rebecca are Rob's friends.
______________________
(d) Rob's flat is near Rachel and Rebecca's.
______________________
(e) Is that Julie's?
______________________?
(f) No, it's Michael's.
______________________

**3. Decide if *'s* = is, or *possession***

(a) Is that Peter'**s** car? possession
(b) John'**s** a doctor. _________
(c) John and Mary'**s** house is in London. _________
(d) My daughter'**s** interested in tennis. _________
(e) The Queen'**s** one of the richest women in the world. _________
(f) Mum and Dad'**s** wedding anniversary is in June. _________

**4. Rewrite the sentences in exercise 3 *without using the name* of the person.**

(a) Is that **Peter**'s car? Is that his car?
(b) **John**'s a doctor. _________
(c) **John and Mary**'s house is in London. _________
(d) **My daughter**'s interested in tennis. _________
(e) **The Queen**'s one of the richest women in the world. _________
(f) **Mum and Dad**'s wedding anniversary is in June. _________

**5. Complete the sentences with *a*, *the* or *nothing***

My parents live in **(a)** ___a___ small house. **(b)** _______ house has only one garage but they have two cars, **(c)** _______ Ford and **(d)** _______ Volkswagen. **(e)** _______ Ford is quite new and **(f)** _______ Volkswagen is older. So they keep **(g)** _______ Ford in **(h)** _______ garage.

My brother is **(i)** _______ businessman. He works in **(j)** _______ London, but he lives in **(k)** _______ Henley, near **(l)** _______ River Thames.

His wife is **(m)** _______ teacher in **(n)** _______ school in **(o)** _______ Henley. They have **(p)** _______ eight year old son, Marcus.

**6. Correct the mistakes you find in these sentences**

(a) Johnny wants to be doctor when he grows up.
Johnny wants to be a doctor......

(b) Oh no, it's raining. Can you lend me a umbrella?
_______________

(c) He often gives she flowers.
_______________

(d) Is that hers house?
_______________

(e) Can you give me your address?
_______________

(f) A pet is an animal who lives in your house.
_______________

(g) River Nile is the longest in the world.
_______________

(h) I don't want to speak to him.
_______________

(i) What's the answer to question 7?
_______________

(j) He travels all over world.
_______________

(k) The Prime Minister is the person which governs England. _______________

(l) I'd love to meet a Queen of England.
_______________

(m)I make breakfast for our children.
_______________

(n) That's mine car, over there.
_______________

**7. Choose *who* or *which***

(a) A clerk is a person __who__ works in a bank or an office.
(b) I like food _______ tastes good.
(c) A wife is a woman _______ is married.
(d) That's the man _______ works in my office.
(e) She's the woman _______ lives next door.
(f) A tram is a type of bus _______ uses electricity.
(g) A fountain pen is a pen _______ uses liquid ink.
(h) Beaujolais is a wine _______ comes from France.
(i) _______ is your favourite book?

## Part four: (Units 13–17) Amounts

**Answers ➤page 141➤**

**1. Complete the dialogues using these words:** ***too/enough/much/many/some/any/have/has/got***

Richard: 'Which hotel do you think we should stay in – the Grand or the Seafront?'
Judy: '(a) _____ the Grand got a swimming-pool?'
Richard: 'No, but it's (b) _____ a sauna.'
Judy: 'How (c) _____ does it cost?'
Richard: '£52 a night. I think that's (d) _____ expensive! The Seafront is cheaper.'

Shopkeeper: 'Can I help you?'
Customer: 'I'd like (e) _____ apples please.'
Shopkeeper: 'How (f) _____ would you like?'
Customer: 'Four please.'

Jane: '(g) _____ you got (h) _____ money?
Dick: 'Yes...'
Jane: 'Can I borrow (i) _____ please?'
Dick: 'How (j) _____ do you want?'
Jane: '£15?'
Dick: 'Sorry, I haven't got (k) _____'

Theresa: 'How (l) _____ children have you (m) _____?
Sheila: 'Four – two boys and two girls. What about you?'
Theresa: 'I haven't got (n) _____'

John: 'What's your town like?'
David: 'Well, I think it's (o) _____ small. There isn't much to do.'
John: 'Are there (p) _____ cinemas or theatres?'
David: 'No, there are (q) _____ pubs though.'

**2. Choose *is* or *are*.**

(a) How many strawberries _____ there?
(b) There _____n't enough eggs.
(c) There _____ some coffee in the jar.
(d) Rice _____ quite cheap.
(e) Tomatoes _____ very good for you.
(f) Bread _____ delicious.
(g) How much flour _____ there?
(h) There _____ six eggs in this cake.
(i) _____ there any sugar?

**3. Complete the dialogues with *too/much/many/enough***

Dad: 'How are you getting on at school, Jim?'
Jim: 'Ok, but there's (a) ______ ______ homework.'
Dad: 'How (b) ______ homework do you get?'
Jim: 'About an hour a night.'
Dad: 'That isn't (c) ______! You should do at least two hours! I'm going to speak to your teacher.....'

Sarah: 'Do you like your new job, Jane?'
Jane: 'It's OK, but the hours are (d) ______ long – I work from 8.00–6.30.'
Sarah: 'How (e) ______ do you get paid?'
Jane: 'Not (f) ______!'

Julie: 'Oh no! I'm making a cake and I haven't got (g) ______ eggs!'
Mark: 'How (h) ______ do you need?'
Julie: 'Four and I've only got two.'

**4. Choose the correct *word* to complete the text**

Julian lives in a big house near the sea. He (a) (*have/has*) got a swimming-pool. He (b) (*have/has*) got (c) (*many/a lot of*) money but he (d) (*hasn't/haven't*) got (e) (*many/much*) friends.

Peter and June live in a flat. The flat (f) (*haven't/hasn't*) got (g) (*some/any*) central heating and it's very cold in winter. They (h) (*haven't/hasn't*) got (i) (*much/many*) money but they still enjoy life.

## Part five: (Units 18–19) Talking about now

**Answers ➤page 141➤**

**1. Write sentences describing what *is happening* in the picture**

***Example:***
(a) The sun/shine — *The sun is shining*

(b) Grandma/sit on the sofa ____________
(c) The dog and cat/eat ____________
(d) The baby/cry ____________
(e) Grandad/lie down ____________
(f) Dad/read a book ____________
(g) The children/play ____________
(h) Grandad/sleep ____________
(i) Mum/write a letter ____________

**2. Make *questions* for the following *answers***

| |
|---|
| ***Example:*** <br> Who/cry? <br> Who's crying ? The baby. |

(b) Who/read a book?
__________? Dad

(c) What/Dad/read?
__________? A book

(d) Who/sit on the sofa?
__________? Grandma

(e) The children/play?
__________? Yes, they are

(f) What/Mum/write?
__________? A letter

(g) Dad/read a newspaper?
__________? No, he isn't

(h) Grandad/sleep?
__________? Yes, he is

**3. Write *short answers* to these questions**

| |
|---|
| ***Example:*** <br> (a) Is the baby crying? Yes, it is |

(b) Is Grandma writing a letter? __________
(c) Is the sun shining? __________
(d) Are the children lying down? __________
(e) Is Dad sleeping? __________
(f) Are the cat and dog eating? __________

**4. Make questions with the *present simple* or *present continuous* to match the answers.**

| |
|---|
| ***Example:*** <br> (a) What/languages/you/speak <br> What languages do you speak? German, Japanese and Italian |

(b) What/the children/do?
__________? They're in the garden, I think.

(c) What/Nick/do?
__________? He's a nurse.

(d) How many CD's/you/have?
__________? About two hundred.

(e) What/you/drink?
__________? Orange juice. It's delicious. Would you like some?

(f) What time/you/usually get up?
__________? During the week at about 7.30, but later at the weekend.

(g) What/you/listen to? The new Oasis album. If you don't like it, we can listen to something else.
__________?

**5. Choose *present simple* or *present continuous* to complete the sentences.**

| |
|---|
| ***Example:*** <br> (a) 'It's so hot this summer that all the plants in the garden *die/are dying* are dying |

(b) 'Peter *runs/is running* in the park every day.'
(c) 'I can't answer the door, I *talk/I'm talking* on the phone!'
(d) 'Sshh! Quiet! The baby *sleeps/is sleeping*.'
(e) 'Where *do you go/are you going* this afternoon?' 'Shopping. Do you want anything?'
(f) 'Where's Grandma?' 'She *sits/is sitting* on the sofa.'
(g) 'What *do you eat/are you eating*?' 'Pizza. Do you want some?'
(h) 'What *is Mike doing?/does Mike do!*' 'He's a teacher.'

**6. Correct any *spelling* mistakes you find.**

*Example:*
(a) Sarah's writting a letter to Jim   writing

(b) John's really tired. He's lieing down.
(c) You naughty boy! Why are you hitting your sister?
(d) The children are swiming in the sea.
(e) It's a beautiful day, the sun's shineing.
(f) Who are you talking to?
(g) I'm telephonning my mother.

## Part six: (Units 20–22) Prepositions

Answers ➤page 142➤

**1. Look at the pictures and decide if the statements are *true* or *false*. If they are *false* – correct the statement.**

(a) The dog is on the table
False - the dog is under the table

(b) The chair is opposite the TV ____________

(c) The cup is next to the oranges ____________

(d) The CD is under the book ____________

(e) The bus is behind the chair ____________

(f) The post office is next to the bank ____________

(g) The clock is in front of the picture ____________

(h) The dog is opposite the chair ____________

(i) The apples are in the box ____________

**2. Look at the maps and complete the directions using a *preposition of movement: (across, round, into, under, over, through, down, along, past, up)***

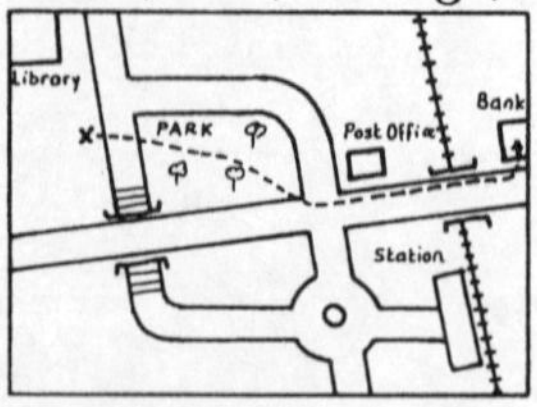


Go (a) across the road, (b) ________ the park, (c) ________ the Post Office, (d) ________ the railway bridge and (e) ________ the building on your left.

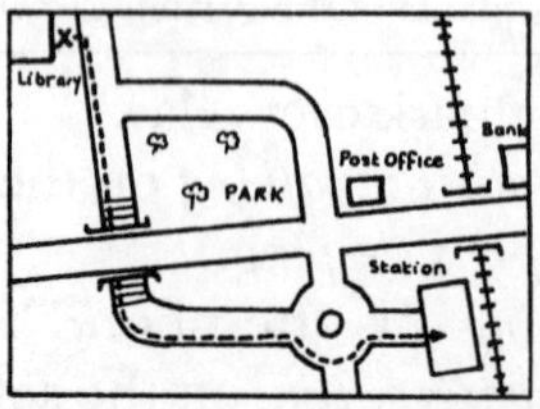


Go (f) ________ the road, (g) ________ the steps, (h) ________ the subway, (i) ________ the steps, (j) ________ the roundabout and (k) ________ the railway station.

**3. Choose the *correct word* to complete the dialogue**

A: How do I get (a) (from/*in*) the railway station (b) (*into/to*) the library?
B: The library? It's quite a long way. Go (c) (*along/past*) the road, (d) (*under/round*) the roundabout, (e) (*over/under*) the subway, (f) (*past/up*) the park and it's the building on your left.
A: Is there a bus?
B: Yes, you could get (g) (*on/down*) a number 12 bus and get (h) (*in/off*) opposite the park.

**4. Complete the following sentences with *in/at/on* or *nothing***

(a) Andy's birthday is on the 27th September.
(b) The train leaves _____ 10.30pm.
(c) Louise is going to Spain _____ next week.
(d) England won the World Cup _____ 1966.
(e) John and Alison went to the cinema _____ last night.
(f) Steve's cleaning his car _____ the moment.
(g) Are you having a party _____ your birthday?
(h) The Beatles were very popular _____ the 1960s.

**5. Correct the mistakes in *some* of these sentences**

(a) At the future, there will be more computers.
X in the future
(b) I usually get home from work 6.00.
(c) All the shops are closed on Christmas Day.
(d) Sue's going to visit her grandmother in the weekend.
(e) Maria Jose is coming to England in next month.
(f) Life was very different in the 18th Century.
(g) It's very cold in night now.
(h) On the past not many people had telephones.

**6. 'The' or 'nothing'? Write 'the' if *necessary* in these sentences**

(a) Sarah always goes running in the morning.
(b) On _____ Valentine's Day, Sheila got four cards!
(c) At _____ midnight it started raining.
(d) I'm studying English at _____ moment.
(e) On _____ Saturdays I stay in bed late.

## Part seven: (Units 23–25) Talking about the past I

Answers ➤page 143➤

**1. Choose *was* or *were***

> ***Example:***
> (a) She was/were an only child   She was an only child

(b) I rang Justin and Sue but they *was/were* away on holiday.
(c) The bank *was/were* in the main square.
(d) *Was/Were* you at home last night?
(e) No, I *was/were* out.
(f) We *was/were* really excited about going on holiday.

**2. Complete the sentences using the past simple tense**

| |
|---|
| ***Example:*** |
| (a) I <u>was</u> (be) happy as a child |

(b) There ________ (be) any cars when Grandfather ________ (be) a child.
(c) Alexander Bell ________ (invent) the telephone.
(d) Patricia ________ (go) to Spain last year.
(e) She ________ (swim) across the English Channel!
(f) The English ________ (not win) the Battle of Hastings in 1066.
(g) Queen Victoria ________ (have) nine children.
(h) 'I ________ (think) the film was great.' 'Really? I ________ (not like) it much.'
(i) I ________ (lose) my wallet yesterday.
(j) Sophie ________ (not go) to the party because she ________ (be) ill.
(k) They ________ (sing) the National Anthem when the Queen ________ (arrive).

**3. Make these sentences *negative***

| |
|---|
| ***Example:*** |
| (a) The play was very good — <u>The play wasn't very good</u> |

(b) Ian passed all his exams.
________________________

(c) Leeds United won the football match.
________________________

(d) I knew her address.
________________________

(e) The train stopped in Frankfurt.
________________________

(f) Cars were expensive in the 1960s.
________________________

(g) After school, Laura went to university.
________________________

(h) He brought her flowers.
________________________

(i) She was very friendly.
________________________

(j) We spoke Greek all evening.
________________________

(k) I gave up smoking.
________________________

**4. Make *questions* from the following *answers***

| |
|---|
| ***Example:*** |
| (a) John Logie Baird invented the television. — What <u>did John Logie Baird invent</u>? |

(b) Claire and Nick went to Madeira on holiday. — Where ________________?
(c) Chopin and Marie Curie were Polish. — What nationality ________________?
(d) Prince Charles married Diana Spencer in 1981. — Who ______ Prince Charles ________?
(e) He bought the car because he likes the colour. — Why ________________?
(f) Rio de Janeiro was the capital of Brasil in the 1950s. — When ________________?
(g) Alexander Kwasniewski became president of Poland in 1995. — When ________________?
(h) Queen Victoria died in 1901. — When ________________?
(i) He was in Cairo in June. — When ________________?

**5. Correct the mistakes you find.**

| |
|---|
| ***Example:*** |
| (a) Nick not watched the football match on tv last night — <u>Nick didn't watch the football match on tv last night</u> |

(b) When died King Henry VIII?
(c) My parents weren't very rich when they were young.
(d) Did you went to the party last night?
(e) 'Did you enjoy the film?' 'Yes, it were great.'
(f) I finished reading that book last night.
(g) Last year on holiday the weather didn't be good.
(h) I didn't gave her a present for her birthday.
(i) Ate you toast for breakfast?

**6. Correct any *spelling* mistakes you find.**

> *Example:*
> (a) I marryed him last year. married

(b) I payed a lot of money for that!
(c) He finally stopped smoking.
(d) John carried Amanda's bags.
(e) We traveled all over Europe.
(f) 'I'm tired' said Maria'.
(g) Jonny and Duncan plaied football yesterday.

## Part eight: (Units 26–31) Adding meaning

**Answers ➤page 144➤**

**1.** Chisako is a Japanese student staying with an English family. **Complete the conversations with her English host, Mrs Jenkins.**
**Use: *would/can/may/have to/should***

Mrs Jenkins: 'Hello, dear. Did you have a good day at the college?'
Chisako: 'Yes, thankyou.'
Mrs Jenkins: '(a) Would you like a cup of tea?'
Chisako: 'Yes, please. (b) _________ I have a sandwich too?'
Mrs Jenkins: 'Well, we're going to have dinner in half an hour, so you (c) _________n't eat too much now. (d) _________ you like a biscuit?'
Chisako: 'OK. Thankyou. I (e) _________ do some homework before dinner so (f) _________ I take the tea up to my room?'
Mrs Jenkins: 'Yes – careful you don't spill it!'

*Later...*
Mrs Jenkins: '(g) _________ you pass the potatoes, please?'
Chisako: 'Here you are (h) _________ you like some carrots too?'
Mrs Jenkins: 'Thankyou. You (i) _________ eat more vegetables, dear – they're good for you.'
Chisako: 'Yes, I know......I (j) _________ like to go out tonight (k) _________ I have a key?'
Mrs Jenkins: 'OK. Where are you going? You (l) _________n't stay out late, it isn't safe.'
Chisako: 'To the cinema. My friend will bring me home so I don't (m) _________ walk in the dark, don't worry.'

**2. Complete the sentences with *may/might/have to/can/could/can't/would***

(a) 'Where would you like to sit? Near the window?'
(b) '_______ you sing?' 'I like singing – but I'm terrible!'
(c) 'Where are you going this weekend?' 'I'm not sure yet. I _______ go to Wales.'
(d) The only problem with my new job is that now I _______ get up really early.
(e) I was a very intelligent child. I _______ read before I went to school.
(f) _______ I read that magazine when you've finished with it?
(g) I want a secretary who _______ type properly!
(h) Sorry, I _______ go home now. It's getting very late.
(i) _______ you like to go out this weekend?
(j) _______ you lend me some money?
(k) I think she _______ like him but it's difficult to know.
(l) '_______ you drive when you were a teenager?' 'No, I learnt when I was 24.'
(m) In England you _______ wear a seatbelt in the backseat of a car or the police will make you pay a fine.
(n) She _______ speak three languages now – Portuguese, French and Polish.
(o) I _______ read that notice – the letters are too small!
(p) _______ I use your phone, please?
(q) What _______ you like for dinner?

**3. Complete the horoscopes.**
**Use: *should or might***

*Sagittarius*
Work: You (a) should be very careful. Someone (b) _______ want your job!
Money: You (c) _______ need to borrow some money if you spend too much this month.
Love: You (d) _______ think more about your partner's feelings.

*Capricorn*
Work: You (e) _______ be working too hard. If you are, take more time off.
Money: You (f) _______n't spend so much! You will be very poor at the end of the month.
Love: You (g) _______ meet the love of your life.

*Aquarius*
Work: You (h) _______ get a new job this month – if you're lucky.
Money: You (i) _______ try to save your money. Next month you (j) _______ need it!
Love: You (k) _______ stop thinking about someone you can't have.

**4. Choose the correct word**
(a) You *should/might* eat more – you're too thin. should
(b) He's really musical. He *can/may* play four or five instruments.
(c) *Would/Can* you like to sit down?
(d) I *might/can* go swimming this weekend – if the weather's good.
(e) A nurse *would/has* to work very hard.
(f) *Can/would* I sit here, please?
(g) You *should/can* stop smoking – it's very bad for you.
(h) I *would/can* like to go to Mexico.
(i) You *have to/should* drive on the left in Britain.
(j) I think he *should/would* work harder. He's really lazy.

**5. Correct the mistakes you find**
(a) Waiter! I'd likes the menu please. I'd like
(b) Do you can swim?
(c) He haves to work very late.
(d) They should exercise more.
(e) It might rains tomorrow.
(f) May I going out tonight?
(g) English is very difficult. I have work so hard!
(h) What woulds he like?

## Part nine: (Units 32–33) Talking about the past II

**Answers ➤page 144➤**

**1. Complete the following sentences using the *past continuous tense***
(a) I (play) was playing chess.
(b) John and Barbara (walk) __________ in the park.
(c) __________ he __________ (visit) his parents?
(d) You (eat) __________ breakfast.
(e) Alan (not swim) __________
(f) __________ they __________ (listen) to the radio?'
(g) Kate (not watch) __________ the television.
(h) We (make) __________ dinner.
(i) The sun (not shine) __________
(j) __________ it __________ (rain)?
(k) Richard (drive) __________ to town.

**2. Look at the time lines and make sentences using *when***

(a) 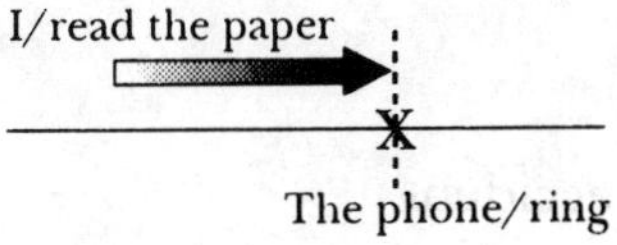


I was reading the paper when the phone rang

(b) 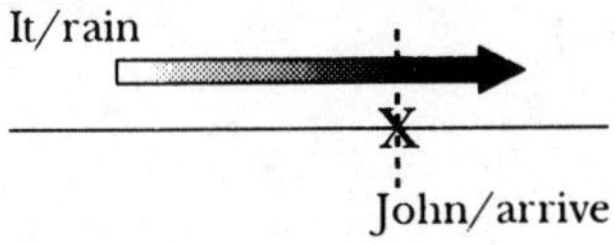


(c) 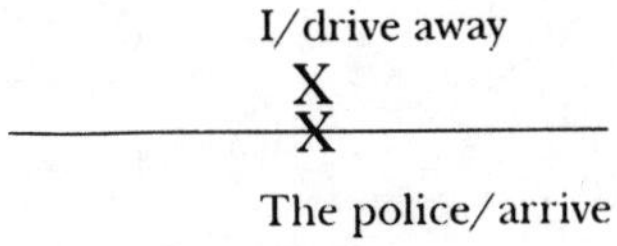


(d) 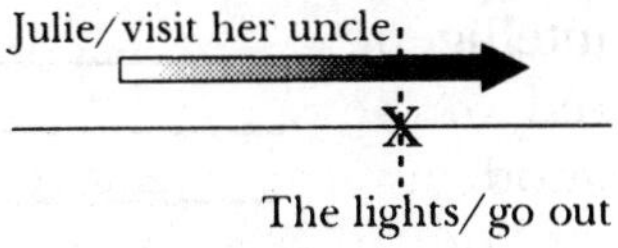


(e) 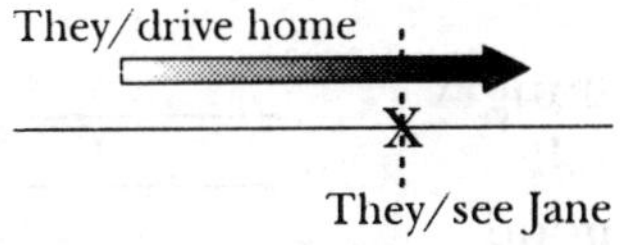


(f) 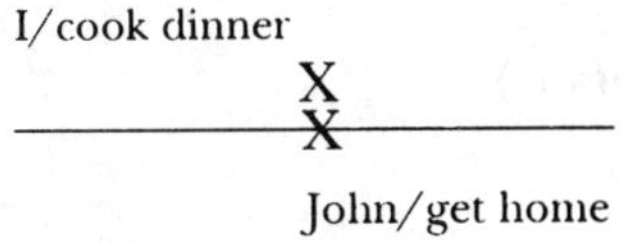


(g) 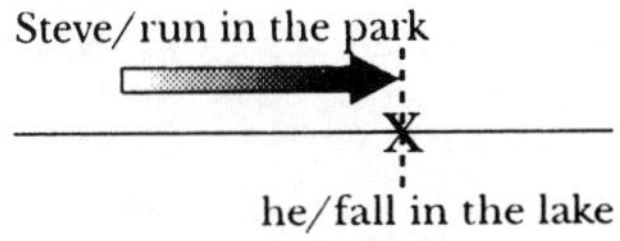


(h) 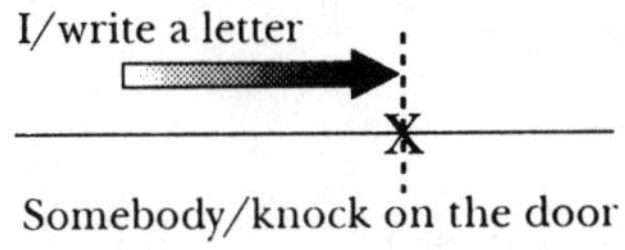


(i) 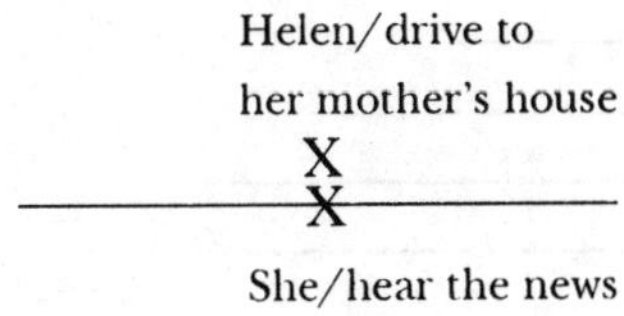


(j) 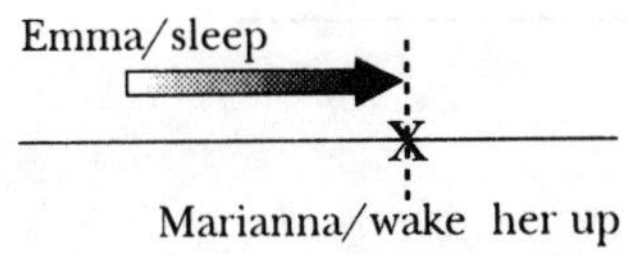

3. **Choose *past simple* or *past continuous* to complete the sentences**
(a) While Claire was cooking dinner, I (*was laying/laid*) the table. laid
(b) As they were dancing, a strange man (*was coming/came*) to talk to them.
(c) Nick (*slept/was sleeping*) when the storm started.
(d) Sarah was reading when the doorbell (*was ringing/rang*)
(e) Alison and Alex (*walked/were walking*) along the street when they saw an accident.
(f) I (*bought/was buying*) a hamburger while the children were swimming.
(g) Eric (*fell asleep/was falling asleep*) during the film but he woke up at the end.
(h) The sun (*shone/was shining*) when the plane landed.
(i) Jill (*waited/was waiting*) for a train when the rain started.

## Part ten: (Units 34–37) Describing Answers ➤page 145➤

1. **Write the *comparative form* of these adjectives**

| | | | | | |
|---|---|---|---|---|---|
| (a) big | bigger | (d) rich | ______ | (g) intelligent | ______ |
| (b) small | ______ | (e) fat | ______ | (h) red | ______ |
| (c) exciting | ______ | (f) shy | ______ | (i) good | ______ |

2. **Write the *superlative form* of these adjectives**

| | | | | | |
|---|---|---|---|---|---|
| (a) quick | the quickest | (d) early | ______ | (g) hungry | ______ |
| (b) far | ______ | (e) hot | ______ | (h) tall | ______ |
| (c) poor | ______ | (f) lazy | ______ | (i) good | ______ |

3. ***Compare* the two things in each question using the adjectives in brackets ( )**
(a) The Empire State Building/The Eiffel Tower (*high*)
The Empire State Building is higher than the Eiffel Tower
(b) The Nile/The Thames (*long*) ______
(c) Paris/Warsaw (*expensive*) ______
(d) Mandarin Chinese/French (*difficult*) ______
(e) Tokyo/London (*big*) ______
(f) A car/a bicycle (*fast*) ______
(g) A trumpet/a flute (*noisy*) ______
(h) An armchair/a stool (*comfortable*) ______

4. **Rewrite the sentences so they mean the *opposite*.**
(a) He's the most untidy person I know. He's the tidiest person I know
(b) That football team is the best in the world. ______
(c) It's one of the largest cities in South America. ______
(d) He's the most interesting man I've ever met. ______
(e) Who is the oldest? ______
(f) She must be the ugliest woman in the world! ______
(g) Which is the quietest room? ______
(h) I bought the cheapest ticket. ______

**5. Write the missing *adjective* or *adverb***

(a) good/ well
(b) _______/slowly
(c) bad/_______
(d) tidy/_______
(e) _______/noisily
(f) happy/_______
(g) _______/cleverly
(h) _______/quickly
(i) angry/_______

**6. Choose the correct adjective or adverb to complete the sentences**

(a) He sat down (*heavy/heavily*) heavily
(b) You cook really (*good/well*) _______
(c) He's a (*terrible/terribly*) teacher! _______
(d) The sea was very (*deep/deeply*) _______
(e) Did you have a (*great/greatly*) holiday? _______
(f) This exercise is quite (*easy/easily*) _______
(g) He drank the water (*thirsty/thirstily*) _______
(h) I feel awful – I slept really (*bad/badly*) _______
(i) He's a very (*naughty/naughtily*) child _______
(j) I looked for it very (*careful/carefully*) _______

## Part eleven: (Units 38–40) Talking about the future

**Answers ➤page 146➤**

**1. Choose *be going to* or *will* to complete the following sentences**

(a) Have you got your raincoat? It is going to rain.
(b) Next summer I ___________ visit my relatives in America. It's all arranged.
(c) 'Oh no! Those cars ___________ crash!' 'BANG!!!!'
(d) A: 'What do you want to do tonight?'
B: 'I don't know. I ___________ ring you later, Ok?'
(e) A: 'My plane gets in at 2.30am'
B: 'I ___________ meet you at the airport.'
A: 'Are you sure?'
(f) I'm so happy – I ___________ have a baby!
(g) You're quite good at maths. I expect you ___________ pass the exam.
(h) I couldn't answer *any* of the exam questions! I ___________ fail!
(i) The neighbours ___________ have a party tonight. Shall we go?
(j) She looks very upset and sad. I think she ___________ cry.
(k) The weather next week ___________ (continue) to be sunny.
(l) When I grow up I ___________ (be) a marine biologist.

**2. Correct the mistakes in *some* of these dialogues with *going to* and *will***

(a) A: 'Why are you going into town?'
B: 'I'll buy some food.'
X I'm going to buy some food
(b) A: 'Is that the phone?'
B: 'I'll get it.'
___________________
(c) A: 'Can I have some more pudding?'
B: 'You're going to put on weight.'
___________________
(d) A: 'Why are you saving all your money?'
B: 'I'll buy a car.'
___________________
(e) A: 'Have you got your suncream?'
B: 'Why? Is it going to be hot today?'
___________________
(f) A: 'The film starts at 7.00.'
B: 'OK. I'm going to pick you up at 6.30.'
___________________
(g) A: 'Will you marry me?'
B: 'I'm sorry, I'll marry Julian next month.'
___________________

**3. Choose *present simple* or *present continuous* to complete the following sentences:**
(a) The film (start) starts at 7.30.
(b) I (see) ________ the doctor tomorrow morning.
(c) What time ________ the play ________ (end)?
(d) The conference (start) ________ on May 22nd.
(e) He (meet) ________ Jake later tonight.
(f) What ________ you ________ (do) tomorrow?
(g) I need to go home now because John (ring) ________ me at 8.00.
(h) Lisa and Roger (come) ________ for dinner tomorrow night.
(i) The plane (leave) ________ at 9.00 so we need to be at the airport by 7.00.
(j) Can I borrow your new jacket? I (go) ________ for a job interview tomorrow.

## Part twelve: (Units 41–44) Connecting the past and the present

Answers ➤page 146➤

**1. Write the *past participle* of these verbs:**

| | | | | | | | |
|---|---|---|---|---|---|---|---|
| (a) think | thought | (d) wear | ________ | (g) eat | ________ | (j) have | ________ |
| (b) drink | ________ | (e) write | ________ | (h) go | ________ | (k) get | ________ |
| (c) see | ________ | (f) know | ________ | (i) break | ________ | (l) cut | ________ |

**2. Choose the correct verb *form***
(a) [*I've never been/I never went*] to Brazil. Maybe I'll go next year I've never been
(b) 'When I was six [*I've broken/I broke*] my arm in three places!
(c) 'How long [*have you lived/did you live*] in Leeds?' 'Six years. We left there last year.'
(d) '[*Have you paid/Did you pay*] the telephone bill yet?' 'Sorry, I'll do it tomorrow.'
(e) 'You're very suntanned – [*have you been/did you go*] on holiday?
(f) '[*Have you ever eaten/did you ever eat*] pierogi?' 'What's that?!'
(g) 'It's our wedding anniversary next week. [*We've been married/We were married*] for five years.'
(h) 'How are you getting on with your studying?' 'Not bad. [*I've already read/I already read*] three books.'
(i) 'When you were in Japan [*have you eaten/did you eat*] sushi?'
(j) '[*Have you had/Did you have*] your car long?' 'No, it's still almost new.'
(k) ['*Have you written/Did you write*] to Auntie Mabel yet?' 'No, not yet.'
(l) 'I didn't recognise you! [*Did you dye/have you dyed*] your hair? It's a different colour.'
(m)Oh no! Where's my purse? I think someone [*stole/has stolen*] it!

**3. Complete the sentences with the verb in the *correct tense* – present perfect or simple past**
(a) 'Where's Susan?' 'Her tooth was hurting so she has gone (go) to the Dentist.'
(b) 'There's a lot of washing up in the kitchen.....' 'I ________ already ________ (do) it.'
(c) 'You speak very good Czech. How long ________ you ________ (be) in Czech now?'
(d) 'I ________ (live) in Brazil for two years. It was wonderful.'
(e) 'I ________ never ________ (go) in a balloon – but I would love to do it one day.'
(f) 'What ________ you ________ (do) to your hair?! It looks terrible!'
(g) 'It was Margaret's birthday last week but I am so busy I ________ (not buy) her a present yet.'
(h) 'Have you ever been to the opera?' 'No, but I ________ (go) to the ballet last week.'
(i) 'Look! I ________ (clean) the car. Doesn't it look better?'
(j) 'Oh no! I forgot to write my address on that letter.' 'Sorry, I ________ already ________ (post) it.'

**4. Complete the dialogues using *present perfect* or *simple past***

Mary: 'Hi! How are you, Juliet? I (a) _______ (not see) you for months!'
Juliet: 'Fine. You look good. (b) _______ you _______ (go) on holiday?'
Mary: 'Yes, I (c) _______ (go) to the Caribbean for two weeks. It was wonderful'
Juliet: '(d) _______ you ever _______ (go) to Venezuela? I'm going there next week'
Mary: 'Really? I (e) _______ (not go) there yet but I'm planning to go next year. Where are you going to stay? (f) _______ you _______ (book) a hotel yet?'
Juliet: 'Yes, we (g) _______ already _______ (arrange) everything.'

Mother: 'Are you looking forward to going to the Safari Park, Mark? You (h) _______ never _______ (see) a lion, have you?'
Mark: 'I am looking forward to it but I (i) _______ (see) a lion in the zoo last year.'
Mother: 'Oh, but that's not the same...... Come here, you (j) _______ (not tie) your shoes up properly.'
Mark: 'Mum! I'm late. I've got to go.'
Mother: 'Wait! You (k) _______ (forget) your sandwiches!'

Mr Brown: 'Well, my wife and I (l) _______ (be married) for fifty years now and they've all been happy ones.'
Journalist: '(m) _______ you ever _______ (argue)?'
Mr Brown: 'I don't think we (n) _______ (have) an argument since yesterday.'
Journalist: 'Yesterday?!'

# Further-practice exercises

## Part one: (Units 1–4) Talking about people, places and objects

*(Units 1 & 2)*

**1. Complete these sentences with the *correct form* of the verb to be.**

*Example:*
(a) I **am** an engineer

(b) My brother _____ called Richard.
(c) _____ she Chinese?
(d) _____ we in France?
(e) They _____ both very intelligent.
(f) It _____ a lovely day.

**2. Put the words in order to make QUESTIONS, then write true answers.**

*Example:*
(a) Student/you/are/a? Are you a student? Yes, I am

(b) Teacher/your/is/English? ________________? ________________
(c) English/easy/is? ________________? ________________
(d) The Eiffel Tower/is/in France? ________________? ________________
(e) Your/friend/is/where? ________________? ________________
(f) Your/name/is/what? ________________? ________________

*This/that/these/those (Unit 3)*

**3. Use the pictures to *make sentences* using this/that/these/those and the verb to be.**

*Example:*
This is my dog.
That dog is dangerous.

_____ shoes _____ too high. __________ more comfortable.

What _____ _____ called? It's a rose.

What _____ _____?!

_____ _____ my son.

John! _____ flowers _____ dead!

Who _____ _____ girls?

_____ _____ my babies.

*Singular and plural (Unit 4)*

**4. Make these sentences singular**

*Example:*
These are my sisters This is my sister

a) Those people are English.
________________
(b) The factories are very noisy.
________________
(c) The buses are always late!
________________
(d) My keys are on the table.
________________
(e) These are my children.
________________
(f) Where are the men?
________________

**5. Write the *plural* of these words (careful with spelling!)**

(a) holiday holidays
(b) cat ________
(c) baby ________
(d) daughter ________
(e) church ________
(f) woman ________
(g) class ________
(h) girl ________
(i) house ________

## Part two: (Units 5–7) Talking about routines and habits

### *Unit 5: Present simple tense*

**1. Complete the text about what Sheila does every day.**
Use these verbs: see/get up/have (x 2)/be/arrive/like/leave/help/walk/catch/make/go/live

Sheila ________ a dentist. She ________ her work but she ________ a long way from her surgery so she usually ________ quite early. She ________ three children so she ________ them get dressed and ________ them breakfast. They ________ to school, it isn't far. Then she ________ the house at about 7.30. She ________ to work by train and then ________ a bus. She usually ________ at about 8.30, ________ a cup of coffee and ________ her first patient at 9.00.

**2. Complete the text about what Jane does every day.**
Use these verbs: go/finish/love/watch/stay/start/work

Jane ________ in a cinema. She ________ work at 3.00 in the afternoon, when the first film is on, and ________ about 11.00 at night. She ________ her job because she ________ all the new films free! But she ________ to bed very late. So, in the mornings, she ________ in bed until 10.00 or 11.00.

### *Unit 6: Present simple auxiliaries*

**3. Read about Alfredo's daily routine. Then write questions and short answers.**
Alfredo is a disc jockey. He works for a radio station in Milan. He starts work at 7.00 in the morning so he usually goes to bed quite early. He thinks his job is very interesting but he hates getting up so early. He only sees his friends at the weekends but they listen to him on the radio.

*Example:*
(a) What/Alfredo do?
What does Alfredo do? He's a disc-jockey

(b) He/work in Rome?
________? ________
(c) What time/he/start work?
________? ________
(d) He/go to bed late?
________? ________
(e) He/think his job is interesting?
________? ________
(f) He/like getting up early?
________? ________
(g) When/his friends/see Alfredo?
________? ________
(h) His friends/listen to him on the radio?
________? ________

**4. Correct these statements about Alfredo with a full sentence.**

*Example:*
(a) Alfredo works in Madrid No, he doesn't work in Madrid

(b) He starts work at 9.00
________
(c) He goes to bed late
________
(d) He hates his job
________
(e) He likes getting up early
________
(f) His friends see Alfredo every day
________

### *Unit 7: Adverbs 1: adverbs of frequency*

**5. Rewrite these sentences using the adverb in brackets ( )**

| |
|---|
| ***Example:*** |
| (a) Alfredo gets up early (always) Alfredo always gets up early |

(b) Alfredo sees his friends during the week (never) ____________________

(c) Sheila is late for work (rarely) ____________________

(d) Jane enjoys her job (usually) ____________________

(e) Sheila has a cup of coffee in the morning (always) ____________________

(f) Sheila's children are naughty (often) ____________________

(g) Alfredo is tired (usually) ____________________

(h) Jane gets up early (never) ____________________

(i) Alfredo's friends listen to him on the radio (often) ____________________

(j) Jane watches new films first (always) ____________________

## Part three: (Units 8–12) Referring to people, places and objects

### *(Units 8–10)*

**1. Complete the film review with the correct *pronoun* or *possessive adjective***

Many people know Shakespeare's play Romeo and Juliet, but this film *'William Shakespeare's Romeo and Juliet'* is something new. The Director sets the story in modern day America. Romeo meets Juliet at a party and **(a)** (*he/him/his*) falls in love with **(b)** (*she/her/hers*) immediately **(c)** (*She/her/hers*) also loves **(d)** (*he/him/his*). But there's a problem **(e)** (*he/him/his*) family hate **(f)** (*she/her/hers*) and **(g)** (*she/her/hers*) family hate his. Unfortunately **(h)** (*they/their/theirs*) love affair cannot work. Everybody is against **(i)** (*they/them/their*).....

**2. Complete the letter with the correct *pronoun* or *possessive adjective***

Dear Duncan,

Hi! How are **(a)** (*you/your/yours*)? **(b)** (*I/me/my*) am very busy at the moment. **(c)** (*We/us/our*) are moving house next week and there is a lot to do. Now we have two children **(d)** (*we/our/ours*) old house is very small and **(e)** (*we/us/our*) need more space. The new house has four bedrooms and **(f)** (*it's/its*) much nicer. The children are very excited because **(g)** (*they/them/their*) will have **(h)** (*they/their/theirs*) own bedrooms. **(i)** (*I/me/my*) hope **(j)** (*they/them/their*) bedrooms will be tidier now **(k)** (*they/them/their*) have more space.

### *(Unit 11)*

**3. Complete the text with *a* or *the* – then solve the puzzle!**

**(a)** ____ policeman is walking past **(b)** ____ house when he hears a shout. 'Michael! Don't kill me!' **(c)** ____ policeman rushes into **(d)** ____ house and he sees **(e)** ____ dead body on the floor. There are three people standing near **(f)** ____ body – **(g)** ____ doctor, **(h)** ____ lawyer and **(i)** ____ engineer. **(j)** ____ policeman arrests **(k)** ____ engineer. How does he know who **(l)** ____ murderer is? *(answer: the doctor and lawyer are **women**)*

### *(Unit 12)*

**4. Match the words and the definitions. Then write sentences using *who, which that* to define these people and things**

| | | |
|---|---|---|
| (a) Feijoada | | 1. writes plays |
| (b) A baker | is someone... | 2. people eat in England for Sunday dinner |
| (c) A watch | | 3. works on an aeroplane |
| (d) A fork | is something | 4. people eat in Brazil |
| (e) An air steward | | 5. peole use to eat with. |
| (f) A playwright | | 6. tells the time |
| (g) Yorkshire Pudding | | 7. makes bread and cakes |

(a) Feijoada is something which/that people eat in Brazil
(b) ____________________
(c) ____________________
(d) ____________________
(e) ____________________
(f) ____________________
(g) ____________________

## Part four: (Units 13–17) Amounts

*(Unit 13)*

**1. Complete the dialogue using *have/has(n't) got***

Estate Agent: 'I've got the perfect house for you, sir!'
Customer: '______ it ______ three bedrooms?'
Estate Agent: 'Well, in fact, it ______ ______ four.'
Customer: 'Is it expensive? I ______ ______ much money.'
Estate Agent: 'No, it's very reasonable. Only £53,000.'
Customer: '______ you ______ the keys? Can I go and see it?'
Estate Agent: 'Certainly. I think I ______ ______ some free time this afternoon, if you like.'

*(Unit 14)*

**2. Write *a* or *some* before these nouns**

(a) ______ milk
(b) ______ paper
(c) ______ newspaper
(d) ______ rain
(e) ______ mushrooms
(f) ______ yoghurt
(g) ______ tomato
(h) ______ bread
(i) ______ money
(j) ______ toast
(k) ______ soap
(l) ______ cup of tea
(m) ______ coffee
(n) ______ cheese
(o) ______ chocolate

*(Unit 15)*

**3. Complete the sentences with *some* or *any***

(a) Have you got ______ orange juice?
(b) There aren't ______ potatoes.
(c) I haven't got ______ money.
(d) There are ______ eggs in the fridge.
(e) I'd like to listen to ______ music.
(f) Have you got ______ cigarettes?
(g) He usually meets ______ friends at the weekend.
(h) Why doesn't he have ______ friends?
(i) Sorry, we don't have ______ milk today.

*(Unit 16)*

**4. Complete the questions with *much* or *many***

(a) How ______ does it cost?
(b) How ______ times a week do you go swimming?
(c) How ______ bedrooms has your house got?
(d) How ______ chocolate do you eat in a week?
(e) How ______ cake would you like?
(f) How ______ hours do you work?
(g) How ______ people do you know?
(h) How ______ water is there?
(i) How ______ sandwiches are there?
(j) How ______ bread is there?

*(Unit 17)*

**5. Rewrite these complaints using *too/too much/too many/not enough***

(a) I don't like this really hot weather. — The weather is ______ hot.
(b) My flat isn't very warm. — My flat is ______ warm ______
(c) I work from 8.00am – 7.00pm. — The hours are ______ long.
(d) It's very noisy in here. — There's ______ noise!
(e) I've eaten a lot of chocolate – I feel sick! — I've eaten ______ chocolate
(f) It rains all the time here! — It's ______ wet.
(g) There aren't many people at this party – it's boring! — There are ______ people
(h) I've eaten lunch but I'm still hungry! — I have ______ eaten ______

## Part five: (Units 18–19) Talking about now

*(Unit 18)*

**1.** *Example:*
(a) It/snow It's snowing

(b) The children/throw snowballs ________
(c) They/wear hats ________
(d) The/play in the snow ________
(e) The sun/shine ________
(f) Two children/carry bags ________

*(Unit 19)*

**2. Complete the sentences about the pictures with *present simple* or *present continuous***

Sean (be) is a doctor
He (work) _____ in a hospital
He (play) _____ football
He (wear) _____ shorts
At work he (wear) _____ a white coat

Jimmy (be) _____ 26
He (drive) _____ his new car
He (listen) _____ to music
He (like) _____ rock music
He (clean) _____ his car every Saturday

Roger and Lisa (be) _____ teachers
They (teach) _____ English
They (have) _____ dinner
They often (eat) _____ in restaurants
They (like) _____ good food!

Jose (be) _____ Spanish
She (live) _____ in Barcelona
She (like) _____ Barcelona because
the sun always (shine) _____
Unfortunately, today it (rain) _____

## Part six: (Units 20–22) Prepositions

*(Unit 20)*

**1.** Sheila's kitchen is very untidy! She doesn't know where her things are. **Look at the picture and answer the questions to help her find them.**

**Use the following words:** ***in, on, under, near, behind, in front of, opposite, next to***

(a) Where's the cat? It's under the newspaper
(b) Where's Sheila's book? ____________
(c) Where's the milk? ____________
(d) Where's the telephone? ____________
(e) Where are the apples? ____________
(f) Where's the dog? ____________
(g) Where are her keys? ____________
(h) Where's the cheese? ____________
(i) Where's Sheila's bag? ____________
(j) Where are the onions? ____________
(k) Where are Sheila's shoes? ____________
(l) Where's the shopping list? ____________

**2. Look at the picture of Sheila's kitchen again. Are the following statements** ***true or false?*** **If they are** ***false*** **correct the statement**

(a) The toy car is under the hi-fi.
False - the toy car is on the hi-fi
(b) The radio is near the telephone. ____________
(c) The saucepan is on the cooker. ____________
(d) The bananas are on the saucepan. ____________
(e) The shoes are in the fridge. ____________
(f) The plant is behind the book. ____________
(g) The vacuum cleaner is next to the cupboard. ____________
(h) The bread is opposite the keys. ____________

*(Unit 21)*

**3. Look at Louise' diary and complete the sentences using** ***in/at/on*** **or** ***nothing***

(a) _On_ Monday morning _at_ 9.00 Louise has got a meeting.
(b) She's got another meeting _____ 3.00 _____ Tuesday.
(c) John's birthday is _____ Wednesday and they're having dinner _____ the evening.
(d) _____ noon _____ 13th April, she's having lunch with the Directors.
(e) _____ the morning _____ Saturday she's playing tennis.
(f) _____ Easter Sunday _____ the afternnon she's visiting her grandmother.
(g) _____ next week is her parents' wedding anniversary.
(h) She isn't working _____ the weekend.
(i) On Friday she finishes her job. _____ the future she won't work so hard!

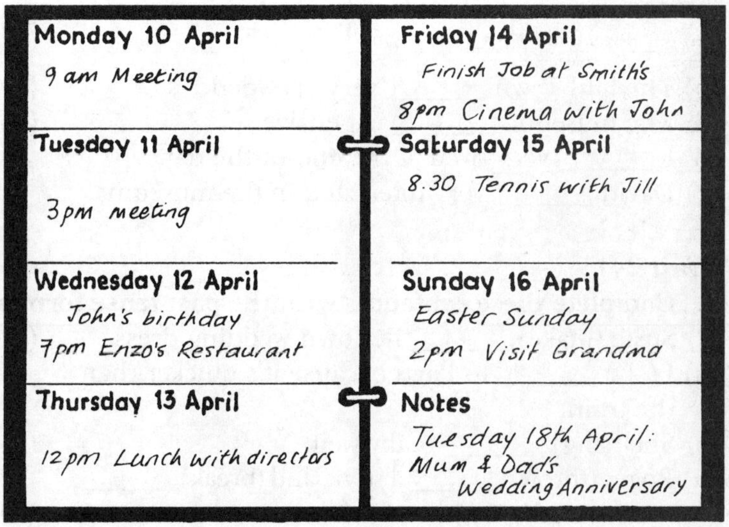
Monday 10 April
9 am Meeting
Tuesday 11 April
3pm meeting
Wednesday 12 April
John's birthday
7pm Enzo's Restaurant
Thursday 13 April
12pm Lunch with directors
Friday 14 April
Finish Job at Smith's
8pm Cinema with John
Saturday 15 April
8.30 Tennis with Jill
Sunday 16 April
Easter Sunday
2pm Visit Grandma
Notes
Tuesday 18th April:
Mum & Dad's
Wedding Anniversary

*(Unit 22)*

**4. Look at the picture and complete the directions with the following words:**
***across, round, from, to, into, under, on, over, through, down, along, past, out of, up, off***

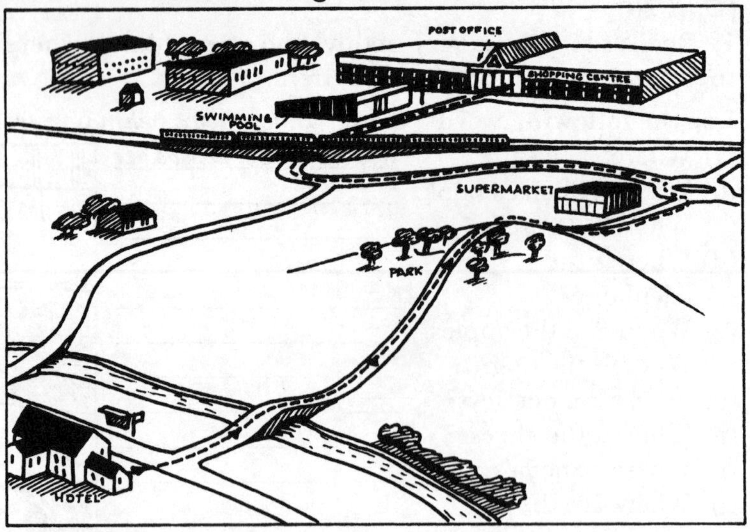


A: Excuse me, how do I get _to_ the post office ________ this hotel?
B: 'Well, go ________ of the hotel, ________ the road, ________ the bridge, ________ the hill, ________ the park, ________ the hill, ________ the supermarket, ________ the road, ________ the roundabout, ________ the railway bridge and ________ the shopping centre. The post office is on the left.
A: That sounds complicated. Is there a bus?
B: Yes, get ________ a number 29 and get ________ next to the swimming pool.

## Part seven: (Units 23–25) Talking about the past I

*(Unit 23)*

**1.** Julie has just been on holiday to Prague.
**Complete the questions her friend Lisa asks her about her holiday. Use *was/were***

*Example:*
(a) Where/the hotel? In the Old Town _Where was the hotel?_

| | | |
|---|---|---|
| (b) /it nice? | Yes, lovely. | ________ |
| (c) /the weather good? | Not bad. It rained a bit. | ________ |
| (d) /the museums good? | Yes, very interesting. | ________ |
| (e) What/the food like? | Delicious. I ate so much! | ________ |
| (f) /you on your own? | No, I went with David. | ________ |

**2. Complete these sentences using *wasn't/weren't***

*Example:*
(a) The weather _wasn't_ very good

(b) The Old Town ______ very crowded.
(c) The museums ______ expensive.
(d) I ______ very tired at the end of the day.
(e) David ______ very interested in the museums.
(f) We ______ in Prague for very long – just a week.
(g) The other guests in the hotel ______ very friendly.

*(Unit 24)*

**3. Complete these sentences with the past tense form of the *irregular* verb in brackets ( )**

(a) Susie (make) ______ her own wedding dress.
(b) I (fly) ______ to Paris because it's quicker than the train.
(c) She (sing) ______ really well.
(d) Roger (throw) ______ a stone and (break) ______ the window!
(e) I (write) ______ to her about a week ago.
(f) Last night (I go) ______ to a party and (lose) ______ my umbrella. I think someone (steal) ______ it.
(g) He (drink) ______ six cups of coffee and didn't sleep all night!
(h) I (build) ______ this house myself. It (take) ______ me six years.
(i) She (pay) ______ the bill and (leave) ______.

**4. Complete these sentences with the past tense form of the *regular* verb in brackets. *Be careful with spelling!***

(a) I really (enjoy) _______ the film.
(b) He (carry) _______ the heaviest bag.
(c) The car (stop) _______ at the traffic lights.
(d) He (study) _______ really hard to pass his exam.
(e) I (try) _______ to walk but it was too far.
(f) They (plan) _______ to go to Buenos Aires but in the end they couldn't.

***(Unit 25)***

5. In 1996 Stephen lived in Brno, in the Czech Republic. **Complete the questions about his experiences.**

(a) *Why/go/there?*
Why did you go there? — I had a job as an English Teacher
(b) *Where/teach?*
_______________? — In a small school in the centre
(c) *teach children?*
_______________? — Yes, from eight years old to fifteen
(d) *enjoy it there?*
_______________? — Yes, it's a beautiful town.
(e) *learn Czech?*
_______________? — No, it was very difficult.
(f) *make Czech friends?*
_______________? — Yes, people were very friendly.
(g) *What/do in your spare time?*
_______________? — I went walking in the countryside.

**6. Use the information above to answer these questions with *short answers***

(a) Did Stephen work in Brno? Yes, he did
(b) Did he teach in a large school? _______
(c) Did he teach children? _______
(d) Did he teach adults? _______
(e) Did he enjoy it there? _______
(f) Did he speak good Czech? _______
(g) Did he make Czech friends? _______

## Part eight: (Units 26–31) Adding meaning

***(Unit 26)***

**1. Choose *like* or *would like***

(a) '*Do you/Would you* like a drink?' 'No, thanks.' Would you
(b) '*Do you/Would you* like to sit down?'
(c) 'I think *I'd like/I like* a cup of tea – I'm thirsty'
(d) '*He'd like/he likes* listening to very loud music. I hate it!'
(e) 'It's raining. *Do you/would you* like to borrow my umbrella?'
(f) '*I don't like/wouldn't like* swimming much. It's usually too cold in England.'
(g) 'My parents *would like/like* to meet you. Shall I introduce you?'

**2. Complete the dialogues using *would like* (to + infinitive) *or like* (+ing)**

(a) A: '*Would* you *like to go* (go) to the cinema next week? There's a new thriller on.'
B: 'Well, I __________ (go) to the cinema but I hate thrillers! I __________ (see) comedies better.'

(b) A: 'Do you __________ (eat) out in restaurants?'
B: 'Yes, I love it! I really __________ (eat) Indian food.'
A: '__________ you __________ (go) out for an Indian meal tonight?'
B: 'Yes, please!'

(c) A: 'I _____ you _____ (meet) my friends. Why don't we all go out for a drink next week?'
B: 'Oh, I'm really shy. I don't __________ (meet) new people.'

*(Unit 27)*

**3. What do you *say*?**

(a) You are cold and want to *borrow* some gloves from your friend.
*Can I borrow some gloves, please?*

(b) You are in class and haven't got a pen. You want to *borrow* one.
______________________________?

(c) You want someone to *close* the door.
______________________________?

(d) You are in a shop and you want to *pay by cheque*
______________________________?

(e) You need 10p to make a phone-call. You want a friend to *lend* it to you.
______________________________?

(f) You want to *turn on the television* in your friend's house.
______________________________?

(g) You want someone to *telephone* you later.
____________________?

**4. Complete the dialogues**

(a) A: *May/Can* I use the phone?
B: Certainly

(b) A: Are you going to the party?
B: Well, __________ you give me a lift?

(c) A: My phone number's 7273456.
B: Wait.... __________ you lend me a pen?

(d) A: __________ I read that magazine when you've finished with it?
B: Of course.

(e) A: __________ you tell me the time please?
B: It's exactly 6.00.

(f) A: __________ we sit here?
B: Sorry, there's only one seat free.

*(Unit 28)*

5. Look at the picture of Debbie's room. **Make six sentences about what she *can* do**

(a) *She can play the guitar*
(b) ____________________
(c) ____________________
(d) ____________________
(e) ____________________
(f) ____________________
(g) ____________________

**6. Debbie is eighteen now. Write sentences about what *you think* she *could/couldn't* do when she was twelve?**

(a) *She could play the guitar*
(b) ____________________
(c) ____________________
(d) ____________________
(e) ____________________
(f) ____________________
(g) ____________________

*(Unit 29)*

**7. Use the verbs to write about what you *have to do* in different places**

*wear a tie* *wait in a queue* *be quiet* *buy a ticket* *drive on the left*
*wait until the light turns green* *wear a hat*

(a) In a cinema you have to buy a ticket
(b) In a library ____________
(c) At the traffic lights ____________
(d) In an expensive restaurant ____________
(e) On roads in England ____________
(f) In many swimming pools ____________
(g) In the bank you often ____________

**8.** Last year Jim was still at school. Now he is working in a supermarket.
**Write sentences about last year and now using *has to/had to (+)* and *doesn't have to/didn't have to (-)***

When Jim was at school:
(a) He had to do homework (+)
(c) He ____________ get up very early (-)
(e) He ____________ work on Saturdays (-)
(g) He ____________ study French (+)
(i) He ____________ wear a uniform (+)

Now he's working in a supermarket:
(b) He doesn't have to do homework
(d) He ____________ get up at 6.00 (+)
(f) He ____________ work on Saturday mornings (+)
(h) He ____________ study French (-)
(i) He *still* ____________ wear a uniform! (+)

*(Unit 30)*

**9.** Here are some sentences giving advice about travelling abroad. **Rewrite the sentences using *should/shouldn't***

(a) It's a good idea to take out insurance.
You should take out insurance
(b) It's a good idea to write your address on your luggage. ____________
(c) It *isn't* a good idea to take very heavy luggage.
____________
(d) It's a good idea to buy a guidebook.
____________
(e) It *isn't* a good idea to carry too much cash.
____________
(f) It's a good idea to learn to speak a little of the language ____________

**10. Complete the answers to some 'problem page' letters using *should(n't) + one of these verbs:***

*eat* *listen* *try* *tell* *stop* *make* *cook* *walk* *smoke* *expect*

You (a) ________ to your 'friends'. They are being very cruel. But you (b) ________ to take more exercise. You (c) ________ to school rather than take the bus and you (d) ________ more fruit and less chocolate.

I think you (e) ________ your friend that she (f) ________ smoking. Obviously it is making her ill. Tell her that if she wants to be healthy and able to run fast she (g) ________ at all.

Your parents (h) ________ you eat meat if you want to be vegetarian but you (i) ________ them to cook two meals every night. You (j) ________ your own dinner.

*(Unit 31)*

**11. Rewrite these sentences using *may (not)* or *might(n't)***

(a) Perhaps she's on holiday.
She might/may be on holiday

(b) Perhaps he doesn't like me.
________________

(c) Perhaps he will pass the exam.
________________

(d) Perhaps they live in Scotland.
________________

(e) Perhaps I'll go out tonight.
________________

(f) Perhaps I'll stay at home.
________________

(g) Perhaps he is a doctor.
________________

(h) Perhaps they speak Swahili.
________________

(i) Perhaps she doesn't speak English.
________________

(j) Perhaps they don't live here.
________________

(k) Perhaps we are lost.
________________

## Part nine: (Units 32–33) Talking about the past II

*(Unit 32)*

1. Elaine and John work for the same company but last week Elaine was on a business trip in Dublin while John was working in the office in London. **Look at the pictures and complete the sentences about what they were doing *last Wednesday*.**

9am
Elaine/have breakfast
*John/drive to work*
At 9am Elaine was having breakfast
and John was driving to work

10am
Elaine/visit an exhibition
*John/write letters*
________________
________________

3pm
Elaine/meet clients
*John/do the accounts*
________________
________________

12.30pm
Elaine/have lunch
*John/have a meeting with a Director*
________________
________________

6pm
Elaine/have dinner with the Director of the Dublin office
*John/drive home*
________________
________________

*(Unit 33)*

2. Elaine didn't have a very good journey home from Dublin. In fact, she had a lot of problems. **Look at the pictures and use *when* and the *past simple* or *past continuous* to describe what happened.**

rain/leave hotel
It was raining when she
left the hotel

drive to the airport/taxi break down
________________
________________

stand in the check-in queue/someone steal her handbag
________________
________________

Talk to the police/the plane leave without her

______________________

______________________

sit on the plane/spill her drink

______________________

______________________

wait for her luggage/someone tell her it was lost

______________________

feel really tired and annoyed/get home

______________________

______________________

**3.** Later Elaine told the story to her husband. **Complete her story using the *past simple* and *past continuous*.**
'The journey home was terrible. First it (rain) __was raining__ when I left the hotel, so I got wet. Then the taxi (break down) ____________ on the way to the airport. Then, while I was waiting in the check-in queue someone (steal) ____________ my handbag so I had to go to the police. And then I (miss) ____________ my plane because I was talking to the police for so long! I was really angry. The, I finally got on another plane. I (begin) ____________ to relax a bit when I spilt my orange juice everywhere! We got to London at last and I (wait) ____________ for my luggage when a man came and told me it was lost! 'It might be in Rome.' he said. So you can understand why I (feel) ____________ unhappy and tired when I got home!'

## Part ten: (Units 34–37) Describing

***(Units 35 and 36)***

**1. Compare the *three* things in each question using a *comparative* and a *superlative*.**

(a) 1. The Thames 2. The Amazon 3. The Nile
(*long*) __The Amazon is longer than The Thames.__
__The Nile is the longest.__

(b) 1. a bicycle 2. a motorbike 3. a car
(*fast*) ______________________
______________________

(c) 1. silver 2. gold 3. platinum
(*precious*) ______________________
______________________

(d) 1. a grape 2. an orange 3. a grapefruit
(*big*) ______________________
______________________

(e) 1. Norway 2. England 3. Thailand
(*hot*) ______________________
______________________

(f) 1. coca-cola 2. fruit juice 3. water
(*healthy*) ______________________
______________________

(g) 1. newspaper 2. magazine 3. book
(*expensive*) ______________________
______________________

**2. *Complete* the quiz questions with *superlatives* and then *match* them with the *answers*.**

(a) What is (*new*) __the newest__ national TV Channel in Britain?
(b) Which is (*big*) ____________ second ____________ city in Britain?
(c) Which restaurant in London is owned by three of (*famous*) ____________ American film stars?
(d) What is (*young*) ____________ age you can marry in Britain?
(e) What is Britain's (*popular*) ____________ tourist attraction?
(f) When was (*bad*) ____________ fire in the history of London?
(g) Which is (*expensive*) ____________ hotel in London?

1. 1666
2. Blackpool Beach
3. Birmingham
4. Channel Five __(✓)__
5. Planet Hollywood
6. 16
7. Claridge's

*(Units 34 and 37)*

**3. Decide if these words are *adjectives* or *adverbs***

| | | | | |
|---|---|---|---|---|
| Large adjective | poor ________ | patiently ________ | magic ________ | immediately ________ |
| new ________ | slowly ________ | angry ________ | comfortable ________ | angrily ________ |

**4. Use the adjectives and adverbs *from exercise 3* to complete the story**

Once upon a time there was a very poor fisherman and his wife. One day the fisherman caught a fish which spoke to him. 'Let me go, fisherman.' it said, 'I am a ________ fish.' So the fisherman let him go. He returned home to his wife but when he told her the story she was very ________. 'Why didn't you ask him to give us a ________ house instead of this small hut we live in?' she asked, 'Go back and ask him for a house.' So the fisherman went back to the lake, called the fish and told him what his wife had said. 'Go home' said the fish, 'she has it already'. When the fisherman got home his wife was in a lovely ________ house.

But two weeks later his wife said, 'This house is very small and not very ________. Go and ask the fish for a castle. 'The fisherman didn't want to but he went back to the fish and asked him for a castle. 'Go home,' said the fish, ________ 'she has it already.'

When the fisherman got home his wife was very happy with her new castle but the next day she said 'Now I live in a castle I want to be Queen. Go and ask the fish.' The fisherman went to ask the fish. 'Go home', said the fish, 'She is Queen already.'

But when the fisherman got home his wife was watching the sun ________ going down. 'Why can't I do that?' she asked. 'Go back to the fish ________ and tell him I want to be Master of the Universe!' The fisherman went back to the fish and asked him but the fish said ________, 'Go home. Your wife is back in her small hut.'

## Part eleven: (Units 38–40) Talking about the future

*(Unit 38)*

**1. Complete the dialogues with *present simple* or *present continuous* to talk about the future**

A: 'When (meet) are you meeting Mr Johnson?'
B: 'At lunchtime. We (have) ____________ lunch in Quaglino's'
A: 'Lucky you! (meet) ________ you ________ him at the restaurant?'
B: 'No, he (come) _____ here. He (give) ________ me a lift.'

C: 'What time (leave) ________ the train ________?'
D: 'Twelve o'clock. So hurry up!'
C: 'Where (meet) ________ we ________ the others?'
D: 'On the platform.'

E: 'When (go) ________ you ________ back to University?'
F: 'Well, term (start) ________ on October 3rd but I (go) ________ back a few days early'
E: 'Why?'
F: 'I (move) ________ in to my new flat on September 30th.'

*(Unit 39)*

**2.** Ola works in the office of a language school.
**Look at Ola's list of things to do today and write sentences about what she is *going to do***

**To do**
type some letters
pay the teachers
telephone the Director
check the registers
check how many students there are in each class

(a) She's going to type some letters
(b) ____________________
(c) ____________________
(d) ____________________
(e) ____________________

**3. Now complete the dialogues between Ola and the teachers, using *going to* and *will*.**

Teacher 1: 'Ola? Are we going to get paid today?'
Ola: 'Yes, I ____________ pay you all this afternoon, don't worry.'

Teacher 2: 'Ola? How many students are there in class B501?'
Ola: 'Can I tell you later? I ____________ check how many students there are this afternoon. OK?'

Teacher 3: 'Ola? Those plants look almost dead!'
Ola: 'Oh! O.K. I ____________ give them some water.'

Teacher 4: 'Ola? Is the Director coming here today?'
Ola: 'No, but I ____________ ring him later. Do you want me to pass on a message?'

Teacher 5: 'Ola! The phone's ringing. Shall I answer it?'
Ola: 'No, it's OK. I ____________ answer it.'

Ola: 'Have you completed your registers properly?'
Teacher 6: 'Er.....'
Ola: 'Well, I ____________ check them this afternoon.'

*(Unit 40)*

**4. Write a sentence to describe what *is going to* happen in each picture**

(a) They're going to dance

(b) ____________________

(c) ____________________

(d) ____________________

(e) ____________________

(f) ____________________

**5. Complete the conversation with the gypsy using *will*.**

Gypsy: 'You (have) will have a long and happy life'
Client: 'When (get married) ________ I ________?'
Gypsy: 'Oh, you (not marry) ________ early. You (meet) ________ your husband when you are about thirty.'
Client: 'What (be) ________ his job ________?'
Gypsy: 'He (be) ________ a businessman.'
Client: '(have) ________ we ________ any children?'
Gypsy: 'Yes, you (have) ________ six children.'
Client: 'Six?!'

## Part twelve: (Units 41–44) Connecting the past and the present

*(Unit 41)*

**1. Look at the table and write sentences about what the people *have done/have never done***

(a) Dick/climbed Mount Everest — Dick has climbed Mount Everest
(b) Sandra/be on television — Sandra has never been on television
(c) Julie and Dave/climb Mount Everest ________
(d) Dick/write a book ________
(e) Sandra/meet Prince Charles ________
(f) Julie and Dave/be on television ________
(g) Dick/have an accident ________
(h) Sandra/write a book ________
(i) Julie and Dave/meet Prince Charles ________

| | climb Mount Everest | write a book | meet Prince Charles | be on television | have an accident |
|---|---|---|---|---|---|
| Dick | ✓ | ✗ | ✗ | ✓ | ✓ |
| Sandra | ✗ | ✓ | ✓ | ✗ | ✗ |
| Julie and Dave | ✗ | ✗ | ✗ | ✓ | ✓ |

**2. Write questions using *ever* and *short answers* using the information in the table.**

(a) Dick/meet Prince Charles? — Has Dick ever met Prince Charles? — No, he hasn't
(b) Sandra/be on television? ________ ________
(c) Julie and Dave/write a book? ________ ________
(d) Sandra/have an accident? ________ ________
(e) Dick/be on television? ________ ________
(f) Julie and Dave/have an accident? ________ ________

*(Unit 42)*

**3. *It's now 1997.* Write sentences about *how long*, using *for* and *since***

(a) He got married in 1987 (*be married*)
He's been married for ten years
He's been married since 1987

(b) He went to live in Ecuador twelve years ago (*live*)
________
________

(c) They became teachers in 1989 (*be*)
________
________

(d) I bought a computer a year ago (*have*)
________
________

(e) She learnt to play the piano when she was six. Now she's seventeen (*play*)
________
________

(f) I learnt to speak Japanese three years ago (*speak*)
________
________

(g) It started being sunny last week (*be sunny*)
______________________
______________________

(h) The shop opened two years ago (*be open*)
______________________
______________________

(i) We went to University three years ago (*be at*)
______________________
______________________

**4. Write questions for the situations in *exercise 3* using *How long....?***

(a) How long has he been married?
(b) ______________________
(c) ______________________
(d) ______________________
(e) ______________________
(f) ______________________
(g) ______________________
(h) ______________________
(i) ______________________

***(Unit 43)***

**5.** Look at the two pictures of Mike. **What can you see has *changed* in the second picture? Write sentences using these verbs:**

*shave his beard* | *grow his hair* | *put on weight*
*get older* | *start wearing a tie* | *buy some new clothes*
*stop wearing an earring* | *get married* | *become smarter*

(a) He's shaved his beard
(b) ______________________
(c) ______________________
(d) ______________________
(e) ______________________
(f) ______________________
(g) ______________________
(h) ______________________
(i) ______________________

**6. Write questions and short answers about Mike in the *second picture***

(a) cut his hair? Has he cut his hair? No, he hasn't
(b) grow a moustache? ______________ ______
(c) put on weight? ______________ ______
(d) start wearing a tie? ______________ ______
(e) lose weight? ______________ ______
(f) get married? ______________ ______
(g) shave his beard? ______________ ______

***(Unit 44)***

**7.** Paul is in town. He has a list of things to do. **Write sentences about what he *has already done* and what he *hasn't done yet***

- post the letters ✓ (a) He's already posted the letters
- pay in the cheque ✓ (b) ______________________
- take out some cash ✓ (c) ______________________
- buy some bread and milk ✓ (d) ______________________
- get some petrol for the car (e) ______________________
- take the dog to the vet (f) ______________________
- pay the electricity bill (g) ______________________
- buy some aspirin (h) ______________________

**8. Write *questions* and *short answers* about what Paul has done (using 'yet')**

(a) Has Paul posted the letters yet? Yes, he has
(b) ______________________ ______
(c) ______________________ ______
(d) ______________________ ______
(e) ______________________ ______
(f) ______________________ ______
(g) ______________________ ______
(h) ______________________ ______

# Appendix 1: List of irregular verbs

| INFINITIVE | PAST SIMPLE | PAST PARTICIPLE | INFINITIVE | PAST SIMPLE | PAST PARTICIPLE |
|---|---|---|---|---|---|
| be | was/were | been | lend | lent | lent |
| beat | beat | beaten | let | let | let |
| become | became | become | lose | lost | lost |
| begin | began | begun | make | made | made |
| bite | bit | bitten | mean | meant | meant |
| blow | blew | blown | meet | met | met |
| break | broke | broken | must | had to | had to |
| bring | brought | brought | pay | paid | paid |
| build | built | built | put | put | put |
| burn | burnt (burned) | burnt (burned) | read/ri:d/ | read/red/ | read/red/ |
| buy | bought | bought | ride | rode | ridden |
| can | could | been able | ring | rang | rung |
| catch | caught | caught | rise | rose | risen |
| choose | chose | chosen | run | ran | run |
| come | came | come | say | said | said |
| cost | cost | cost | see | saw | seen |
| cut | cut | cut | sell | sold | sold |
| do | did | done | send | sent | sent |
| draw | drew | drawn | shine | shone | shone |
| drink | drank | drunk | show | showed | shown |
| drive | drove | driven | sing | sang | sung |
| eat | ate | eaten | sit | sat | sat |
| fall | fell | fallen | sleep | slept | slept |
| feel | felt | felt | speak | spoke | spoken |
| find | found | found | spend | spent | spent |
| fly | flew | flown | stand | stood | stood |
| forget | forgot | forgotten | steal | stole | stolen |
| get | got | got (AmEng gotten) | swim | swam | swum |
| | | | take | took | taken |
| give | gave | given | teach | taught | taught |
| go | went | gone (or 'been')* | tell | told | told |
| | | | think | thought | thought |
| have | had | had | throw | threw | thrown |
| hear | heard | heard | understand | understood | understood |
| hold | held | held | wake | woke | woken |
| hurt | hurt | hurt | wear | wore | worn |
| keep | kept | kept | win | won | won |
| know | knew | known | write | wrote | written |
| leave | left | left | | | |

**see Unit 41*

# Appendix 2: Communicative Activities.... 'Practise with a friend...'

At the end of most Units are 'Practise with a friend' activities, providing the opportunity for communicative oral practice (following on from controlled practice). Reference from the Unit to this Appendix is given.

The activities in this Appendix are in Unit sequence. Where an activity requires that friend 'B' is looking at different material to friend 'A' ('information gap' activities), where to find the friend 'B' material is clearly indicated.

## Unit 3: this/that/these/those (page 7)

**Draw a plan of your room with furniture. Like this:**

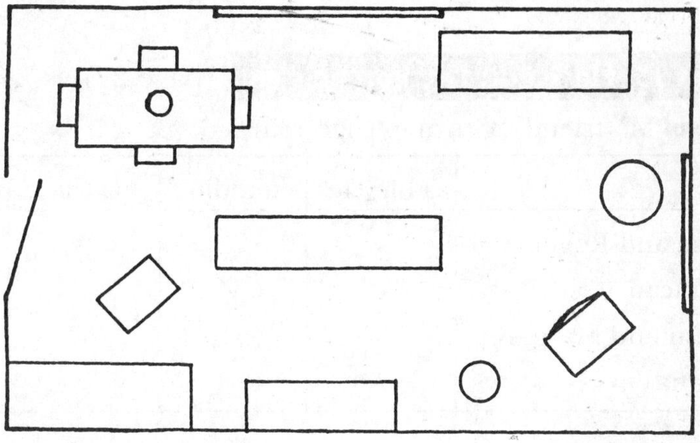

Tell your friend about it and ask questions

***Example:***
A: '**This** is my TV.'
B: 'What are **those**?'
A: 'Armchairs'
B: 'Is **that** a lamp?...'

## Unit 4: Singular and plural nouns (page 9)

***Friend 'A' picture*** (friend 'B' picture, see page 135)

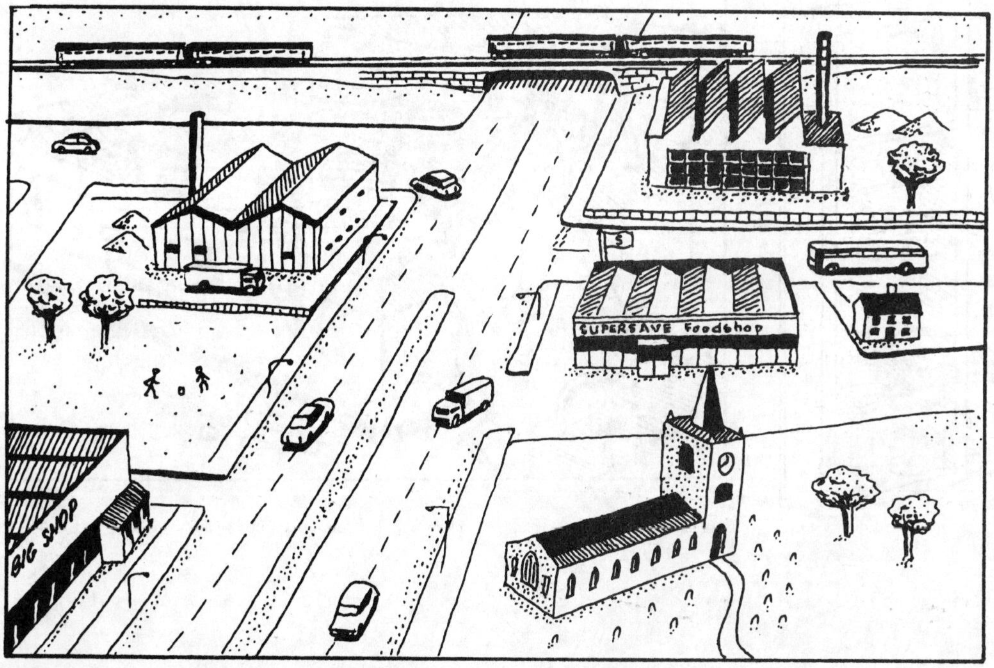

## Unit 6: Present simple auxiliaries: do/does (page 13)

***Train information: Friend 'A'*** (friend 'B' turn to page 135)

A: You want to travel to **Prague**. Your friend has the information. Ask questions to find out.
What time/it/leave?
When/it/arrive?
How much/it/cost?
/you/need/a reservation?
/it/stop/in Berlin?

| |
|---|
| The train to **Rome** leaves at 6.00 in the morning. It arrives at 7.00 in the evening. It stops in Trieste and Bologna. It costs US$89 second class and US$129 first class. You need a reservation. |

## Unit 13: Have got: I've got/he's got (page 27)

***Friend 'A'*** (friend 'B' turn to page 135)

| **A:** | a bicycle | a radio | a cat | children | a house | a camera |
|---|---|---|---|---|---|---|
| Lisa and Roger | ✓ | | ✗ | | ✓ | |
| Duncan | ✓ | ✓ | ✗ | | | |
| John and Margaret | | | ✓ | ✓ | | ✗ |
| Fiona | ✗ | | ✗ | | ✗ | |

## Unit 15: 'Some' and 'any' (page 31)

***Friend 'A'*** (friend 'B' turn to page 136)

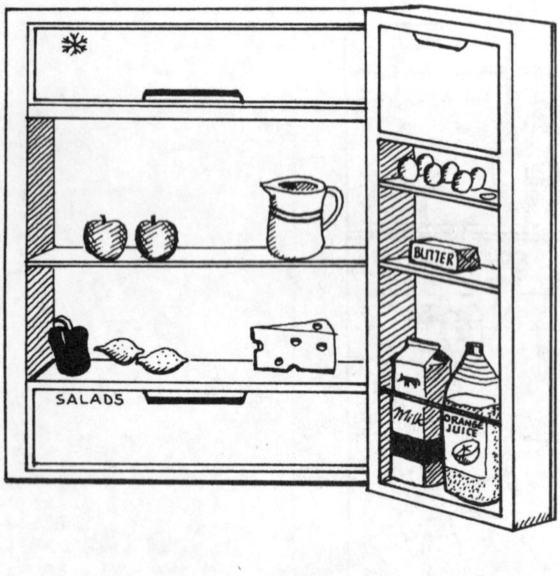


## Unit 16: Much/many/a lot (page 33)

***Friend 'A'*** (friend 'B' turn to page 136)

## Unit 17: 'Too' and 'not enough' (page 35)

Play this game: Throw the two dice and make a sentence about the **picture** using the **word**

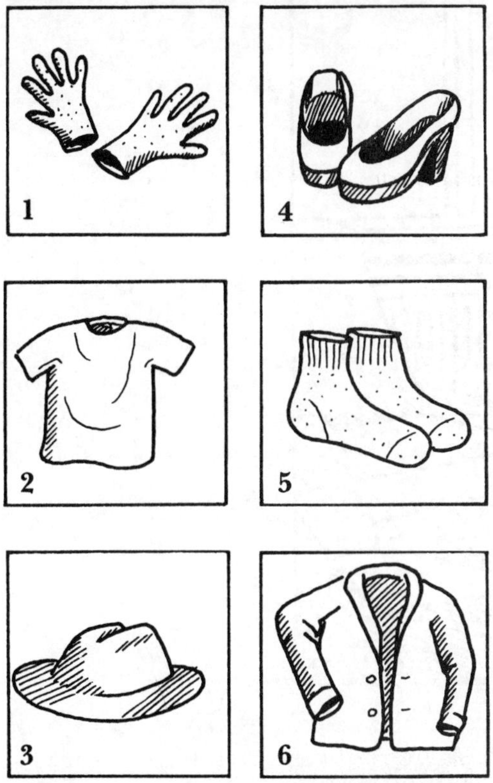


***Examples:***

Friend A:

 = 1 (gloves)

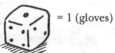

 = 3 big (enough)

'They aren't big enough'

Friend B:

 = 4 (shoes)

 = 2 expensive (too)

'They are too expensive'

1. small (too)
2. expensive (too)
3. big (enough)
4. big (too)
5. cheap (enough)
6. colourful (enough)

## Unit 18: Present Continuous Tense (page 37)

***Friend 'A'*** (friend 'B' turn to page 137)

## Unit 20: Prepositions of place: in/on/next to (page 41)

***Friend 'A'*** (friend 'B' turn to page 137)

## Unit 22: Prepositions of movement: up/down (page 45)

How many *logical* combinations can you make with these **places** and these **prepositions**? Who can make the most?

*Places*

| | | | |
|---|---|---|---|
| the river | the school | the stairs | the wall |
| the town | the cinema | the hotel | the bridge |

*Prepositions*

| | | | | |
|---|---|---|---|---|
| across | into | down | over | on |
| along | out of | past | round | |

***Example:***

A: '**Past** the school'
B: '**Over** the town'
A: 'That's not logical!'
B: 'Yes, in an aeroplane!'

## Unit 25: Past simple auxiliary: did/didn't (page 51)

***Information about Shakespeare: Friend 'A'*** (friend 'B' turn to page 138)

**A: Read the text and answer your friend's questions**

William Shakespeare was born on (approximately) 23rd April 1564 in Stratford-upon-Avon. His father was a glove-maker. Shakespeare went to school in Stratford, at the local Grammar School. When he was eighteen he married Anne Hathaway. She was twenty-six. They had three children: a daughter, Susannah and twins, Judith and Hamnet. He spent a lot of his life away from his family, working in London. When he died in 1616, he left most of his money to his daughter, Susannah. He left Anne his second-best bed!

**Ask your friend these questions about *their* text**

When/Shakespeare/come to London?
What/he/do in London?
How many plays/he/write?
/He/only write plays?
What/he/call his theatre?
What/he/do in 1596
When/he/return to Stratford?
What day/he/die?

## Unit 26: Would like (page 53)

**Ask questions about these things using: *Do you like...? Would you like...?***

orange juice go/going to the theatre cooking come to a party dancing/to dance
play/playing tennis going on holiday writing letters go/going out to dinner

| Choose from these answers: | | | | | |
|---|---|---|---|---|---|
| Yes, please | No, thank you | Yes, I do | No, I don't | Yes, I'd love to | Sorry, I can't |

***Examples:***

A: '**Do you like** orange juice?'
B: 'No, I don't.'

B: '**Do you like** going to the theatre?'
A: 'Yes, I do.'

B: '**Would you like** to go to the theatre on Saturday?'
A: 'Yes, I'd love to.'

## Unit 29: Obligation (have to) (page 59)

**Write down five things you *have to do now* that you *didn't have to* do when you were a child.**

*Example:* clean the house ______ ______ ______ ______

**Now write down five things you *don't have to* do now that you *had to do* when you were a child.**

*Example:* go to bed very early ______ ______ ______ ______

**Now tell your friend about them.**

***Example:***

A: 'Now I have to clean the house. I didn't have to clean the house when I was a child.'
B: 'Oh, I had to clean the house when I was a child – but now my husband does it!'

## Unit 30: Advising: should/shouldn't (page 61)

**How often do you do these things? Every day? Sometimes? Never?**

exercise eat chocolate study English smoke eat fruit and vegetables
read in English drink wine go for a walk watch English films relax speak English

**Tell your friend how often and listen to their advice!**

***Example:***

A: 'I never exercise.'
B: 'You **should** exercise more.'

A: 'And I smoke.'
B: 'You **shouldn't** smoke. It's very bad for you.'

A: 'But I eat lots of fruit every day.'
B: 'That's good.'

## Unit 31: Possibility (may/might) (page 63)

You and your friend are going on holiday. Here are some things that **might/may** happen:

rain get lost be sunny run out of money (have no more) be expensive
be cheap be dangerous be fun meet some interesting people
see some beautiful things get ill

**Talk with your friend. Make sentences** about what **might/may** happen on your holiday using these ideas (and your own ideas)

A is very *optimistic*. B is very *pessimistic*.

***Example:***

A: 'It **may** be fun.'
B: 'We **might** run out of money.'

## Unit 32: Past continuous (page 65)

Ask your friend about what they were doing at these times yesterday:

8.00am 12.00pm 4.00pm 6.00pm 7.00pm 10.00pm

> ***Example:***
> A: 'What **were** you **doing** at 8.00?'
> B: '**I was reading** the newspaper.'

## Unit 33: Past continuous and past simple (page 67)

***Friend 'B'***: turn to page 138.

You each have ten sentence beginnings. Read a sentence *beginning* to your friend. They must *complete* the sentence.

> ***Examples:***
> A: 'As I **was walking** through the park.....' ⟶ B: '...I **saw** a boy fall off a bicycle'
> B: 'She **was wearing** a big hat when......' ⟶ A: '...the wind **blew** it off her head'

**A:**

1. As I was walking through the park......
2. While it was raining......
3. When I was out shopping......
4. As I was eating dinner......
5. They were sleeping when......
6. As he was watching television......
7. I was walking to work when......
8. He was out jogging when......
9. When he was living in Peru......
10. They were feeling very happy when......

## Unit 34: Adjectives I (page 69)

**Look at the pictures for one minute.** Try to remember the objects and *think of an adjective to describe them.* Then *cover* the page and try to remember as many as you can - *with an adjective.* Who can remember more?

> ***Example:***
> A: A black cat, a big watch...
> B: A fast car...

## Unit 36: Superlatives (page 73)

Choose three cities in your country (or countries). Compare them using these adjectives in the **superlative** form.

big polluted exciting beautiful modern expensive interesting
small dangerous relaxing nice hot cold cheap boring noisy

> ***Example:***
> A: 'St Petersburg is the **most beautiful** and the **oldest**'
> B: 'Moscow is the **most dangerous**'

## Unit 40: Going to/Will – II (page 81)

Talk together about the picture. Make sentences about what you **can see *is* going to happen** and what you **think *will* happen.**

## Unit 41: Present perfect I: experience (page 83)

Use these verbs (or others you know) to ask questions, using **Have you ever......?**

be break buy cut drink drive eat fall forget give
have meet read see speak steal take wear

If the answer is **'Yes, I have'**, ask another question using **When, Where, Why, What + simple past**

| | | |
|---|---|---|
| ***Examples:*** | '**Have you ever** eaten sushi?' | '**Have you ever** worn a fur hat?' |
| | 'No, I haven't' | 'Yes, I have.' |
| | | 'Where **did** you **wear** it?' |
| | | 'In Siberia! It was very cold.' |

## Unit 43: Present perfect III: present result (page 87)

Look at the picture and try to find *at least nine things* that you can see that Roger *has done* in the kitchen today.

| |
|---|
| ***Example:*** |
| He *has swept* the floor. |

## Unit 44: Present perfect IV: 'yet' and 'already' (page 89)

***Round the world trip: Friend 'A'*** (friend 'B' turn to page 138)

**A:** You are on a Round the World Trip. Look at the map below and see where you've **already been** and where you **haven't been yet**. Your friend must try to find out where you are now. They can ask questions: '**Have** you **been** to Bali yet?' and you can tell them some information '**I've already been** to Bombay.' ***But don't tell them where you are now!***

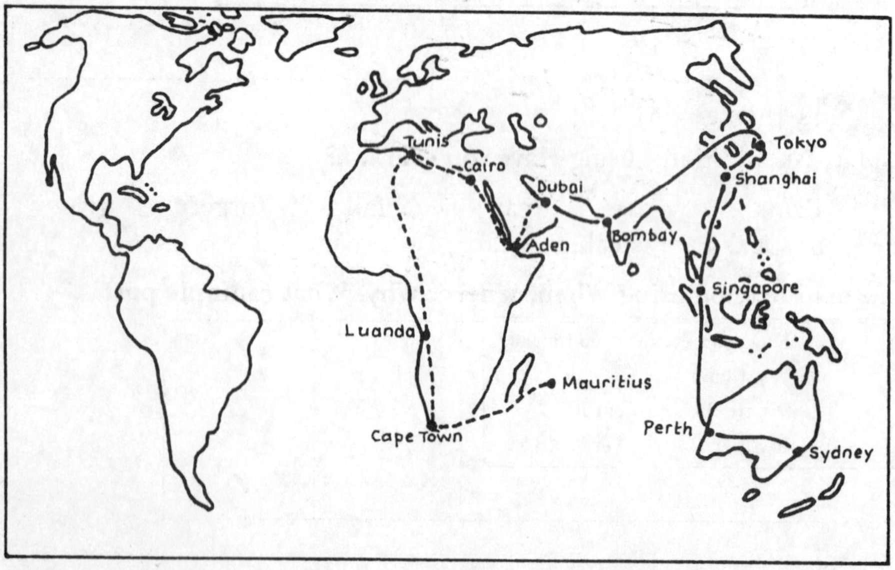

# Friend 'B' material

## Unit 4: Singular and plural nouns (page 9)

(friend 'A' turn to page 127)

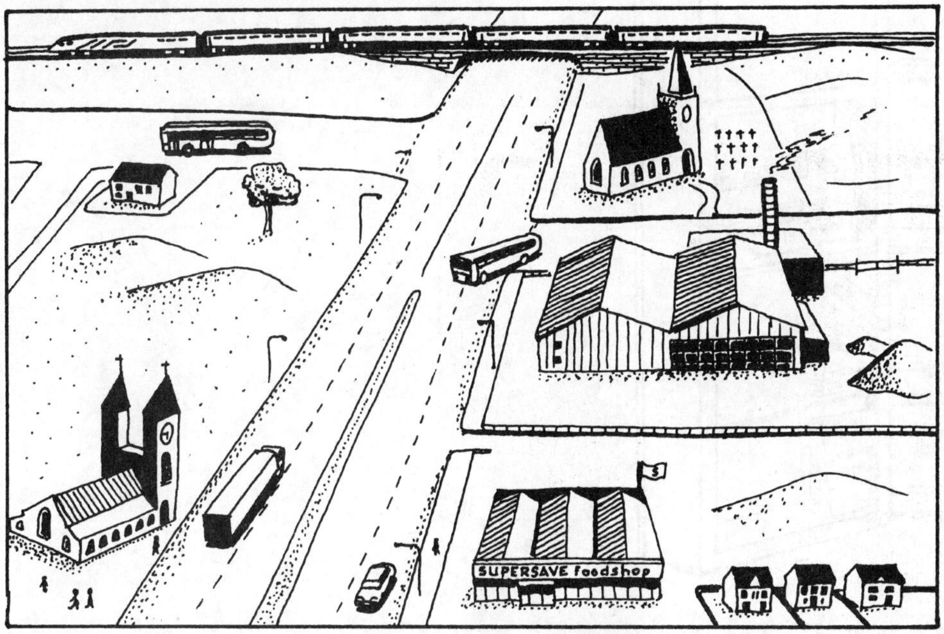


## Unit 6: Present simple auxiliaries: do/does (page 13)

***Train information friend 'B'*** (friend 'A' turn to page 128)

**B:** You want to travel to **Rome**. Your friend has the information. Ask questions to find out.
When/it/leave?
What time/it/arrive?
How much/a first class ticket/cost?
/you/need/a reservation?
/it/stop/in Trieste?

| |
|---|
| The train to **Prague** leaves at 8.00 in the evening. It arrives at 6.30 in the morning. It stops in Berlin and Bratislavia. It costs US$70 second class and US$95 first class. You don't need a reservation. |

## Unit 13: Have got: I've got/he's got (page 27)

***Friend 'B'*** (friend 'A' turn to page 128)

| **B:** | a bicycle | a radio | a cat | children | a house | a camera |
|---|---|---|---|---|---|---|
| Lisa and Roger | | ✓ | | ✗ | | ✓ |
| Duncan | | | | ✓ | ✓ | ✗ |
| John and Margaret | ✗ | ✗ | | | ✓ | |
| Fiona | | ✓ | | ✗ | | ✓ |

## Unit 15: 'Some' and 'any' (page 31)

***Friend 'B'*** (friend 'A' turn to page 128)

## Unit 16: Much/many/a lot (page 33)

***Friend 'B'*** (friend 'A' turn to page 128)

## Unit 18: Present Continuous Tense (page 37)

***Friend 'B'*** (friend 'A' turn to page 129)

## Unit 20: Prepositions of place: in/on/next to (page 41)

***Friend 'B'*** (friend 'A' turn to page 130)

## Unit 25: Past simple auxiliary: did/didn't (page 51)

***Information about Shakespeare: Friend 'B'*** (friend 'A' turn to page 130)

**B: Read the text and answer your friend's questions**

No-one knows exactly when Shakespeare came to London but he quickly became a very successful playwright and actor. He wrote at least 37 plays as well as poetry. He and his colleagues built their own theatre, called the Globe. In 1596 he bought the largest house in Stratford, New Place, as a family home. He returned to Stratford a few years before his death and died on the same day he was born, April 23rd – St George's Day.

**Ask your friend these questions about *their* text**

When/Shakespeare/born?
What/his father/do?
Where/Shakespeare/go to school?
When/he/marry Anne Hathaway?
How old/she?
How many children/they/have?
Who/he/leave most of his money to when he died?
What/he/leave his wife?

## Unit 33: Past continuous and past simple (page 67)

***Friend 'B'*** (friend 'A' turn to page 132)

**B**

1. She was wearing a big hat when......
2. While the plane was landing......
3. They were eating icecream when......
4. As she was crossing the road......
5. While I was talking to him......
6. As they were dancing......
7. I was lying on the beach when......
8. They were swimming in the sea when......
9. Were you listening when......?
10. As I was going to work this morning......

## Unit 44: Present perfect IV; 'yet' and 'already' (page 89)

***Round the world trip: Friend 'B'*** (friend 'A' turn to page 134)

**B:** You are on a Round the World Trip. Look at the map below and see where you've **already** been and where you haven't been yet. Your friend must try to find out where you are now. They can ask questions: 'Have you been to Bali yet?' and you can tell them some information 'I've already been to Buenos Aires.' ***But don't tell them where you are now!***

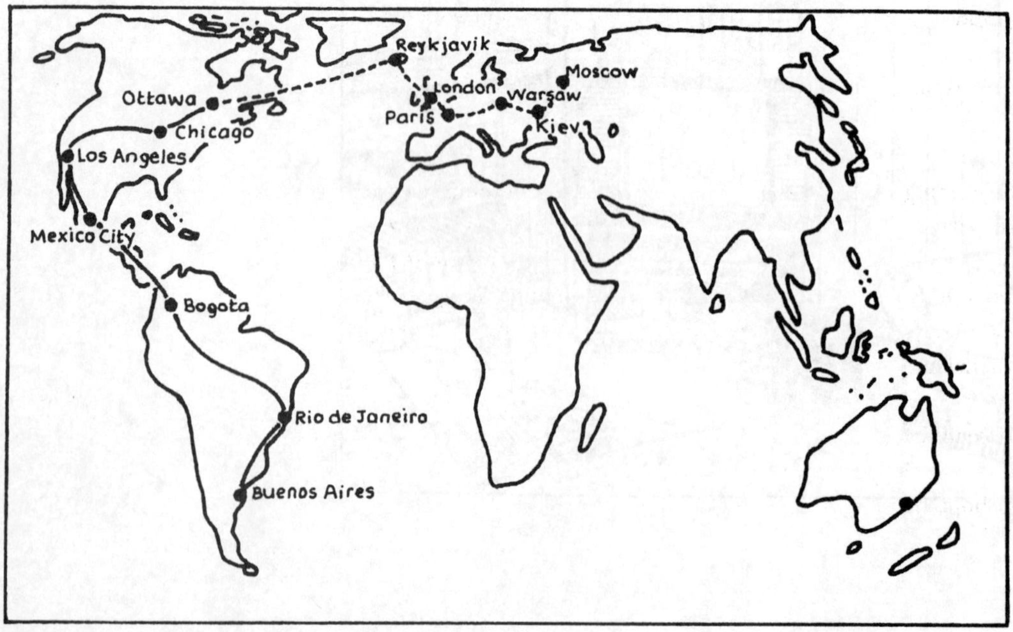

# Appendix 3: Test-yourself answers and study/revision guide

## Answers to Test-yourself exercises (see page 94)

### *Part one: (Units 1–4) Talking about people, places and objects*

| | | Study/revise Unit 1 | 2 | 3 | 4 |
|---|---|---|---|---|---|
| 1. (a) | What is (what's) this? | • | • | | |
| (b) | Are these expensive? | • | • | | |
| (c) | Is this the Post Office? | | | • | |
| (d) | Are we late? | • | • | | |
| (e) | Is that your sister? | | | • | |
| (f) | Are they German? | • | • | | |
| (g) | Are these her shoes? | | | • | |
| 2. (a) | Are | • | • | | |
| (b) | this | | | • | |
| (c) | isn't | • | • | | |
| (d) | that | | | • | |
| (e) | is | • | • | | |
| 3. (a) | Those children are very intelligent | | | • | • |
| (b) | Are these your bags? | | | • | • |
| (c) | These are English dictionaries | | | • | • |
| (d) | Are these cheese sandwiches? | | | • | • |
| (e) | The buses are red | | | | • |
| (f) | These are your keys | | | • | |

| | | Study/revise Unit 1 | 2 | 3 | 4 |
|---|---|---|---|---|---|
| 4. (a) | Correct | • | • | | |
| (b) | I like **children** | | | | • |
| (c) | I **am** an artist | • | • | | |
| (d) | Are **those** your sisters? | | | • | |
| (e) | Correct | • | | | |
| (f) | Correct | | | • | • |
| (g) | We aren't very happy. (**no'?'**) | • | • | | |
| (h) | Correct | | | • | |
| (i) | **He's/he is** my boyfriend | • | • | | |
| (j) | Correct | | | • | • |
| (k) | Correct | | | • | • |
| (l) | Is **this your** husband? | • | • | • | |
| 5. (a) | We **are** French | • | • | | |
| (b) | **These** are my parents | | | • | |
| (c) | What **is** your name? | • | • | | |
| (d) | The people **are** happy | | | | • |
| (e) | Yes, it **is** | • | • | | |
| (f) | The men **are** in the pub | | | | • |
| (g) | Are you a student? No, **I'm** not. | • | • | | |
| (h) | What's **that**? | | | • | |

### *Part two: (Units 5–7) Talking about routines and habits*

| | | Study/revise Unit 5 | 6 | 7 |
|---|---|---|---|---|
| 1. (b) | The Japanese **make** very good cars | • | | |
| (c) | I **live** in Devon | • | | |
| (d) | Yuko **wants** to go to England | • | | |
| (e) | In the winter he **goes** skiing | • | | |
| (f) | Suzanne and Jo **have** breakfast at 8am | • | | |
| (g) | Renata **finishes** work at 6pm | • | | |
| (h) | She **studies** French in the evening | • | | |
| (i) | Sarah **gets up** at 6am every day | • | | |
| 2. (b) | Tony and Vicky **don't live** in Italy | | • | |
| (c) | We **don't get up** early on Sundays | | • | |
| (d) | Jorge **doesn't study** medicine at University | | • | |
| (e) | I **don't stay** late at the office in the evenings | | • | |
| (f) | Helen **doesn't like** going shopping | | • | |

| | | Study/revise Unit 5 | 6 | 7 |
|---|---|---|---|---|
| 3. (b) | How much does a ticket cost? | | • | |
| (c) | Do you like living in London? | | • | |
| (d) | Does she work for Toyota? | | • | |
| (e) | Where do Kate and Ian study? | | • | |
| (f) | When does the plane arrive in New York? | | • | |
| 4. (b) | Sarah **sometimes** gets up early | | | • |
| (c) | Sheila **never** drives | | | • |
| (d) | They are **always** happy | | | • |
| (e) | Emma **rarely** smokes | | | • |
| (f) | I **often** go running | | | • |

| | | Study/revise Unit 5 | 6 | 7 |
|---|---|---|---|---|
| 5. (b) | Jo never drinks wine | | | • |
| (c) | Nick sometimes goes to watch a football match | | | • |
| (d) | I often go swimming | | | • |
| (e) | Debbie rarely goes to the Disco | | | • |
| (f) | Jim is always hungry | | | • |
| 6. (b) | Jean and Brian **always go** to Spain on holiday | | | • |
| (c) | The buses **are never** late | | | • |
| (d) | When the sun **shines**, I go swimming in the sea | • | | |
| (e) | Correct | | • | |
| (f) | What time **does** Mr Koshura **get up**? | | • | |
| (g) | Richard **finishes** work at 5.30 | • | | |
| (h) | What **does** Steven do at the weekend? | | • | |
| (i) | He **plays** football | • | | |
| (j) | Alison never **goes** to the cinema | | | • |

## *Part three: (Units 8–12) Referring to people, places and objects*

| | | Study/revise Unit 8 | 9 | 10 | 11 | 12 |
|---|---|---|---|---|---|---|
| 1. (b) | No, but I like **her** | • | | | | |
| (c) | **We** don't live in **our** old house now. | • | • | | | |
| (d) | Is that car **yours**? | | | • | | |
| (e) | No, it's **hers** | | | • | | |
| (f) | **Their** daughter is a doctor | | • | | | |
| (g) | Where does **she** live? | • | | | | |
| (h) | Where is **her** house? | | • | | | |
| (i) | Please write to **me** soon | • | | | | |
| (j) | That book isn't **mine** | | | • | | |
| (k) | I don't think that house is **theirs** | | | • | | |
| 2. (b) | What floor is **his** flat on? | | • | | | |
| (c) | **They** are **his** friends | • | • | | | |
| (d) | **His** flat is near **theirs** | | • | • | | |
| (e) | Is that **hers**? | | | • | | |
| (f) | No, it's **his** | | | • | | |
| 3. (b) | is | | • | | | |
| (c) | possession | | • | | | |
| (d) | is | | • | | | |
| (e) | is | | • | | | |
| (f) | possession | | • | | | |
| 4. (b) | **He's** a doctor | • | | | | |
| (c) | **Their** house is in London | | • | | | |
| (d) | **She's** interested in tennis | • | | | | |
| (e) | **She's** one of the richest women in the world | • | | | | |
| (f) | **Their** wedding anniversary's in June | | • | | | |
| 5. (b) | **The** house has only one garage | | | | • | |
| (c) | **a** Ford | | | | • | |
| (d) | **a** Volkswagen. | | | | • | |
| (e) | **The** Ford is quite new | | | | • | |
| (f) | **the** Volkswagen is older. | | | | • | |
| (g) | **the** Ford | | | | • | |
| (h) | **the** garage. | | | | • | |
| (i) | **a** businessman. | | | | • | |
| (j) | **(nothing)** London | | | | • | |
| (k) | **(nothing)** Henley | | | | • | |
| (l) | **the** River Thames. | | | | • | |
| (m) | **a** teacher | | | | • | |
| (n) | **a** school | | | | • | |
| (o) | **(nothing)** Henley. | | | | • | |
| (p) | **an** eight year old son | | | | • | |
| 6. (b) | Oh no, it's raining. Can you lend me **an** umbrella? | | | | • | |
| (c) | He often gives **her** flowers | | • | | | |
| (d) | Is that **her** house? | | • | | | |
| (e) | **Correct** | • | • | | | |
| (f) | A pet is an animal **which** lives in your house | | | | | • |
| (g) | **The** River Nile is the longest in the world | | | | • | |
| (h) | **Correct** | • | • | | | |
| (i) | **Correct** | | | | • | |
| (j) | He travels all over **the** world | | | | • | |
| (k) | The Prime Minister is the person **who** governs England. | | | | | • |
| (l) | I'd love to meet **the** Queen of England | | | • | | |
| (m) | **Correct** | • | • | | | |
| (n) | That's **my** car, over there. | | | • | | |

| | | Study/revise Unit 8 | 9 | 10 | 11 | 12 |
|---|---|---|---|---|---|---|
| 7. (b) | I like food **which** tastes good | | | | | • |
| (c) | A wife is a women **who** is married. | | | | | • |
| (d) | That's the man **who** works in my office | | | | | • |
| (e) | She's the woman **who** lives next door | | | | | • |
| (f) | A tram is a type of bus **which** uses electricity | | | | | • |
| 7. (g) | A fountain pen is a pen **which** uses liquid ink | | | | | • |
| (h) | Beaujolais is a wine **which** comes from France | | | | | • |
| (i) | **Which** is your favourite book? | | | | | • |

## *Part four: (Units 13–17) Amounts*

| | | Study/revise Unit 13 | 14 | 15 | 16 | 17 |
|---|---|---|---|---|---|---|
| 1. (a) | Has | • | | | | |
| (b) | got | • | | | | |
| (c) | much | | | | • | |
| (d) | too | | | | | • |
| (e) | some | | | • | | |
| (f) | many | | | | • | |
| (g) | have | • | | | | |
| (h) | any | | | • | | |
| (i) | some | | | • | | |
| (j) | much | | | | • | |
| (k) | enough | | | | | • |
| (l) | many | | | | • | |
| (m) | got | | | | • | |
| (n) | any | | | • | | |
| (o) | too | | | | | • |
| (p) | any | | | • | | |
| (q) | some | | | • | | |
| 2. (a) | are | | • | | • | |
| (b) | are | | • | | | |
| (c) | is | | • | | | |
| (d) | is | | • | | | |
| (e) | are | | • | | | |
| (f) | is | | • | | | |
| (g) | is | | • | | • | |
| (h) | are | | • | | | |
| (i) | is | | • | | | |
| 3. (a) | too much | | | | | • |
| (b) | much | | | | • | |
| (c) | enough | | | | | • |
| (d) | too | | | | | • |
| (e) | much | | | | • | |
| (f) | enough | | | | | • |
| (g) | enough | | | | | • |
| (h) | many | | | | • | |
| 4. (a) | has | • | | | | |
| (b) | has | • | | | | |
| (c) | a lot of | | | | • | |
| (d) | hasn't | • | | | | |
| (e) | many | | | | • | |
| (f) | hasn't | • | | | | |
| (g) | any | | | • | | |
| (h) | haven't | • | | | | |
| (i) | much | | | | • | |

## *Part five: (Units 18–19) Talking about now*

| | | Study/revise Unit 18 | 19 |
|---|---|---|---|
| 1. (b) | Grandma's sitting on the sofa | • | |
| (c) | The dog and cat are eating | • | |
| (d) | The baby's crying | • | |
| (e) | Grandad's lying down | • | |
| (f) | Dad's reading a book | • | |
| (g) | The children are playing | • | |
| (h) | Grandad's sleeping | • | |
| (i) | Mum's writing a letter | • | |
| 2. (b) | Who's reading a book? | • | |
| (c) | What's Dad reading? | • | |
| (d) | Who's sitting on the sofa? | • | |
| (e) | Are the children playing? | • | |
| (f) | What's Mum writing? | • | |
| (g) | Is Dad reading a newspaper? | • | |
| (h) | Is Grandad sleeping? | • | |

| | Study/revise Unit 18 | 19 |
|---|---|---|
| 3. (b) No, she isn't | • | |
| (c) Yes, it is | • | |
| (d) No, they aren't | • | |
| (e) No, he isn't | • | |
| (f) Yes, they are | • | |
| 4. (b) What are the children doing? | | • |
| (c) What does Nick do? | | • |
| (d) How many CDs do you have? | | • |
| (e) What are you drinking? | | • |
| (f) What time do you usually get up? | | • |
| (g) What are you listening to? | | • |
| 5. (b) Peter runs in the park every day | | • |
| (c) I can't answer the door, I'm talking on the phone! | | • |
| (d) Sshh! Quiet! The baby is sleeping | | • |
| (e) 'Where are you going this afternoon?' 'Shopping. Do you want anything?' | | • |
| (f) 'Where's Grandma?' 'She is sitting on the sofa' | | • |
| (g) 'What are you eating?' 'Pizza. Do you want some?' | | • |
| (h) 'What does Mike do?' 'He's a teacher.' | | • |
| 6. (b) lying | • | |
| (c) Correct | • | |
| (d) swimming | • | |
| (e) shining | • | |
| (f) Correct | • | |
| (g) telephoning | • | |

## *Part six: (Units 20–22) Prepositions*

| | Study/revise Unit 20 | 21 | 22 |
|---|---|---|---|
| 1. (b) True | • | | |
| (c) False – the cup is **near** the oranges | • | | |
| (d) True | • | | |
| (e) False – the bus in **in front of** the car | • | | |
| (f) True | • | | |
| (g) False – the clock is **next to** the picture | • | | |
| (h) False – the dog is **behind** the chair | • | | |
| (i) True | • | | |
| 2. (b) through | | | • |
| (c) past | | | • |
| (d) over | | | • |
| (e) into | | | • |
| (f) along | | | • |
| (g) down | | | • |
| (h) under | | | • |
| (i) up | | | • |
| (j) round | | | • |
| (k) into | | | • |
| 3. (b) to | | | • |
| (c) along | | | • |
| (d) round | | | • |
| (e) under | | | • |
| (f) past | | | • |
| (g) on | | | • |
| (h) off | | | • |
| 4. (b) at | | • | |
| (c) nothing | | • | |
| (d) in | | • | |
| (e) nothing | | • | |
| (f) at | | • | |
| (g) on | | • | |
| (h) in | | • | |
| 5. (b) I usually get home from work **at** 6.00 | | • | |
| (c) Correct | | • | |
| (d) Sue's going to visit her grandmother **at the weekend** | | • | |
| (e) Maria Jose is coming to England **next month** | | • | |
| (f) Correct | | • | |
| (g) It's very cold **at** night now | | • | |
| (h) **In** the past not many people had telephones | | • | |

| | | Study/revise Unit 20 | 21 | 22 |
|---|---|---|---|---|
| 6. (b) | **On Valentines Day**, Sheila got four cards! | | • | |
| (c) | **At midnight** it started raining | | • | |
| (d) | I'm studying English at **the** moment | | • | |
| (e) | **On Saturdays** I stay in bed late | | • | |

## *Part seven: (Units 23–25) Talking about the Past I*

| | | Study/revise Unit 23 | 24 | 25 |
|---|---|---|---|---|
| 1. (b) | I rang Justin and Sue but they **were** away on holiday | • | | |
| (c) | The bank **was** in the main square | • | | |
| (d) | **Were** you at home last night? | • | | |
| (e) | No, I **was** out | • | | |
| (f) | We **were** really excited about going on holiday | • | | |
| 2. (b) | There **weren't** any cars when Grandfather **was** a child | • | | |
| (c) | Alexander Bell **invented** the telephone | | • | |
| (d) | Patricia **went** to Spain last year | | • | |
| (e) | She **swam** across the English Channel! | | • | |
| (f) | The English **didn't win** the Battle of Hastings in 1066 | | | • |
| (g) | Queen Victoria **had** nine children | | • | |
| (h) | 'I **thought** the film was great.' 'Really? I didn't like it much.' | | • | • |
| (i) | I **lost** my wallet yesterday | | • | |
| (j) | Sophie **didn't go** to the party because she **was** ill | • | | |
| (k) | They **sang** the National Anthem when the Queen **arrived** | | • | |
| 3. (b) | Ian didn't pass all his exams | | | • |
| (c) | Leeds United didn't win the football match | | | • |
| (d) | I didn't know her address | | | • |
| (e) | The train didn't stop in Frankfurt | | | • |
| (f) | Cars weren't expensive in the 1960s | • | | |
| (g) | After school, Laura didn't go to University | | | • |
| (h) | He didn't bring her flowers | | | • |
| (i) | She wasn't very friendly | • | | |
| (j) | We didn't speak Greek all evening | | | • |
| (k) | I didn't give up smoking | | | • |

| | | Study/revise Unit 23 | 24 | 25 |
|---|---|---|---|---|
| 4. (b) | Where did Claire and Nick go on holiday? | | | • |
| (c) | What nationality were Chopin and Marie Curie? | • | | |
| (d) | Who did Prince Charles marry in 1981? | | | • |
| (e) | Why did he buy the car? | | | • |
| (f) | When was Rio de Janeiro the capital of Brazil? | • | | |
| (g) | When did Aleksander Kwasniewski become the president of Poland? | | | • |
| (h) | When did Queen Victoria die? | | | • |
| (i) | When was he in Cairo? | • | | |
| 5. (b) | When **did** King Henry VIII **die**? | | | • |
| (c) | Correct | • | | |
| (d) | Did you **go** to the party last night? | | | • |
| (e) | 'Did you enjoy the film?' 'Yes, it **was** great' | • | | |
| (f) | Correct | | • | |
| (g) | Last year on holiday the weather **wasn't** good | • | | |
| (h) | I didn't **give** her a present for her birthday | | | • |
| (i) | **Did** you **eat** toast for breakfast? | | | • |
| 6. (b) | I **paid** a lot of money for that! | | • | |
| (c) | Correct | | • | |
| (d) | Correct | | • | |
| (e) | We **travelled** all over Europe | | • | |
| (f) | Correct | | • | |
| (g) | Jonny and Duncan **played** football yesterday | | • | |

## *Part eight: (Units 26–31) Adding meaning*

| | | Study/revise Unit 26 | 27 | 28 | 29 | 30 | 31 |
|---|---|---|---|---|---|---|---|
| 1. (b) | Can/Could/May | | • | | | | |
| (c) | should | | | | | • | |
| (d) | Would | • | | | | | |
| (e) | have to | | | | • | | |
| (f) | can/could/may | | • | | | | |
| (g) | Can/Could | | • | | | | |
| (h) | Would | • | | | | | |
| (i) | should | | | | | • | |
| (j) | would | • | | | | | |
| (k) | Can/Could/May | | • | | | | |
| (l) | should | | | | | • | |
| (m) | have to | | | | • | | |
| 2. (b) | can | | | • | | | |
| (c) | might | | | | | | • |
| (d) | have to | | | | • | | |
| (e) | could | | | • | | | |
| (f) | Can/May | | • | | | | |
| (g) | can | | | • | | | |
| (h) | have to | | | | • | | |
| (i) | would | • | | | | | |
| (j) | can/could | | • | | | | |
| (k) | might | | | | | | • |
| (l) | could | | | • | | | |
| (m) | have to | | | | • | | |
| (n) | can | | | • | | | |
| (o) | can't | | | • | | | |
| (p) | can | | • | | | | |
| (q) | would | • | | | | | |

| | | Study/revise Unit 26 | 27 | 28 | 29 | 30 | 31 |
|---|---|---|---|---|---|---|---|
| 3. (b) | might | | | | | | • |
| (c) | might | | | | | | • |
| (d) | should | | | | | • | |
| (e) | might | | | | | | • |
| (f) | should | | | | | • | |
| (g) | might | | | | | | • |
| (h) | might | | | | | | • |
| (i) | should | | | | | • | |
| (j) | might | | | | | | • |
| (k) | should | | | | | • | |
| 4. (b) | can | | | • | | | |
| (c) | Would | • | | | | | |
| (d) | might | | | | | | • |
| (e) | has to | | | | • | | |
| (f) | can | | • | | | | |
| (g) | should | | | | | • | |
| (h) | would | • | | | | | |
| (i) | have to | | | | • | | |
| (j) | should | | | | | • | |
| 5. (b) | **Can** you swim? | | | • | | | |
| (c) | He **has** to work very late | | | | • | | |
| (d) | Correct | | | | | • | |
| (e) | It might **rain** tomorrow | | | | | | • |
| (f) | May I **go** out tonight? | | • | | | | |
| (g) | English is very difficult. I have **to** work so hard! | | | | • | | |
| (h) | What **would** he like? | • | | | | | |

## *Part nine: (Units 32–33) Talking about the past II*

| | | Study/revise Unit 32 | 33 |
|---|---|---|---|
| 1. (b) | John and Barbara **were walking** in the park. | • | |
| (c) | **Was** he **visiting** his parents? | • | |
| (d) | You **were eating** breakfast. | • | |
| (e) | Alan **wasn't swimming**. | • | |
| (f) | **Were** they **listening** to the radio? | • | |
| (g) | Kate **wasn't watching** the television. | • | |
| (h) | We **were making** dinner. | • | |
| (i) | The sun **wasn't shining**. | • | |
| (j) | **Was** it **raining**? | • | |
| (k) | Richard **was driving** to town. | • | |

| | | Study/revise Unit 32 | 33 |
|---|---|---|---|
| 2. (b) | It **was raining** when John **arrived**. | | • |
| (c) | I **drove away** when the police **arrived**. | | • |
| (d) | Julie **was visiting** her uncle when the lights **went out**. | | • |
| (e) | They **were driving** home when they **saw** Jane. | | • |
| (f) | I **cooked** dinner when John **got** home. | | • |
| (g) | Steve **was running** in the park when he **fell** in the lake. | | • |
| (h) | I **was writing** a letter when somebody **knocked** on the door. | | • |
| (i) | Helen **drove** to her mothers house when she **heard** the news. | | • |
| (j) | Emma **was sleeping** when Marianna **woke** her up. | | • |

| | | Study/revise Unit 32 | 33 |
|---|---|---|---|
| 3. (b) | As they were dancing, a strange man **came** to talk to them. | | • |
| (c) | Nick **was sleeping** when the storm started. | | • |
| (d) | Sarah was reading when the doorbell **rang**. | | • |
| (e) | Alison and Alex **were walking** along the street when they saw an accident. | | • |
| (f) | I **bought** a hamburger while the children were swimming. | | • |
| (g) | Eric **fell asleep** during the film but he woke up at the end. | | • |
| (h) | The sun **was shining** when the plane landed. | | • |
| (i) | Jill **was waiting** for a train when the rain started. | | • |

## *Part ten: (Units 34–37) Describing*

| | | Study/revise Unit 34 | 35 | 36 | 37 |
|---|---|---|---|---|---|
| 1. (b) | smaller | | • | | |
| (c) | more exciting | | • | | |
| (d) | richer | | • | | |
| (e) | fatter | | • | | |
| (f) | shyer | | • | | |
| (g) | more intelligent | | • | | |
| (h) | redder | | • | | |
| (i) | better | | • | | |
| 2. (b) | the furthest | | | • | |
| (c) | the poorest | | | • | |
| (d) | the earliest | | | • | |
| (e) | the hottest | | | • | |
| (f) | the laziest | | | • | |
| (g) | the hungriest | | | • | |
| (h) | the tallest | | | • | |
| (i) | the best | | | • | |
| 3. (b) | The Nile is **longer** than the Thames | | • | | |
| (c) | Paris is **more expensive** than Warsaw | | • | | |
| (d) | Mandarin Chinese is **more difficult** than French | | • | | |
| (e) | Tokyo is **bigger** than London | | • | | |
| (f) | A car is **faster** than a bicycle | | • | | |
| (g) | A trumpet is **noisier** than a flute | | • | | |
| (h) | An armchair is **more comfortable** than a stool | | • | | |
| 4. (b) | That football team is the **worst** in the world | | | • | |
| (c) | It's one of the **smallest** cities in South America | | | • | |
| (d) | He's the most **boring/uninteresting** man I've ever met | | | • | |
| (e) | Who is the **youngest**? | | | • | |
| (f) | She must be the **most beautiful** woman in the world! | | | • | |
| (g) | Which is the **noisiest** room? | | | • | |
| (h) | I bought the **most expensive** ticket | | | • | |
| 5. (b) | **slow**/slowly | • | | | |
| (c) | bad/**badly** | | | | • |
| (d) | tidy/**tidily** | | | | • |
| (e) | **noisy**/noisily | • | | | |
| (f) | happy/**happily** | | | | • |
| (g) | **clever**/cleverly | • | | | |
| (h) | **quick**/quickly | • | | | |
| (i) | angry/**angrily** | | | | • |
| 6. (b) | You cook really **well** | • | | | • |
| (c) | He's a **terrible** teacher! | • | | | • |
| (d) | The sea was very **deep** | • | | | • |
| (e) | Did you have a **great** holiday? | • | | | • |
| (f) | This exercise is quite **easy** | • | | | • |
| (g) | He drank the water **thirstily** | • | | | • |
| (h) | I feel awful – I slept really **badly** | • | | | • |
| (i) | He's a very **naughty** child | • | | | • |
| (j) | I looked for it very **carefully** | • | | | • |

## *Part eleven: (Units 38–40) Talking about the future*

| | Answer | Study/revise Unit 38 | 39 | 40 |
|---|---|---|---|---|
| 1. (b) | Next summer **I'm going to** visit my relatives in America. It's all arranged. | | • | |
| (c) | 'Oh no! Those cars **are going to** crash!' 'BANG!!!!' | | | • |
| (d) | A: 'What do you want to do tonight?' B: 'I don't know. **I'll** ring you later, Ok?' | | • | |
| (e) | A: 'My plane gets in at 2.30 am' B: '**I'll** meet you at the airport.' A: 'Are you sure?' | | • | |
| (f) | I'm so happy – **I'm going to** have a baby! | | | • |
| (g) | You're quite good at maths. I expect you'**ll** pass the exam. | | | • |
| (h) | I couldn't answer any of the exam questions! **I'm going to** fail! | | | • |
| (i) | The neighbours **are going to** have a party tonight. Shall we go? | | • | |
| (j) | She looks very upset and sad. I think she'**s going to** cry | | | • |
| (k) | The weather next week **will continue** to be sunny | | | • |
| (l) | When I grow up **I'm going to be** a marine biologist. | | • | |

| | Answer | Study/revise Unit 38 | 39 | 40 |
|---|---|---|---|---|
| 2. (b) | Correct | | • | |
| (c) | You'll put on weight | | | • |
| (d) | I'm going to buy a car | | • | |
| (e) | Correct | | | • |
| (f) | I'll pick you up | | • | |
| (g) | I'm going to marry Julian | | • | |
| 3. (b) | **I'm seeing** the doctor tomorrow morning | • | | |
| (c) | What time **does** the play **end**? | • | | |
| (d) | The conference **starts** on May 22nd | • | | |
| (e) | He **is meeting** Jake later tonight | • | | |
| (f) | What **are** you **doing** tomorrow? | • | | |
| (g) | I need to go home now because John **is ringing** me at 8.00 | • | | |
| (h) | Lisa and Roger **are coming** for dinner tomorrow night | • | | |
| (i) | The plane **leaves** at 9.00 so we need to be at the airport by 7.00 | • | | |
| (j) | Can I borrow your new jacket? **I'm going** for a job interview tomorrow. | • | | |

## *Part twelve: (Units 41–44) Connecting the past and the present*

| | Answer | Study/revise Unit 41 | 42 | 43 | 44 |
|---|---|---|---|---|---|
| 1. (b) | drunk | • | | • | • |
| (c) | seen | • | | | • |
| (d) | worn | • | | | |
| (e) | written | • | • | | |
| (f) | known | • | • | | |
| (g) | eaten | • | | • | • |
| (h) | gone/been | • | | | • |
| (i) | broken | • | | • | |
| (j) | had | • | • | | • |
| (k) | got | • | | | |
| (l) | cut | | | • | |
| 2. (b) | I broke | • | | | |
| (c) | have you lived | | • | | |
| (d) | Have you paid | | | | • |
| (e) | Have you been | | | • | |
| (f) | Have you ever eaten | • | | | |
| (g) | We've been married | | • | | |
| (h) | I've already read | | | | • |
| (i) | did you eat | • | | | |
| (j) | Have you had | | • | | |
| (k) | have you written | | | | • |
| (l) | Have you dyed | | | • | |
| (m) | has stolen | | | • | |

| | Answer | Study/revise Unit 41 | 42 | 43 | 44 |
|---|---|---|---|---|---|
| 3. (b) | I've already done it | | | | • |
| (c) | have you been | | • | | |
| (d) | I lived | | • | | |
| (e) | I've never been | • | | | |
| (f) | What have you done | | | • | |
| (g) | haven't bought | | | | • |
| (h) | I went | • | | | |
| (i) | I have cleaned | | | • | |
| (j) | I've already posted it | | | | • |
| 4. (a) | haven't seen | | • | | |
| (b) | Have you been | | | • | |
| (c) | went | | | • | |
| (d) | Have you ever been | • | | | |
| (e) | I haven't been | | | | • |
| (f) | Have you booked a hotel | | | | • |
| (g) | We've already arranged everything | | | | • |
| (h) | have never seen | • | | | |
| (i) | I saw | • | | | |
| (j) | haven't tied | | | • | |
| (k) | have forgotten | | | • | |
| (l) | have been married | | • | | |
| (m) | Have you ever argued | • | | | |
| (n) | have had | | • | | |

# Appendix 4: Answers and explanations to Unit 'Teaching' pages

*Note: Handscript indicates what is expected to have been filled in*

## *Unit 1: Present tense of the verb 'to be' (is/am/are)*

**Meaning**

I am Susan
I am from London

I am John
My name is Steve
We are friends

His name is Carlos
He is from Mozambique

This is the International School
It is in Manchester

You are in Class 2a

They are from Rome
They are Italian

This is Claire
She is a student

**Form**

I'm from London
You're in my class
She's from Poland
He's a student
It's in London
We're German
They're from Denmark

She's not from Poland
She isn't from Poland
We're not German
We aren't German

He's not a student
He isn't a student
They're not from Denmark
They aren't from Denmark

It's not in London
It isn't in London
I'm not from London
(only one possibility here - we DON'T say 'I amn't')

---

## *Unit 2: Verb 'to be': questions (Am I?/Are you?/Is he?)*

**Meaning**

(a) 'Is he French? – 3 No he isn't
(b) 'Are we friends now?' – 5 No we're not
(c) 'Where are you from?' – 6 Spain
(d) 'What's your name?' – 4 Keiko
(e) 'Is she from Japan?' – 2 Yes, she is
(f) 'Are you a model?' – 1 No, I'm not

**Form**

**I/you**
'Am I boring?' — 'No, you aren't/you're not'
'Are you tired?' — 'Yes, I am'
**He/She/It**
'Is she your sister?' — 'Yes, she is.'
'Is he from Venezuala?' — 'No, he isn't./he's not'
**We**
'Are we late?' — 'No, we aren't./we're not'
**They**
'Are they married?' — 'Yes, they are'

**Rules**

Normally we put the verb 'to be' after the subject, but to make questions with the verb 'to be' we put the verb before the subject

| | | |
|---|---|---|
| ***Example:*** | Subject + Verb | Verb + Subject |
| | [You're Polish = **Are** you Polish?] | |

To make negative short answers we contract but to make positive short answers we do NOT contract

**Example:** [No, **I'm not**/Yes, **I am**]

Negative short answers can contract two different ways (except No, I'm not)*

***Example:*** [No, **he's not** or No, **he isn't**]

*see Unit 1

**Question words**

1. (a) Is she very rich?
   (b) Why is she very rich?
2. (a) Is Warsaw in Poland?
   (b) Where is Warsaw?
3. (a) Are they both 16?
   (b) How old are they?
4. (a) Are we late?
   (b) Why are we late?

## *Unit 3: This/that/these/those*

### Meaning

(a) = (2); (b) = (1); (c) = (1); (d) = (2)

### Form

| | | | |
|---|---|---|---|
| This **is** the bathroom | 'This' and 'that' are **singular** | These **are** my children | 'These' and 'those' are **plural** |
| That'**s** the kitchen | | Those **are** my bags | |
| This room'**s** beautiful | | These apples **are** green | |
| That bag'**s** mine | | Those chairs **are** uncomfortable! | |

Remember that only **'that's** normally contracts. So we *don't* write **this's**.

**Negative statements and questions**

| | | |
|---|---|---|
| This is your room | This isn't your room | Is this your room? |
| That's your daughter | That isn't your daughter | Is that your daughter? |
| These are his keys | These aren't his keys | Are these his keys? |
| Those are our bicycles | Those aren't our bicycles | Are those our bicycles? |
| This room is beautiful | This room isn't beautiful | Is this room beautiful? |
| That room is John's | That room isn't John's | Is that room John's? |
| These curtains are very nice | These curtains aren't very nice | Are these curtains very nice? |
| Those chairs are uncomfortable | Those chairs aren't uncomfortable | Are those chairs uncomfortable? |

Note: We can use this/that/these/those *next* to a noun - This room is beautiful, or put the noun *after* the verb 'to be' – This is your room

---

## *Unit 4: Singular and plural nouns*

### Meaning

1. In picture (a) there is **a** dictionary. In picture (b) there are **two** dictionaries.
2. In picture (a) there is **a** teacher. In picture (b) there are **two** teachers.
3. In picture (a) there are **two** keys. In picture (b) there is **a** key.
4. In picture (a) there are **three** desks. In picture (b) there is **a** desk.
5. In picture (a) there are **five** people. In picture (b) there are **ten** people.
6. In picture (a) there is **a** pen. In picture (b) there are **three** pens.
7. In picture (a) there are **two** buses. In picture (b) there is **a** bus.
8. In picture (a) there are **two** women. In picture (b) there are **four** women.
9. In picture (a) there is **a** man. In picture (b) there are **two** men.
10. In picture (a) there are **two** sandwiches. In picture (b) there is **a** sandwich.
11. In picture (a) there is **a** book (not the dictionary). In picture (b) there are **nine** books (not the dictionaries).
12. In picture (a) there are **two** children. In picture (b) there are **four** children.

We use the plural form when there is *more than one* [2, 3, 4, 5, 6 ...]

### Form

| | SINGULAR | PLURAL |
|---|---|---|
| (a) | book | **books** |
| | **desk** | desks |
| | table | **tables** |
| | **teacher** | teachers |
| | pen | **pens** |

**RULE:** Most nouns add '**s**' in the plural

| | SINGULAR | PLURAL |
|---|---|---|
| (b) | **bus** | buses |
| | sandwich | **sandwiches** |

**RULE:** When the last SOUND of the noun is/s/S/tS/dz/we add '**es**' in the plural

| | SINGULAR | PLURAL |
|---|---|---|
| (c) | dictionary | **dictionaries** |

**RULE:** When the noun ends consonant + y the 'y' changes to '**ies**'

| | SINGULAR | PLURAL |
|---|---|---|
| (d) | **key** | keys |

**RULE:** When the noun ends vowel + y the 'y' does NOT change to -ies, we add '**s**' [Like rule (a)]

| | SINGULAR | PLURAL |
|---|---|---|
| (e) | man | **men** |
| | **woman** | women |
| | person | **people** |
| | child | **children** |

**RULE:** Some nouns (not only these four) are *irregular.* A good dictionary will help you with these.

## *Unit 5: Present simple tense*

### Meaning

We use the present simple tense to talk about things that are generally true.

### Form

| | be | make | work | go | finish | have | play | study |
|---|---|---|---|---|---|---|---|---|
| **I** | am | make | work | go | finish | have | play | study |
| **you** | are | make | work | go | finish | have | play | study |
| **he/she/it** | is | makes | works | goes | finishes | has | plays | studies |
| **we** | are | make | work | go | finish | have | play | study |
| **they** | are | make | work | go | finish | have | play | study |

After he/she/it we usually add -s to the verb

**Spelling**

INFINITIVE HE/SHE/IT

(a) work works
make makes
get up gets up
live lives
**RULE:** Most verbs add 's after he/she/it

(b) finish finishes
watch watches
**RULE:** When the last SOUND of the verb is/s/S/tS/dz/ we add -es after he/she/it

(c) study studies
**RULE:** When the verb ends consonant +y the 'y' changes to ies

(d) play plays
**RULE:** When the verb ends vowel +y the 'y' does NOT change to -ies, we add -s [Like Rule a]

(e) go goes
have has
be is
**RULE**: Some verbs (not many) are irregular

---

## *Unit 6: Present simple auxiliaries*

### Meaning

QUESTIONS
What time does the train leave?
Where do I buy a ticket?
When do we arrive in Paris?
Does this train go to Berlin?
Do we stop at Munich?

NEGATIVES
Sorry, I don't know
This train doesn't go to Paris

SHORT ANSWERS
Yes, we do

### Form

**Look at your examples and complete the rules**

- To make a **question** in the present simple tense with most verbs (go, arrive etc) we use:
[QUESTION WORD] + do OR does + SUBJECT + INFINITIVE
What/When/Why etc you/he/I etc go/arrive/etc [NOT goes, arrives]

- To make a **negative** in the present simple tense with most verbs we use:
SUBJECT + don't OR doesn't + INFINITIVE
I/She/it etc go/like/arrive etc

- To make a **short answer** in the present simple tense with most verbs we use:
YES/NO + SUBJECT + do OR does (positive) / don't OR doesn't (negative)
Yes, I do
No, it doesn't

- When the subject is **I, you, we, they,** we use do (positive) or don't (negative)
- When the subject is **he, she, it,** we use does (positive) or doesn't (negative)

## *Unit 7: Adverbs 1: adverbs of frequency*

**Meaning**

Mr Jones is **never** at home in the evenings
He **always** eats caviar and drinks champagne
He **often** goes on holiday
He **rarely** takes exercise
He **sometimes** smokes a cigar

Mr Smith is **always** at home in the evenings
He **often** runs in the park
He **never** drives a car
He **rarely** goes on holiday
He **sometimes** goes to watch a football match

| ALWAYS 100% | OFTEN | SOMETIMES | RARELY | NEVER 0% |
|---|---|---|---|---|

**Form**

The VERB in sentence (a) is '**stay**'
The VERB in sentence (b) is '**is**' (the verb 'to be')

With a verb like stay/go/drink etc the *frequency adverb* (never, always etc) **usually*** goes **before** the verb.
With the verb 'to be' (is/are etc) the *frequency adverb* **usually*** goes **after** the verb.

[*'Usually' because sometimes a different word order is possible but this one is *always correct*]

---

## *Unit 8: Subject and object pronouns*

**Meaning**

(a) I = **John**
(b) you = **Barbara**
(c) me = **John**
(d) you = **John**
(e) me = **Barbara**
(f) you = **John**
(g) They = **Barbara's family**
(h) us = **John and Barbara**
(i) we = **John and Barbara**
(j) them = **Barbara's family**
(k) she = **Barbara's mother**
(l) him = **Barbara's father**
(m) he = **Barbara's father**
(n) her = **Barbara's mother**
(o) you = **John and John's family**
(p) it = **the ring**
(q) I = **Barbara**
(r) it = **the ring**

**Form**

(a) I = **subject**
(b) you = **object**
(c) me = **object**
(d) you = **subject**
(e) me = **object**
(f) you = **subject**
(g) They = **subject**
(h) us = **object**
(i) we = **subject**
(j) them = **object**
(k) she = **subject**
(l) him = **object**
(m) he = **subject**
(n) her = **object**
(o) you = **subject**
(p) it = **subject**
(q) I = **subject**
(r) it = **object**

Notice that *'you'* and *'it'* can be both subject *and* object pronouns

| SUBJECT PRONOUNS | OBJEC T PRONOUNS |
|---|---|
| I | **me** |
| **you** | you |
| he | **him** |
| **she** | her |
| it | **it** |
| **we** | us |
| you | **you** |
| **they** | them |

## *Unit 9: Possessive adjectives and 's*

### Meaning

| Possessive adjective | | ...'s |
|---|---|---|
| (a) my | = | Mary's |
| (b) your | = | Debbie's |
| (c) his | = | Great-grandfather's |
| (d) her | = | Harry's wife's/Edith's |
| (e) their | = | Harry and Edith's |
| (f) its | = | the dog's |
| (g) our | = | Mary and Debbie's |

| | | |
|---|---|---|
| (a) is | (d) is | (g) possession |
| (b) is | (e) possession | (h) is |
| (c) possession | (f) is | |

### Form

| | |
|---|---|
| I | my |
| you | your |
| he | his |
| she | her |
| it | its |
| we | our |
| they | their |

*Notice that 'her' has the same form as the object pronoun (Unit 8)*

---

## *Unit 10: Possessive pronouns*

### Meaning

Whose is this?
I think it's hers

Is this his?

These are ours

Richard? Is this yours?

I think these are theirs

Look! Jane's is here now.

This isn't mine

Where are yours?

### Form

| Possessive adjective + noun | Possessive pronoun |
|---|---|
| my suitcase(s) | mine |
| your bag(s) | yours |
| his suitcase(s) | his |
| her bag(s) | hers |
| our bag(s) | ours |
| their suitcase(s) | theirs |
| | |
| 's + noun | 's |
| Jane's bag(s) | Jane's |

## Unit 11: Articles

### Meaning

Peter lives in O London. It's a big city. It's the capital of O Britain. It's an expensive city but Peter has a good job. He's a lawyer. He has a big house near the Thames. The house was very expensive but it's beautiful.

1. London and Britain are places — **So, we generally use nothing with places**
2. The Thames is a river — **So, we use 'the' with the names of rivers**
3. Lawyer is a job — **So, we use 'a' [or 'an'] with jobs**
4. There is only one capital of Britain — **So, we use 'the' when there is only one**
5. There are many big cities in Britian
   There many any expensive cities
   There are many good jobs
   There are many big houses — **So, we use 'a' when we talk about *one of many***
6. The first time the text talked about Peter's house it was one of many [He has a big house], but the second time [The house was very expensive] you knew *which* house.
   **So, when we know *which* thing we mean we use 'the'.**

### Form and Pronunciation

We use an when the first SOUND of the next word is a vowel sound.[ae/e/i/i:/au etc]
We use a when the first SOUND of the next word is a consonant. [b/d/f/t/g/h etc]

Remember it is the first **sound** and maybe not the first **letter**.

Sometimes the letter 'u' is pronounced /ju:/so we DON'T use 'an' [Example: university]
Sometimes the letter 'h' is silent so we DO use 'an' [Example: hour]

---

## Unit 12: Relative pronouns (who/which/that)

### Meaning

A person **who** has children is *a parent*
An animal **that** has a very long nose is *an elephant*
A house **which** only has one floor is *a bungalow*
A man **who** is married is *a husband*
An animal **which** eats grass is *a cow*
A person **that** can play the piano is *a pianist*

- We can use **who** to define (a) - people
- We can use **which** to define (b) - things
- We can use **that** * to define (c) - people and things

(*It is possible to use 'that' for people but we usually prefer 'who')

So, to say more about **what sort of** *person* it is we use who or sometimes that
To say more about **what sort of** *thing* it is we use which or that

### Form

1. A parent is a person. (What sort of person?) – He/She has children
   **A parent is a person who has children**
   What happens to 'he/she'? We replace 'he/she' with who
2. A dictionary is a book (What sort of book?) – Students use it
   **A dictionary is a book that students use**
   What happens to 'it'? We replace 'it' with that

A wife is a woman who has a husband
A mechanic is a person who repairs cars
A Reliant Robin is a car which (or 'that') only has three wheels
Concorde is a plane which (or 'that') goes very fast

## *Unit 13: Have got*

**Form**

| Positive sentences | Negative sentences | Questions | Short answers |
|---|---|---|---|
| I've got | I haven't got | Have I got? | Yes, I have/No, I haven't |
| You've got | You haven't got | Have you got? | Yes, you have/No, you haven't |
| He/She/It's got | He/She/It hasn't got | Has he/she/it got? | Yes, he/she/it has<br>No, he/she/it hasn't |
| We've got | We haven't got | Have we got? | Yes, we have/No, we haven't |
| They've got | They haven't got | Have they got? | Yes, they have/No, they haven't |

Remember: We can use 'have' with 'got' or as a normal present simple verb (see unit 5)

How many has he got? = How many does he have?
He hasn't got it = He doesn't have it
I've got 625,000 = I have 625,000

**Have** you got a big collection? Yes, I have
**Does** he have all the cards he wants? No, he doesn't
**Has** he got more than 100,000 cards? Yes, he has
**Do** you have a complete set? No, I don't

Notice how the answer *matches* the question.

---

## *Unit 14: Countable and Uncountable nouns*

**Meaning**

What can you **count**? Write the noun and the letter
Eggs (b) Cakes (e) Chocolates (g) Bananas (i) Pounds (k)
THESE ARE **COUNTABLE** NOUNS

What **can't** you **count**? Write the noun and the number
Milk (a) Flour (c) Cake (d) Chocolate (f) Bread (h) Money (j)
THESE ARE **UNCOUNTABLE** NOUNS

What can you **sometimes count** and **sometimes not count**- with a ***different meaning***? Write the noun and the letter
Chocolate (f) Chocolates (g) Cake (d) Cakes (e)
SOME NOUNS CAN BE COUNTABLE **AND** UNCOUNTABLE – *WITH A DIFFERENT MEANING*

**Form**

'Banana' is countable
Yes, we **can use a/an** with countable nouns
Yes, we **can use a number** with countable nouns
Yes, we **can make countable nouns plural**

'Milk' is uncountable.
No, we **can't use a/an** with uncountable nouns
No, we **can't use a number** with uncountable nouns
No, we **can't make uncountable nouns plural**

### *Unit 15: 'Some' and 'any'*

**Meaning**

Bob and Marcia can make **Shepherd's Pie** for dinner.

When we say 'some' or 'any' we DON'T know exactly how many potatoes, peppers and onions there are.
*Potatoes, peppers* and *onions* are **countable**
We use **are** with plural countable nouns.

When we say 'some' or 'any' we DON'T know exactly how much rice, pasta and beef there is.
*Rice, pasta* and *beef* are **uncountable**.
We use **is** with uncountable nouns.

We usually* use **some** with *positive* sentences.
We usually* use **any** with *negative* sentences.
We usually* use **any** with *questions*.

[*'usually' because, *with a different meaning*, we can use 'some' in questions and 'any' in positive sentences.
For example:
Would you like **some** tea?
**Any**thing you can do, I can do better]

**Form**

Complete the table with **is/are** **some/any/a**

| | COUNTABLE NOUNS | UNCOUNTABLE NOUNS |
|---|---|---|
| **Positive** | *Singular*<br>There **is a** pepper<br>*Plural*<br>There **are some** peppers | There **is some** rice |
| **Negative** | *Singular*<br>There **isn't a** pepper<br>*Plural*<br>There **aren't any** peppers | There **isn't any** rice |
| **Questions** | *Singular*<br>**Is** there **a** pepper?<br>*Plural*<br>**Are** there **any** peppers? | **Is** there **any** rice? |

### *Unit 16: Much/many/a lot*

**Meaning**

Cigarettes are **countable**. (We can say *a* cigarette, *three* cigarettes)
Cigars are **countable**.
With countable nouns the question is **How many...?**

Wine is **uncountable** (We say *some* wine)
Perfume is **uncountable**
With uncountable nouns the question is **How much...?**

For more information on countable/uncountable see Unit 14

**Form**

COUNTABLE

| positive | negative |
|---|---|
| **a lot of**<br>cigarettes | **not a lot of**<br>cigarettes<br>*or*<br>**not many**<br>cigarettes |

UNCOUNTABLE

| positive | negative |
|---|---|
| **a lot of**<br>perfume | **not a lot of**<br>perfume<br>*or*<br>**not much**<br>perfume |

### *Unit 17: 'Too' and 'not enough'*

**Meaning**

Is the size of the class (number of students) OK? No
Is it more than is good or less than is good? More than is good
So, the class is *too* big

Is the size of the room OK? No
Is it more than is good or less than is good? Less than is good
So, the room is*n't* big *enough*

Is the number of students OK? No
Is it more than is good or less than is good? More than is good
So, there are *too* many students

Is the amount of noise OK? No
Is it more than is good or less than is good? More than is good
So, there is *too* much noise

Is the number of chairs OK? No
Is it more than is good or less than is good? Less than is good
So, there are*n't enough* chairs

Is the amount of light OK? No
Is it more than is good or less than is good? Less than is good
So, there is*n't enough* light

When there is *more* than is good we use too
When there is *less* than is good we use not enough

**Form**

**With adjectives:**
The class is *too* big/The room is*n't* big *enough*

TOO
'Too' comes before the adjective
ENOUGH
'Enough' comes after the adjective
'Not' comes before the adjective

We use 'much' and 'many' - with 'too'.

---

### *Unit 18: Present continuous tense*

**Meaning**

| | | | |
|---|---|---|---|
| Does she speak French? | Yes [generally] | Is she speaking Polish? | No [not at the moment] |
| Is she speaking French? | No [not at the moment] | Does she speak Chinese? | Yes [generally] |
| Does she speak Polish? | Yes [generally] | Is she speaking Chinese? | Yes [at **this** moment] |

'She speaks French' means (b) - generally, around now but maybe not at this exact moment.
'She's speaking Chinese' means (a) - now, at this *exact* moment.

**Form**

**Present continuous sentences:**
I/eat/dinner = I'm eating dinner
You/look/well = You're looking well
She/speak/Chinese = She's speaking Chinese
He/drink/coffee = He's drinking coffee
It/rain = It's raining
We/sit/down = We're sitting down
They/feel/ill = They're feeling ill

**The present continuous is formed:** I am eat*ing* dinner
Subject + verb 'to be' + verb +ing

**Spelling**
Remember that we usually add *-ing* to the infinitive of the verb. *But sometimes the spelling changes.*

A. bite - biting
smoke - smoking [We take away the 'e']
write - writing

B. lie - lying
die - dying [The 'ie' becomes 'y']

C run - running
hit - hitting [When we have consonant (bcdfgh etc) + vowel (aeiou) + consonant at
swim - swimming the end of the word we double the last consonant]

***…ble and present continuous***

| | |
|---|---|
| **John's a journalist** | **Tom's a teacher** |
| **He writes for a national newspaper** | **He teaches small children** |
| **He's interviewing someone** | **He's thinking about going home** |

…out the present but sentences **(b)**, **(d)** and **(f)** emphasize NOW.
These sentences are **present continuous.**

Sentences **(a)**, **(c)**, **(e)**, **(g)**, **(h)** and **(i)** are about the present *in general.*

These sentences are **present simple**.

---

***Unit 20: Prepositions of place: in/on/next to***

**Meaning**

It's **in front of** the fire
It's **next to** a box
It's **on** a cushion

It's **under** the table
It's **opposite** the dog
It's **near** my feet

It's **next to** my feet
It's **behind** the chair
It's **opposite** the television

It's **in front of** the television
It's **near** the bowl
It's **in** a box

**Form**

Which preposition is this? **next** to
Which preposition is this? in **front** of
Can we say opposite to? **No, we usually say 'It's opposite the bank'**

## *Unit 21: Prepositions of time: in/at/on*

### Meaning and Form

***AT***

We use **at** for:

the time of day: **at 6.00, at midnight, at noon**
festivals of more than one day: **at Christmas, at Easter**
mealtimes: **at tea time**
and three more you need to remember: **at the weekend***, **at night, at the moment**

*In American English you can say on the weekend

***IN***

We use **in** for:

years, or groups of years: **in 1966, in the 1980s, in the 20th century**
periods of the day: **in the evening, in the afternoon**
seasons: **in (the) summer**
months: **in April**
and two more you need to remember: **in the future, in the past**

***ON***

We use **on** for:

days: **on Saturday, on Friday evening**
special days: **on Christmas Day, on my birthday**
dates: **on 14th May***

* We **write** 'on 14th May' but we **say** 'On *the* 14th *of* May'

***NO PREPOSITION***

When there is an *adjective* (this/next etc) we *don't* use a preposition: **next week, last night.**

| AT | IN | ON |
|---|---|---|
| at Christmas | in **the** future* | on Friday |
| at **the** moment | in April | on Tuesday morning |
| at 11.00 | in **the** 15th Century | on 25th December (but we *say* the) |
| at midnight | in **the** morning | on Valentine's Day |
| at **the** weekend | in (**the**) winter (possible with and without *the*) | on Saturdays |

*We can also say 'In future..' when we mean 'From this moment on...'
Example: 'You're late again. In future, please come on time.'

---

## *Unit 22: Prepositions of movement*

### Meaning

**out of** the barracks

**up** the hill

**past** the post-office

**from** the barracks **to** the river

**down** the hill

**across/over** the road

**across/over** the bridge

**through** the park

**under** the railway bridge

**along** the river-bank

**round** the statue

Then jump **on** this box

and jump **off** the box – 20 times!

Then you can go **into** the barracks and rest

### *Unit 23: Past simple tense of verb 'to be': was/were*

**Form**

| SIMPLE PRESENT | | | SIMPLE PAST | | |
|---|---|---|---|---|---|
| **Positive** | **Negative** | **Question** | **Positive** | **Negative** | **Question** |
| I am | I'm not | Am I..? | I was | I wasn't | Was I..? |
| You are | You aren't | Are you..? | You were | You weren't | Were you..? |
| He is | He isn't | Is he..? | He was | He wasn't | Was he..? |
| She is | She isn't | Is she..? | She was | She wasn't | Was she..? |
| It is | It isn't | Is it..? | It was | It wasn't | Was it..? |
| We are | We aren't | Are we..? | We were | We weren't | Were we..? |
| They are | They aren't | Are they..? | They were | They weren't | Were they..? |

---

### *Unit 24: Past simple tense*

**Meaning**

was - be
made - make
decorated - decorate
got - get

lit - light
rose - rise
were - be

built - build
stayed - stay
flew - fly

**Form**

'Decorate' and 'stay' are regular verbs. So, to form the past tense of regular verbs we add -ed to the infinitive
**Example**: stay – stayed
Notice that if there is already an 'e' on the end of the word we do *NOT* add *another* 'e'
**Example**: decorate – decorated

***The irregular verbs:***

| Infinitive | Past Simple | Infinitive | Past Simple |
|---|---|---|---|
| begin | began | | |
| break | broke | buy | bought |
| can | could | do | did |
| drink | drank | go | went |
| have | had | say | said |
| see | saw | take | took |
| write | wrote | | |

*Spelling*
(a) ied
(b) d
(c) consonant

## *Unit 25: Past simple auxiliary: did/didn't*

### Meaning

1. When **did** the Normans invade Britain?
2. When **did** Queen Victoria die?
3. **Did** King George I speak English?
4. What **did** John Logie Baird invent?
5. **Did** Queen Victoria have nine children?
6. Why **did** Edward VIII give up the throne?
7. **Did** the English ever kill their King?

(a) The television (4)
(b) No, **he didn't** (only German) (3)
(c) In 1066 (1)
(d) Yes, **she did** (5)
(e) Because he wanted to marry a divorced woman (6)
(f) In 1901 (2)
(g) Yes, they **did** (Charles the First) (7)

| | |
|---|---|
| Henry the Eighth **didn't have** six wives | FALSE |
| Queen Elizabeth the First **didn't get married** | TRUE |
| The Duke of Wellington **didn't win** the Battle of Waterloo | FALSE |
| Cromwell **didn't win** the Civil War | FALSE |
| The English people **didn't like** Queen Victoria | FALSE |

### Form

**QUESTIONS**

| | [Question word] + | did + | subject + | infinitive+....... |
|---|---|---|---|---|
| 1. | When | did | the Normans | invade Britain? |
| 2. | When | did | Queen Victoria | die? |
| 3. | | Did | King George I | speak English? |
| 4. | What | did | John Logie Baird | invent? |
| 5. | | Did | Queen Victoria | have nine children? |
| 6. | Why | did | Edward VIII | give up his throne? |
| 7. | | Did | the English | ever kill their King? |

**NEGATIVES**

| Subject + | didn't + | infinitive |
|---|---|---|
| Henry VIII | didn't | have six wives |
| The Duke of Wellington | didn't | win the battle of Waterloo |
| Queen Elizabeth the First | didn't | get married |
| Cromwell | didn't | win the Civil War |
| The English people | didn't | like Queen Victoria |

**SHORT ANSWERS**

| Yes/No, + | subject + | did/didn't |
|---|---|---|
| No, | he | didn't |
| Yes, | she | did |
| Yes, | they | did |

---

## *Unit 26: Would like*

### Meaning

Does Bob like chocolate? Yes
Does Bob like apples? Yes, probably
Does Bob want chocolate **now**? No, – because he's on a diet
Does Bob want an apple **now**? Yes

When Ann asks '**Do you like** chocolate?' she is talking about in general.
When Ann asks '**Would you like** some chocolate?' she is talking about now.
Which question **means the same** as 'Do you want...?' (a) or (b) b

Does Susan like going to the theatre? Yes
Does she want to go with Paul on Friday? No
Which question **means the same** as 'Do you want...?' (c) or (d) d

**Form**

| | | | |
|---|---|---|---|
| I would like | I'd like | You would like | Would you like? |
| You would like | You'd like | He would like | Would he like? |
| He would like | He'd like | She would like | Would she like? |
| She would like | She'd like | We would like | Would we like? |
| We would like | We'd like | They would like | Would they like? |
| They would like | They'd like | | |

I like **cooking***
I'd like **to cook** dinner tonight

He likes **watching** television
He'd like **to watch** the football this afternoon

She likes **going to** the cinema
She'd like **to go** and see a film tonight

We like **playing** tennis
We'd like **to play** tennis this afternoon

*In American English it is often possible to say like + to + infinitive 'I like to cook'

---

### *Unit 27: Requests and permissions: can/could/may*

**Meaning**

Sentence **a** ['**Can** you give me a lift?'] is *asking someone to do something.*
Sentence **b** ['**Can** I have some more dessert, please?'] *is asking permission.*

Two words for asking someone to do something: **can** and **could**
**Could** is more formal/polite
John is more polite in the second dialogue because £5 is **a bigger favour** than salt.

Two words for *asking permission:* **can** and **may**
**May** is more formal/polite
The child is more polite in the second dialogue because permission to go to a party is **a bigger favour** than permission to watch tv

**Form**

*Requests (asking for something)*
**'Can/Could you help me?'** is correct.
*Permission*
**'Can/May I smoke?'** is correct.
So, after could/can/may we use the **infinitive**.

---

### *Unit 28: Ability (can/could)*

**Meaning**

*a secretary can type*
*a waiter can add up a bill*
*a cook can make a cake*
*a translator can speak two or more languages*
*a journalist can write*

We use **can/can't** to talk about **the present**
We use **could/couldn't** to talk about **the past**

**Form**

| | PRESENT | PAST |
|---|---|---|
| Question | How many languages can you speak? | Could you speak Italian well then? |
| Positive | I can speak French, German and Italian. | I could speak Italian when I was a child. |
| Positive Short Answer | Yes, I can. | Yes, I could |
| Negative | I can't speak any other languages. | I couldn't speak German until I went to live in Germany. |
| Negative Short Answer | No, I can't. | No, I couldn't. |

The *present tense* form of **can** for I/you/he/she/it/we/they (all persons) is **can**
The *past tense* form of **can** for I/you/he/she/it/we/they (all persons) is **could**

## *Unit 29: Obligation (have to)*

### Meaning

Is it necessary/obligatory for Tom to wear a uniform? Yes
So, Tom has to wear a uniform

Is it necessary/obligatory for Tom to study Latin? No
So, Tom doesn't have to study Latin

Is it necessary/obligatory for Tom's father to wear a hat *now*? No
**Was** it necessary/obligatory for Tom's father to wear a hat when he was at school? Yes
So, Tom's father had to wear a hat when he was at school

Is it necessary/obligatory for Tom's father to eat school dinners now? No
**Was** it necessary/obligatory for Tom's father to eat school dinners when he was at school? No
So, Tom's father didn't have to eat school dinners when he was at school

### Form

Use the examples above to help you complete the table

| | PRESENT | PAST |
|---|---|---|
| NECESSARY | | |
| I | have to study French | had to study Latin |
| You | have to study French | had to study Latin |
| He/She | has to study French | had to study Latin |
| We | have to wear a uniform | had to wear a hat |
| They | have to wear a uniform | had to wear a hat |
| *NOT* NECESSARY | | |
| I | don't have to study Latin | didn't have to study French |
| You | don't have to study Latin | didn't have to study French |
| He/She | doesn't have to study Latin | didn't have to study French |
| We | don't have to wear a hat | didn't have to eat school dinners |
| They | don't have to wear a hat | didn't have to eat school dinners |

**Questions and short answers**

| | | |
|---|---|---|
| He has to study French | Does he have to study French? | Yes, he does/No, he doesn't |
| They have to wear a uniform | Do they have to wear a uniform? | Yes, they do/No, they don't |
| He had to wear a hat | Did he have to wear a hat? | Yes, he did/No, he didn't |
| They had to study Latin | Did they have to study Latin? | Yes, they did/No, they didn't |

---

## *Unit 30: Advising (should/shouldn't)*

### Meaning

- smoke ✗
- eat less fat ✓
- eat fruit ✓
- exercise three times a week ✓
- eat a big meal before you go to bed ✗
- walk up the stairs rather than take the lift ✓
- drive everywhere ✗
- stay awake all night ✗

It isn't a good idea to smoke if you want to be healthy
So, if you want to be healthy you **shouldn't (should not)** smoke

It is a good idea to eat less fat if you want to be healthy.
So, if you want to be healthy, you should eat less fat

- You should eat fruit
- You should exercise three times a week
- You shouldn't eat a big meal before you go to bed
- You should walk up the stairs
- You shouldn't drive everywhere
- You shouldn't stay awake all night

### Form

The present tense form for **should/shouldn't** with I/you/he/she/it/we/they (all persons) is **should**

- I shouldn't smoke is *correct.* [after **should** we use the *infinitive*]

## *Unit 31: Possibility (may/might)*

### Meaning

***Positive***

Is the Princess definitely going to marry Prince Humphrey? **No**
Is she definitely NOT going to marry him? **No**
What word does she use to show she is not sure? **might**

Is the Princess definitely going to marry Prince Alfred? **No**
Is she definitely NOT going to marry him? **No**
What word does she use to show she is not sure? **may**

Do *may* and *might* have the same meaning when talking about possibility? **Yes** – (though some people think **might** is *less* possible than **may**)

***Negative***

Is the Princess definitely NOT going to marry either of the princes? **No**
What word does she use to show she is not sure? **mightn't**

Is the Princess definitely NOT going to marry anyone? **No**
What word(s) does she use to show she is not sure? **may not**

Do *may not* and *mightn't* have the same meaning when talking about negative possibility? **Yes** – (though some people think **mightn't** is *less* possible than **may not**)

### Form

The form of **might/mightn't** for *I/you/he/she/it/we/they* (all persons) is **might/mightn't**

The form of **may/may not** for *I/you/he/she/it/we/they* (all persons) is **may/may not**
It is **not** possible to write **mayn't**

---

## *Unit 32: Past continuous*

### Meaning

What time did Bill start playing the piano? **5.00**
What time did he finish playing the piano? **7.00**

What time did Tom and Tina start visiting? **4.00**
What time did they finish visiting? **6.30**

Sentences **(a)** and **(b)** are **past continuous**.
Sentence **(c)** is **past simple**.

### Form

| **SUBJECT** | + | **VERB TO BE (past)** | + | **VERB+ing** |
|---|---|---|---|---|
| I | | **was** | | read**ing** |
| You | | **were** | | speak**ing** |
| He/She/It | | **was** | | eat**ing** |
| We | | **were** | | play**ing** |
| They | | **were** | | work**ing** |

**Was I reading?**
**Were you speaking?**
**Was he eating?**
**Were we playing?**
**Were they working?**

**I wasn't reading**
**You weren't speaking**
**He wasn't eating**
**We weren't playing**
**They weren't working**

## *Unit 33: Past continuous and past simple*

### Meaning

(a) I was feeling tired = (1)

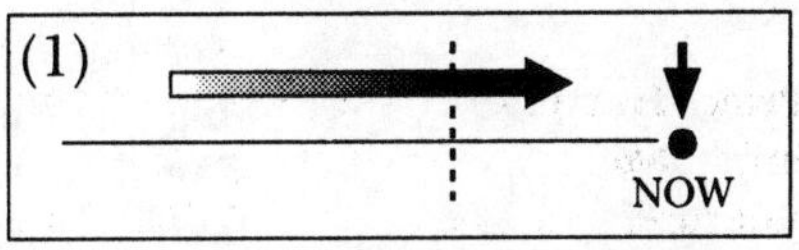


(b) I finally arrived home = (2)

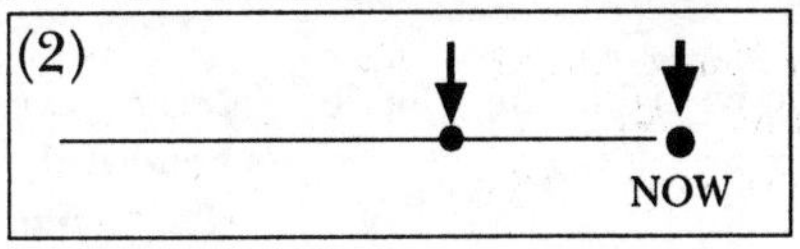


Was he feeling tired before the train arrived in Gloucester **Yes**
Did he *continue* feeling tired after the train arrived in Gloucester? **Yes**
Sentence **a** describes the *background situation.*
Sentence **a** is **past continuous**.
Sentence **b** describes an *action* that happened *during* the background situation.
Sentence **b** is **past simple**.

(c) The car park attendent was sleeping = (1)

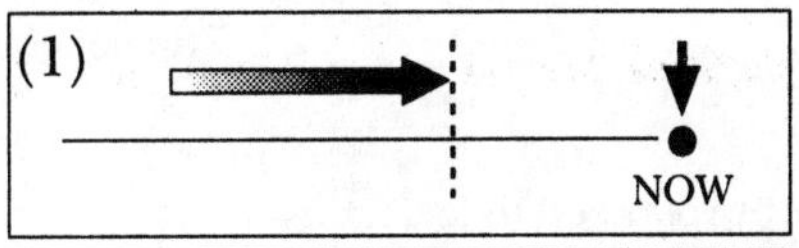


(d) I woke him up = (2)

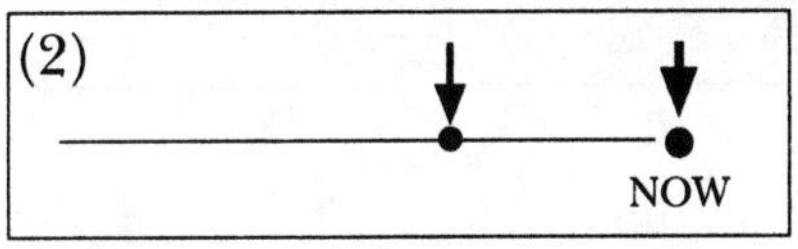


Was the carpark attendent sleeping before the man found him? **Yes**
Did he *continue* sleeping after the man found him? **No**
Sentence **c** describes the *background situation*
Sentence **c** is **past continuous**
Sentence **d** describes an *action* that happened *after* the background situation.
Sentence **d** is **past simple**.

### Form

*Note:-*
We use **when, as** and **while** to *join* past simple and past continuous in one sentence.
**Look at these examples:**

I *was walking* across the car-park **when** I *saw* a yellow clamp.
**When** I *was walking* across the car-park I *saw* a yellow clamp.
**As** I *was walking* across the car-park, I *saw* a yellow clamp.
**While** I *was walking* across the car-park, I *saw* a yellow clamp.

We normally use **when** with *both* past simple and past continuous.
We normally* use **as** with past continuous.
We normally* use **while** with past continuous.

*But it *is* possible to use **as** and **while** with past simple.

---

## *Unit 34: Adjectives I*

### Meaning

| | | | |
|---|---|---|---|
| A **black** cat | A **white** cat | A **fat** man | A **thin** man |
| An **old** house | A **new** house | A **young** woman | An **old** woman |
| He's **happy** | He's **sad** | We're **tall** | We're **short** |

### Form

The adjective goes **before** the noun.
**'a big house'** is correct.

**he's thin**
**they're rich**
**it's cold**
**I'm hungry**

**'big houses'** is the correct plural

## *Unit 35: Comparatives*

**Form**

*One syllable adjectives*

clean cleaner
cheap cheaper
small smaller
near nearer

**Rule:** To make a comparative from adjectives with one syllable we add **-er**

*-y adjectives*

ugly uglier
dirty dirtier

**Rule:** To make a comparative from adjectives with two syllables that **end in y** we change the 'y' to i and add er.

*iregular adjectives*

good better
bad worse
far further

(there aren't many irregular adjectives but you need to learn them)

*Spelling*

big bigger **We double the last letter of the adjective**
hot hotter **We double the last letter of the adjective**
safe safer **We don't need two e's**

*two or more syllable adjectives*

beautiful more beautiful
dangerous more dangerous
boring more boring

**Rule:** To make a comparative from adjectives with two syllables that **DON'T end in y** we use the word more before the adjective.

We often use *'than'* with comparatives. Look at these examples.

**Rio** is a much better place to live *than* **Brasilia.**
It's not true that **Brasilia** is uglier or more boring *than* **Rio.**
**The beaches in Rio** are dirtier *than* **ours.**

---

## *Unit 36: Superlatives*

**Meaning**

Which sentence (a, b or c) compares one roller coaster to a second rollercoaster? b
Write the comparative adjective* in the sentence faster

Which sentence compares one rollercoaster to all the other rollercoasters? c
Write the superlative adjective in the sentence the fastest

Which sentence just describes one rollercoaster? a
Write the adjective** in the sentence fast

*see Unit 35
**see Unit 34

(a) Bolton Towers is £12
(b) Courtney Park is £8
(c) Wondsworth Safari Park is £6

Which is **the most expensive?** Bolton Towers
Which is **the cheapest?** Wondsworth Safari Park
Is Courtney Park **more expensive** than Wondsworth Safari Park? Yes

**Form**

| ADJECTIVE | COMPARATIVE ADJECTIVE | SUPERLATIVE ADJECTIVE |
|---|---|---|
| **One syllable adjectives** | | |
| fast | faster | the fastest |
| cheap | cheaper | the cheapest |
| big | bigger | the biggest |
| near | nearer | the nearest |
| long | longer | the longest |

*To make a superlative adjective from an adjective with one syllable we add* the..............-est

| | | |
|---|---|---|
| **Two syllables or more** | | |
| exciting | more exciting | the most exciting |
| expensive | more expensive | the most expensive |
| educational | more educational | the most educational |
| comfortable | more comfortable | the most comfortable |

*To make a superlative adjective from an adjective with two syllables or more we add* the most...............

| | | |
|---|---|---|
| **Irregular** | | |
| good | better | the best |
| bad | worse | the worst |
| far | further | the furthest |

[*For spelling rules – see Unit 35*]

## *Unit 37: Adverbs II: manner*

### Meaning

| | | | | | |
|---|---|---|---|---|---|
| Night | noun | climbed | verb | Sarah | noun |
| blew | verb | house | noun | run | verb |
| | | candle | noun | went out | verb |
| | | voice | noun | screamed | verb |
| | | said | verb | | |

| | | |
|---|---|---|
| cold | night | (It was a *cold* night) |
| dark | house | (The house was *dark*) |
| long | candle | (She was holding a *long* candle) |
| strange | voice | (She heard a *strange* voice) |
| frightened | Sarah | (Sarah was really *frightened*) |

| | | |
|---|---|---|
| blew | noisily | (The wind blew *noisily* around the house) |
| climbed | slowly | (Sarah climbed the stairs *slowly*) |
| said | quietly | ('Welcome' it said, *quietly*) |
| run | quickly | (She started to run *quickly* down the stairs) |
| went out | suddenly | (*Suddenly* the candle went out) |
| screamed | loudly | (Sarah screamed *loudly*) |

### Form

'quick' is an adjective
'quickly' is an adverb
We usually add ly to an adjective to make an adverb

What happens to the *spelling* when the adjective ends in -y? 'y' changes to 'i'

| ADJECTIVE | IRREGULAR ADVERB |
|---|---|
| I am a **good** tennis player. | I play tennis well |
| This is a **fast** car. | Don't drive so fast. |
| This unit is quite **hard**. | You need to work hard to learn English! |
| I am always **late**. | He arrived late again. |

An **adjective** usually goes before the **noun**.
An **adverb** usually goes after the **verb**.

---

## *Unit 38: Present tenses for future use*

### Meaning

The two TENSES underlined are present simple and present continuous.
*In these examples* they are talking about future TIME.

Sentences a, c, d, e, f, h are talking about *an arrangement between people.*
They are present continuous.

Sentences b, g, i are talking about *an event happening at a specific time/on a specific date.*
They are present simple.

## *Unit 39: Going to/will – I*

### Meaning

Sentences a, b, c, d show what Nick decided **about the future** *before* the conversation with Richard.
He uses going to

Sentences e, f show what Nick decided **about the future** *during* the conversation with Richard.
He uses will

### Form

**Going to**

To make the *going* to future we use SUBJECT (I/you/he etc) + VERB 'TO BE' + GOING TO + INFINITIVE

| | |
|---|---|
| They're going to take the children | Are they going to take the children? |
| He's going to lie on the beach | Is he going to lie on the beach? |
| We're going to visit Disneyland | Are we going to visit Disneyland? |

**Will**

The form of will for I/you/he/she/it/we/they (all persons)* is will.
The **negative** form of will is won't

*Contractions*

| | | | | | |
|---|---|---|---|---|---|
| I will | I'll | You will | You'll | It will | It'll |
| | | He will | He'll | We will | We'll |
| | | She will | She'll | They will | They'll |

I think I'll go to the cinema is the **only** correct sentence.

---

## *Unit 40: Going to/will – II*

### Meaning

Does the gipsy *know* for certain the man will marry a beautiful woman? No
Does the gipsy *know* for certain the man will have five children? No
Does the man *know* for certain that the crystal ball is going to fall? Yes
How does he know? What can he *see*? The ball is nearly falling/on the edge

In the first picture does she *know* for certain that they will have to get some more petrol? No
In the second picture does she *know* for certain that they are going to have to get some more petrol? Yes
How does she know? What can she *see*? The petrol gauge shows 'Empty'

We use will when we are *guessing or predicting* about the future.
We use going to when we can see *now* that something is *certain* to happen in the future.

## *Unit 41: Present perfect I: experience*

### Meaning

Do you know *when* she went to these places? No
What *tense* is 'She's been'? Present perfect
*'Been'* is the *past participle* * of the verb 'to go'*

*There are *two* possible past participles for the verb 'to go' – **been** and **gone**
'She has *been* to Paris' means she has **gone and come back**
'She has *gone* to Paris' means she **is there now.**

'**I've been** there five or six times.' – Do you know *when*? No
What **tense** does she use? Present Perfect or Simple Past? Present Perfect

'I first **went** there in 1985' – Do you know *when*? Yes
What tense does she use? Present Perfect *or* Simple Past? Simple Past

**Did you visit** the Winter Palace when you were in St Petersburg?
Is the interviewer talking about **a definite time** in the past? Yes

**Have** you **been** to Seoul?
Is the interviewer talking about **a definite time** in the past? No

### Form

| | |
|---|---|
| The **positive** form of Present Perfect Simple is | **subject + has or have + past participle (been/visited/eaten etc)** |
| The **negative** form of Present Perfect Simple is | **subject + has or have + not + past participle** |
| The **question** form of Present Perfect Simple is | **have or has + subject + past participle** |
| The **short answer** form of Present Perfect Simple is | **Yes, + subject + has or have** |
| | **No, + subject + hasn't or haven't** |

*Note:*
**Ever and never**

I've *never* been to Moscow
Have you *ever* been to Paris?

We often use 'ever' and 'never' with *this meaning* of Present Perfect Simple.
They **don't** change the meaning but **add emphasis**.

---

## *Unit 42: Present perfect II: time up to now*

### Meaning

Joe *lives* in Venezuela – This is talking about now.
Joe *came* to Venezuela **in 1991** – This is talking about the past.
Joe *has lived* in Venezuela **for six years** – This is talking about now and the past.

Joe *is married* – This is talking about now.
Joe *got married* **in 1993** – This is talking about the past.
Joe *has been married* **since 1993** – This is talking about now and the past.

(a) I've been married since 1993 = 2 (a **point** of time)
(b) I've been married for four years = 1 (a **period** of time)

| since | for |
|---|---|
| last February | a long time |
| 1989 | two months |
| a week ago | a couple of hours |
| I was born | three years |
| yesterday | |
| 9.00 | |

## *Unit 43: Present perfect III: present result*

### Meaning

When did he break his leg? last weekend.
This is talking about the past.

Is his leg still broken now? yes.
This is talking about the present.

He **has broken** his leg – This is talking about a past action with a present result.
This is **the present perfect tense.**

When did he cut his head? last weekend.
This is talking about the past.

Is his head still cut now? yes.
This is talking about the present.

He **has cut** his head – This is talking about a past action with a present result.
This is **the present perfect tense.**

---

## *Unit 44: Present perfect IV: 'yet' and 'already'*

### Meaning

Already means something has happened before now.
Yet means something has *not* happened before now, but it is going to happen.

**ALREADY** DONE
walked along Unter den Linden
visited Checkpoint Charlie
seen Krakow
been skiing in Zakopane
crossed the Charles Bridge in Prague
drunk Czech beer

NOT DONE **YET**
visited Bratislava
eaten goulash
visited the Thermal Baths in Budapest

### Form

'I've **already** been to Czech'
We usually use **already** in *positive sentences.*

SUBJECT + have/has + already + PAST PARTICIPLE

'Have you been to Poland **yet**?'
'I haven't been to Hungary **yet**.'
We usually use **yet** in *questions* and *negative sentences.*

Have/Has + SUBJECT + PAST PARTICIPLE + yet?
Subject + HAVEN'T HASN'T + past participle + yet

**ALREADY** DONE
She's already walked along Unter den Linden
She's already visited Checkpoint Charlie
She's already seen Krakow
She's already been skiing in Zakopane
She's already crossed the Charles Bridge in Prague
She's already drunk Czech beer

NOT DONE **YET**
She hasn't visited Bratislava yet
She hasn't eaten goulash yet
She hasn't visited the Thermal Baths yet

## *Unit 45: Questions Revision 1*

### Meaning

Find two questions asking about someone's plans or arrangements **d e** [Units 38 & 39]
Find one question making a request **f** [Unit 27]
Find one question asking for permission **g** [Unit 27]
Find one question asking politely if someone wants something **i** [Unit 26]
Find one question asking about a non-definite time in the past **c** [Unit 41]
Find one question asking about NOW, this moment **b** [Unit 18]
Find one question asking about ability **a** [Unit 28]
Find three questions asking about the past **c, h, j** [Units 23. 32 & 41]

### Form

| [QUESTION WORD] + | AUXILIARY VERB + | SUBJECT + | MAIN VERB | |
|---|---|---|---|---|
| | Can | you | play | the piano? |
| What | are | you | doing | with that gun?! |
| | Have | you | been | to Paris? |
| What | are | you | going to do | next? |
| | Are | you | meeting | John tomorrow? |
| | Can | I | borrow | £1? |
| | May | I | go | now? |
| Where | were | you | | yesterday? |
| | Would | you | like | a drink? |
| What | were | you | doing? | |

---

## *Unit 46: Questions Revision 2*

### Meaning and Form

A
1. **Do elephants eat leaves?**
2. Where **does he come from?**
3. Where **did you go?**
4. **Did she give up smoking?**
5. **Do they like strong coffee?**
6. How many children **do you have?**

B.
1. **Can tigers run very fast?**
2. Where **are the Galapagos Islands?**
3. What **have you forgotten?**
4. **Is she going to give up smoking?**
5. **Would they like some tea?**
6. **Has he got three cars?**

What **three words** do we use to **make questions** in column A? **do, does, did**
1. **Can** 2. **are** 3. **have** 4. **is** 5. **would** 6. **has**
[Any problems? See Unit 45]

We use **did** to talk about the past
We use **does** with *he, she, it* to talk about the present
We use **do** with *I, you, we, they* to talk about the present

# Appendix 5: Key to Unit 'Practice' pages

## *Unit 1: Present tense of the verb 'to be' (is/am/are)*

1. A. This **is** my brother. He**'s** very tall and thin. He's a teacher too so he **isn't** very rich.

   B. My mother and father **are** quite young. They **are** both photographers. At the moment they **aren't** in England, they **are** on holiday in Africa.

   C. My boyfriend**'s** called Tom. He **isn't** very tall but we **are** very happy together!

   D. My house **is** in London. It**'s** quite old, but it **isn't** very big.

2. Mary and Claudia are my friends
   They're very intelligent
   They aren't (they're not) very rich
   They're actresses

   My father's name's John
   He's a photographer
   He's from Ireland

   My mother's called Hilary
   She's a photographer
   She's 49 years old

3. (a) They**'re** from England
   (b) My house **is** quite old
   (c) Correct
   (d) Correct
   (e) I'm not a student, **I'm** a teacher
   (f) Correct
   (g) Correct
   (h) His name's Peter

---

## *Unit 2: Verb 'to be': questions (Am I?/Are you?/Is he?)*

1. (a) Is Rosa a teacher? — No, she isn't
   (b) Is the International School of English in France? — No, it isn't
   (c) Where is Rosa a doctor? — In Brazil
   (d) Is Rosa forty years old? — No, she isn't
   (e) How old is Rosa? — Thirty two
   (f) Is Rosa married? — Yes, she is
   (g) Is Juliana six? — Yes, she is
   (h) Is Pedro six? — No, he isn't
   (i) How old are the children? — Six and three
   (j) What's her husband's name? — Paulo
   (k) Is Paulo in London now? — No, he isn't
   (l) Where are Paulo and the children? — At school/In Brazil

2. John: Pleased to meet you. My name's John.
   Susan: Sorry, are you my brother's friend?
   John: No, **I'm not**. I'm Catherine's boyfriend.
   Susan: **Are you** a doctor?
   John: No, **I'm not**.
   Susan: Sorry!

   Catherine: Who's that over there?
   Jonathan: That's Michael. He's very famous.
   Catherine: Why **is he** famous?
   Jonathan: He's a singer.

   Mark: Susan's my sister.
   Jane: What's her boyfriend's name?
   Mark: Tom. He's a teacher too.
   Jane: **Are they** married?
   Mark: No, not yet.

   Susan: **Where are** Catherine and Jonathan?
   Mark: In the kitchen.
   Susan: Are they hungry?

## *Unit 3: This/that/these/those*

1. 'This is Maria-Jose.' 'Pleased to meet you.'
What are these in English? Crisps or chips?
Is this your recipe?
These flowers are beautiful
This coffee is excellent!
That's Robert Saunders
Who are those people? Can you introduce me?
That cake is delicious
Who are those children in the garden?
Is that your husband?

2. MJ: This is the REM CD
A: Is that your favourite band?
MJ: Yes, it is
A: Is that their best CD?
MJ: No, it isn't. This is.
A: That's very expensive.

3. MJ: This is a good shop.
These shoes are lovely.
A: Well, I think these are better.
MJ: But these are brown. This shirt is the same colour.
A: OK. Try them on.
MJ: Ahh. These are uncomfortable.
A: So, these are better! And this is a lovely colour.

4. How much are those?
This isn't very good.
This is very cheap!
How much are these?
That's the last one!
These are very fashionable.
Is this the new REM CD?
That isn't fresh!
Why is that so expensive?!
These aren't good for you.
Those aren't English newspapers.
A: These shoes are lovely..
MJ: No, I think those are nicer.

---

## *Unit 4: Singular and plural nouns*

1. (a) There are ten children
(b) There is a teacher
(c) There are two balls
(d) There is a dog
(e) There is a sandwich
(f) There is a bus
(g) There are two houses
(h) There are five girls
(i) There is a book
(j) There are two pens

2. There are 57,800,000 people
There are 23,628,000 women
There are 22,472,000 men
There are 5,967,000 girls
There are 5,733,000 boys
There are 11,700,000 children
There are 28,150 churches
There are 23,000,000 houses
There are 20,700,000 cars
There are 71,000 buses
There are 2,000,000 lorries
There are 160,400 factories

3. (a) There **are** 23,628,000 women in Britain
(b) Correct
(c) In London, the buses are red
(d) Correct
(e) There is an old **man** in the shop
(f) There are 5,733,000 **boys** in Britain
(g) This is my **house**

4. (a) Are the child**ren** happy
(b) The sandwich**es** are fresh
(c) Why are the bus**es** late?
(d) The teacher**s** are tired
(e) There are five church**es** in the town
(f) There are 160,400 factor**ies** in Britain
(g) There are 10 boy**s** and 12 girl**s** in the class

## Unit 5: Present simple tense

1. Devon **is** in the southwest of Britain. The countryside **is** very beautiful and many tourists **go** there in the summer. They **swim** in the sea, **lie** on the beach and **walk** in the hills.
Mr Swinnon **lives** in Torquay. He **works** in a hotel. In the morning he **gets** up early, **goes** for a walk on the beach and then he **cooks** breakfast for the visitors.
'I **love** Devon. We **have** lots of tourists because the sun **shines** all summer.'

2. Portugal **is** in the southwest of Europe. It **has** many kilometres of beaches so the Portuguese **eat** lots of fish. They **make** very good wine too.
Jorge **comes** from Angola but he **lives** in Lisbon, the capital of Portugal. He **studies** medicine at the university. At the weekend he **goes** to the beach and **plays** volleyball. When it **rains** he **watches** football on the t.v.
'I **think** about Angola a lot but I **like** Lisbon. I **have** lots of friends here and we **enjoy** life.

3. St Petersburg is in Russia, near the Baltic Sea. It is a beautiful old city, on forty-four small islands. It snows a lot in the winter and night comes very early, but in the summer the sun never goes down.
Irena works as a tourist guide. She takes visitors to the Hermitage Museum of Art. She gets up early and has breakfast - tea and bread and jam. Then she goes to work and meets the first group of tourists at 9.30am. She works hard and she walks a lot - the Hermitage is very big - 20 kilometres to see everything!
'I **finish** work at 6.00pm and I always feel very tired, so in the evenings I read a book or **listen** to music.'

4. (a) Irena finishes work at 6.00.
(b) Jorge plays volleyball.
(c) Yuko studies hard.
(d) Mr Koshura **works** for Toyota.
(e) Irena goes to work at 9.00
(f) Jorge **has** a lot of friends in Lisbon
(g) Jorge watches football on television

---

## Unit 6: Present simple auxiliaries

1. (a) **When does the train to St Petersburg leave?**
(b) **How much does it cost?**
(c) **When does it arrive?**
(d) **How many countries does it go through?**
(e) **Where do you need to buy a visa?**
(f) **Where do they sell the visas?**
(g) **How much does the visa cost?**

2. (a) **Yes, it does**
(b) **Yes, it does**
(c) **No, it doesn't**
(d) **No, you don't**
(e) **Yes, you do**
(f) **Yes, they do**
(g) **No, it doesn't**

3.

| | |
|---|---|
| When **do** we **arrive** in Vilnius? | Six o'clock |
| **Do** you often **go** to Russia? | Yes, I **do** |
| **Do** you **like** travelling? | I love it! |
| **Does** the train **stop** in Krakow? | No, it **doesn't** |
| How much **does** it **cost** to travel 1st class? | **I don't know** |
| Oh no! I **don't have** a reservation. | Thirty-three hours is a long time to stand up! |
| Where **do** they **check** your passport? | At the border |

4.

| | |
|---|---|
| Do you have a ticket? | Yes, I **do** |
| Where does the train **stop**? | In Poland, Belarus, Lithuania, Latvia and Estonia |
| When **do** we arrive in Grodno? | **I don't** know |
| Does the ticket inspector check the tickets? | Yes, he **does**! |
| I don't speak Russian | I do |
| We don't stop in Krakow | Yes, I **know** |

## *Unit 7: Adverbs 1: adverbs of frequency*

1. (a) Sarah always gets up at 7.30
   (b) She never eats breakfast
   (c) She often has a cup of coffee
   (d) She always drives to work
   (e) She is sometimes late
   (f) The traffic is always bad
   (g) (In the evenings) James often watches old films on the television (in the evenings)
   (h) He always gets up late
   (i) He never goes to bed before 2.00am

2. (a) Peter **always goes** running
   (b) He **often goes** swimming
   (c) He **never eats** meat
   (d) He **is always** very healthy
   (e) He **rarely drinks** beer
   (f) Simon **always gets up** at 5.00
   (g) He **is always** tired

3. Interviewer: What time do you finish work, Julia?
   Julia: Well, I **often finish** about 6.00am, but it is sometimes later. **I often** don't get home until 8.00am - then **I always** go straight to bed!
   Interviewer: What time do you get up?
   Julia: **I usually** get up at about 3.00pm to do some shopping and cooking. I **rarely** get up later that 4.00pm because the children always come home from school then. **I am always** busy in the evening but my husband often helps me to cook the dinner and **he sometimes** puts the children to bed.

---

## *Unit 8: Subject and object pronouns*

1. (a) John loves Barbara but John's friend doesn't like **her** at all
   (b) The ring is beautiful but Barbara doesn't want **it**
   (c) John thinks Barbara's family don't like **him**
   (d) 'We are Barbara's family - why doesn't John visit **us**?'
   (e) 'Barbara's family are strange. I don't like **them** much.'
   (f) 'I love **you**. Why don't you want to marry **me**?'

2. Barbara: John wants **me** to marry **him**. What do you think?
   Barbara's father: Do you love **him**?
   Barbara: **I** don't know. I *like* **him**. Do you like him?
   Barbara's father: Well, **he** never visits **us**... and his family is very strange - **they** talk all the time!

   John: Barbara doesn't want to marry **me**.
   Terry: Good! I don't like **her**. **She** is boring
   John: But, Terry, **she** is very beautiful and **I** love **her**!
   Terry: Maybe, but there are lots of beautiful girls... look at **them**!

3. John loves Barbara but **she** doesn't *love* **him**, **she** *likes* **him**. **He** wants **her** to marry him but **she** doesn't want to marry **him** because **he** doesn't like her family. John thinks **they** are strange. **He** never visits **them** and he thinks **they** don't like him. Maybe **he's** right!

4. (a) Terry thinks Barbara is boring. He doesn't like **her**
   (b) Terry likes the girls in the pub. He thinks **they** are beautiful and he wants to speak to **them**
   (c) Correct
   (d) John loves Barbara and **he** thinks she is beautiful
   (e) 'I love you, do you love **me**?'
   (f) John is unhappy because Barbara doesn't love **him**.

## Unit 9: Possessive adjectives and 's

1. (a) Rose's **John** and **Muriel's** daughter
   (b) Hannah's **Vicky's** sister
   (c) Daniel's **Hannah** and **Vicky's** cousin
   (d) Jonathan's **Ruth** and **Rose's** brother
   (e) Brian's **Ruth's** husband
   (f) Hannah and Vicky **are Jonathan** and **Ann's** daughters
   (g) Muriel's **John's** wife
   (h) Rose's **Jonathan** and **Ruth's** sister

2. (a) Vicky's (**is**) Hannah's (**possession**) sister
   (b) Ruth's (**is**) Brian's (**possession**) wife
   (c) Jonathan's (**is**) a journalist
   (d) Ann's (**is**) Vicky and Hannah's (**possession**) mother
   (e) Katy's (**possession**) sister's (**possession**) name's (**is**) Georgina
   (f) John's (**possession**) son's (**is**) a journalist

3. Ann and **her** husband live near London. They have two children. **Their** names are Hannah and Vicky. They have a cat. **Its** name is Ruby.
   Brian has three children. **His** son's name's Daniel and **his** daughters' names are Katy and Georgina. **Their** cousins' names are Hannah and Vicky.
   John and Muriel live near Oxford. **Their** house is very old.

4. Let me tell you about my family. My father**'s** name**'s** Jonathan and my mother**'s** name**'s** Ann. My father**'s** a journalist. I have one sister, her name**'s** Hannah. She's OK but I like our cat better. Its name**'s** Ruby...

5. (a) Who's Hannah's sister?
   (b) Vicky likes **her** sister Hannah
   (c) Ruby's Vicky and Hannah**'s** cat
   (d) Hannah and Vicky **are** sisters
   (e) Correct
   (f) Brian lives with **his** wife, Ruth
   (g) Correct
   (h) Where's John and Muriel**'s** house?
   (i) 'My name's Georgina. What's **your** name?'

---

## Unit 10: Possessive pronouns

1. (a) Is this **yours?**
   (b) No, I think it's **his**
   (c) Isn't it **hers?**
   (d) This isn't **mine**
   (e) Is it **yours?**
   (f) No, it isn't **mine.**
   (g) Perhaps it's **theirs**
   (h) Have you got **ours?**
   (i) No, I've got **mine** but I don't know where
   (j) **ours** are.
   (k) This isn't **mine**
   (l) No, it's **theirs**

2. (a) This isn't my bag. **Mine** is bigger
   (b) Are these **your** glasses?
   (c) Have you got **our** bags?
   (d) It's **mine**!
   (e) I think **my** bag is lost!
   (f) Can you help me carry **my** bags?
   (g) Is that bag **hers**?
   (h) **Their** bags are heavy

3. (a) **Give me her bag**
   (b) **Is that his?**
   (c) **Their bag is red**
   (d) **Are those theirs?**
   (e) **Hers is over there**
   (f) **Are those his gloves?**
   (g) **Her umbrella is green**
   (h) **His is blue**

4. (a) This isn't **mine**
   (b) Correct
   (c) **My** parents are retired
   (d) Correct
   (e) Correct
   (f) They know our family but we don't know theirs
   (g) Correct
   (h) Your camera is better than **mine**
   (i) Is that **her** coat?

## *Unit 11: Articles*

1. an artist a doctor an electrician a politician a teacher a university professor*
a dentist a secretary a manager a housewife a shop assistant

*Remember that it is the first SOUND that is important /ju:niversiti/

2. (a) O London is (b) a big city. (c) The centre is very busy. (d) O Oxford Street is (e) a good place for shopping. You can also go to (f) a department store, like 'Harrods', (g) a very famous shop.
If (h) the weather is nice, you can go in (i) a boat on (j) the Thames, or walk in (k) a park. It is difficult to find (l) a cheap hotel in (m) O London but, if you are rich you can stay in (n) an expensive hotel like the Park Lane Hilton – with (o) a restaurant on (p) the top floor of (q) the hotel.

3.

| | | |
|---|---|---|
| 1. | (a), (d), (m) | We generally use *nothing* with places |
| 2. | (j) | We use 'the' with the names of rivers |
| 4. | (h), (p) | We use 'the' when there is only *one* |
| 5. | (b), (e), (f), (g), (i), (k), (l), (n),(o) | We use 'a' when we talk about *one of many* |
| 6. | (c) | [We know it's the centre of *London*] |
| | (q) | [We know it's the top floor of *the Park Lane Hotel*] |
| | | When we know *which* thing we mean we use 'the' |

4. How are you? I'm fine. I'm living in O [Rule 1] Warsaw now. I have a [Rule 5] small flat in the [Rule 6] centre. It is very nice. I also have a new job. I'm a [Rule 3] secretary now in a big company. The [Rule 6] company sells computers. I am an [vowel] expert now about computers!
The [Rule 4] weather is very nice now in O [Rule 1] Poland. It's sunny and warm...

---

## *Unit 12: Relative pronouns*

1. (a) I don't like people who are unfriendly
(b) An express is a train that goes fast
(c) I know someone that can play the violin really well
(d) I like children who don't make too much noise!
(e) Do you know the woman that lives upstairs?
(f) I like films which have a happy ending
(g) This book is about a man who falls in love
(h) He has a bicycle that cost £500!

2. (a) A giraffe is an animal that/which has a very long neck
(b) The man who/that works in that office isn't very friendly
(c) Is this the train which/that is always late?
(d) Can you write a sentence which/that uses a relative pronoun?
(e) Do you know the children who/that live in that house?
(f) A suitcase is a big bag which/that you take on holiday
(g) Perfume is something which/that makes you smell nice
(h) A briefcase is a bag which/that business people use.

3. (a) Chips are potatoes that/which are cut and fried
(b) Football is a game that/which has eleven players
(c) A typewriter is a machine that/which writes
(d) A waiter is a person that/who works in a cafe
(e) Tea is a drink that/which people drink in England
(f) A watch is a thing that/which tells the time
(g) A husband is a man that/who is married.

## Unit 13: Have got

1. (a) **How many sisters have you got?**
   (b) **I haven't got any**
   (c) **Has he got a car?**
   (d) **No, he hasn't**
   (e) **I've got a big house in the country**
   (f) **How many bedrooms has it got?**
   (g) **Have you got any pets?**
   (h) **Yes, I've got a dog**
   (i) **They've got three children**
   (j) **Have they got any grandchildren?**
   (k) **Yes, they have**

2. (a) John and Susan **have got** a car
   (b) Emma **has got** children
   (c) Vicky and Tony **haven't got** a television
   (d) Peter **hasn't got** a house
   (e) John and Susan **have got** a dog
   (f) Emma **hasn't got** a flat
   (g) Vicky and Tony **haven't got** a car
   (h) Emma **hasn't got** a car
   (i) Peter **hasn't got** a dog
   (j) John and Susan **have got** a house

3. (a) **Has** Emma **got** a house? **Yes, she has**
   (b) **Has** Peter **got** a dog? **No, he hasn't**
   (c) **Have** Tony and Vicky **got** children? **No, they haven't**
   (d) **Has** Emma **got** a car? **No, she hasn't**
   (e) **Have** John and Susan **got** a television? **No, they haven't**
   (f) **Have** Tony and Vicky **got** a flat? **Yes, they have**
   (g) **Has** Peter **got** children? **Yes, he has**

---

## Unit 14: Countable and Uncountable nouns

1.

| COUNTABLE | UNCOUNTABLE |
|---|---|
| **Eggs** | **Chocolate** |
| **Potatoes** | **Orange juice** |
| **Apples** | **Bread** |
| **Oranges** | **Sugar** |
| **Cakes** | **Wine** |
| **Chocolates** | **Mineral Water** |

2.

| | |
|---|---|
| **an** apple | **a** potato |
| **O** mineral water | **O** sugar |
| **an** orange | **O** orange juice |
| **O** bread | **O** wine |
| | **an** egg |

3.

| | | |
|---|---|---|
| (a) | rice | not possible |
| (b) | egg | **eggs** |
| (c) | banana | **bananas** |
| (d) | bread | not possible |
| (e) | milk | not possible |
| (f) | wine | not possible |
| (g) | potato | **potatoes** |
| (h) | apple | **apples** |
| (i) | money | not possible |
| (j) | pound (£) | **pounds** |
| (k) | orange | **oranges** |
| (l) | orange juice | not possible |
| (m) | flour | not possible |
| (n) | spaghetti | not possible |
| (o) | salt | not possible |
| (p) | sugar | not possible |

In this context it is not possible to say orange juices/milks/wines. BUT, sometimes when you ask for drinks in a cafe you can say for example 'Three orange juices, please'. This is different because you mean 'Three *glasses* of orange juice.' Also with 'sugar' you can say 'Two sugars, please.' when you mean 'Two *spoons* of sugar (in your coffee)'

## Unit 15: 'Some' and 'any'

1. (a) There are some grapefruits
   (b) Are there any eggs?
   (c) Do you have any lemons?
   (d) There aren't any peppers in the fridge
   (e) Give me some apples
   (f) Aren't there any oranges on the table?
   (g) We need some onions

2. (a) There are some onions but there aren't any potatoes
   (b) There is some milk and some water
   (c) There aren't any peppers
   (d) There is an egg
   (e) There are some apples
   (f) There isn't a grapefruit
   (g) There is some rice but there isn't any pasta
   (h) There isn't any cheese or any bread

3. (a) Is there a banana?
   No, there isn't
   (b) Are there any peppers?
   No, there aren't
   (c) Are there any apples?
   Yes, there are
   (d) Is there any milk?
   Yes, there is
   (e) Is there any pasta?
   No, there isn't
   (f) Are there any potatoes?
   No, there aren't
   (g) Is there a grapefruit?
   No, there isn't
   (h) Is there any cheese?
   No, there isn't
   (i) Are there any onions?
   Yes, there are
   (j) Is there an egg?
   Yes, there is

---

## Unit 16: Much/many/a lot

1. (a) How much shampoo have you got?
   (b) How many t-shirts have you got?
   (c) How many books have you got?
   (d) How much vodka have you got?
   (e) How much money have you got?
   (f) How many cassettes have you got?
   (g) How many cigars have you got?
   (h) How much wine have you got?

2. (a) shampoo? A lot
   (b) t-shirts? Not a lot or not many
   (c) books? Not a lot or not many
   (d) vodka? Not a lot or not much
   (e) money? A lot
   (f) cassettes? Not a lot or not many
   (g) cigars? A lot
   (h) wine? Not a lot or not much

3. (a) There is a lot of shampoo
   (b) There aren't many/a lot of cassettes
   (c) There isn't much/a lot of vodka
   (d) There are a lot of cigars
   (e) There is a lot of money
   (f) There aren't many/a lot of books
   (g) There aren't many/a lot of t-shirts
   (h) There isn't much/a lot of wine

4. (a) There are a lot of cigars
   (b) There aren't many books
   (c) Correct
   (d) Correct
   (e) There isn't much/a lot of vodka
   (f) Correct
   (g) How much vodka have you got?
   (h) Correct
   (i) How many books are there?
   (j) Is there much/a lot of wine?

## Unit 17: 'Too' and 'not enough'

1. (a) The class isn't small enough
   (b) The room is too dark
   (c) The teacher isn't experienced enough
   (d) The lessons aren't difficult enough
   (e) The course is too expensive
   (f) My hotel is too far
   (g) The school isn't clean enough
   (h) The lessons are too short

2. (a) There **isn't enough** homework
   (b) There **is too much** homework
   (c) There **aren't enough** books
   (d) There **are too many** breaks
   (e) There **aren't enough** breaks
   (f) There **aren't enough** desks
   (g) There **isn't enough** listening practice
   (h) There **is too much** writing practice

3. Sarah: I don't like London. It's **too** dirty. There's **too much** pollution.
   Jack: But it's very exciting - there are lots of shops
   Sarah: Well, yes, but the shops are **too** expensive for me. I don't have **enough** money and there are **too many** people. Oxford Street is so crowded!
   Jack: What about transport? Don't you like the double-decker buses?
   Sarah: They look nice, but they're not cheap **enough**. It costs me £30 a week to go to work! My house is **too** far from the centre
   Jack: Do you have a nice house?
   Sarah: No, it isn't big **enough**. I live with four students and they have parties every weekend. It's **too** noisy for me
   Jack: So why don't you go out at the weekend? There's so much to do in London! There are lots of theatres and cinemas
   Sarah: Yes, but there are **too many** theatres and cinemas - I can't decide where to go!

---

## Unit 18: Present continuous tense

1. (a) The dog is running
   (b) The children are swimming
   (c) Grandmother's sleeping
   (d) Dad's lying down
   (e) The birds are singing
   (f) Mum and Dad are talking
   (g) Grandfather's eating
   (h) The sun's shining
   (i) The baby's crying
   (j) The tree's dying

2. (a) Q: Who's smoking? A: Dad is
   (b) Q: Who's sleeping? A: Grandmother is
   (c) Q: Who's crying? A: The baby is
   (d) Q: Who's eating? A: Grandfather is
   (e) Q: Who's swimming? (*) A: The children are
   (f) Q: What's dying? A: The tree is
   (g) Q: Who's wearing shorts? A: Dad is
   (h) Q: What are singing? A: The birds are

Remember (*) In this case 'Who' is followed by 'is' even if the answer is plural.

3. (a) Q: Is Grandmother talking? A: No, she isn't
   (b) Q: Where are the children swimming? A: In the lake
   (c) Q: Are the birds singing? A: Yes, they are
   (d) Q: What's Grandfather eating? A: An icecream
   (e) Q: Is the sun shining? A: Yes, it is
   (f) Q: Is the dog sleeping? A: No, it isn't*
   (g) Q: Who's mum talking to? A: Dad
   (h) Q: Is dad writing a letter? A: No, he isn't

[*Sometimes people call their dog 'he' or 'she']

If you have problems with these questions look at Unit 2 - Questions with the verb to be

4. (a) 'Help! The dog is **biting** me!
   (b) Correct
   (c) 'You're **running** too fast for me.'
   (d) 'Mary's **swimming** really well.'
   (e) Correct
   (f) 'Mum's **talking** to Dad'
   (g) 'I love **sleeping** in the afternoon'

## Unit 19: Present simple versus continuous

1. Tim is a mechanic
He mends cars
He is having lunch

Stuart is a postman
He delivers letters
He's running away from a dog!

William is a writer
He writes books
He's reading a book

Jo is a secretary
She types letters
She is answering the phone

Sally is a pilot
She flies planes
She's going home

John is a painter
He paints houses
He's having a cup of tea

2. (a) Japan is in the Pacific Ocean
(b) John has ten cups of tea every day
(c) We can't go out – it's raining
(d) I can't hear you because I'm listening to music
(e) Where's Julia? She's reading a book
(f) I usually get up early
(g) I never eat chocolate – it makes you fat!

3. (a) What does Sally do?
(b) What are you doing?
(c) What languages do you speak?
(d) Where do you usually go on holiday?
(e) How many sisters do you have?
(f) Where are you going now?
(g) What are you eating?

---

## Unit 20: Prepositions of place (in/on/next to)

1. (a) The box is in front of the plant
(b) The chair is opposite the table
(c) The saucer is under the cup
(d) The book is on the table
(e) The plant is behind the television
(f) The cup is on the saucer
(g) The picture is next to the mirror
(h) The cushion is on the sofa
(i) The glass is near the apples

2. (a) The lamp is on the television
(b) True
(c) True
(d) The videos are under the television
(e) The curtains are behind the television
(f) The apples are in front of the calendar
(g) True
(h) The cat is under the table
(i) True

3. (a) The glasses are next to the bottle
(b) The apples are in the bowl.
(c) The radio is on the table
(d) The photograph is next to the lamp
(e) The shoes are on the floor
(f) The calendar is behind the apples
(g) The table is opposite the sofa
(h) The remote control is on the sofa

## Unit 21: Prepositions of time: in/at/on

1. (a) St Valentine's day is **on** 14th February
   (b) St Patrick's day is **in** March
   (c) The British open their presents **on** Christmas Day
   (d) The Queen has two birthdays – one **on** 21st April and the other **on** 14th June
   (e) The British don't have a holiday **on** the Queen's Birthdays
   (f) Some people go to church **at** midnight **on** Christmas Eve
   (g) There is usually a three or four day holiday **at** Easter
   (h) Most people don't work **at** the weekends.

2. (a) **On** Monday morning **at** 9.00 Jane's going to the Dentist
   (b) She's meeting John **at** lunchtime **on** Tuesday
   (c) **In** the evening **on** Valentine's Day she's going out to dinner
   (d) She has a meeting **at** 3.00 **in** the afternoon **on** Thursday
   (e) **On** 16th February she has a meeting **at** noon
   (f) She's having a party **on** her birthday
   (g) She isn't working **at** the weekend
   (h) **On** Sunday she's visiting John's parents
   (i) David's birthday is **next week on** 21st February
   (j) Jane is very busy **at** the moment

3. (a) I was born **in** the 1970's
   (b) Correct
   (c) I can't sleep **at** night
   (d) Are you going on holiday **at** Christmas?
   (e) Correct
   (f) Do you think life will be very different **in** the future?
   (g) Life was different **in the** past
   (h) Correct
   (i) Is it cold in Poland **in** (the) winter?
   (j) I'm learning Spanish **at** the moment
   (k) The telephone rang **at** midnight.
   (l) I'm going on holiday next week.

---

## Unit 22: Prepositions of movement: up/down

1. (a) **Map B**
   (b) **Map A**
   (c) **Map C**
   (d) **Map D**

2. (a) Go **across** the road
   (b) How do I get **from** the post-office **to** the bank?
   (c) Go **into** the hotel
   (d) Get **on** the bus
   (e) Go **down** the hill
   (f) Go **along** the road
   (g) Go **through** the shopping centre
   (h) Go **past** the supermarket
   (i) Go **under** the subway

3. A: 'How do I get **from** the school **to** the post office?'
   B: 'Go **out of** the school, **along** the road, **round** the roundabout, then turn left. Go **across/over** the bridge and it's the building on your left.'
   A: 'Is it a long way?'
   B: 'About half an hour. You could get **on** a number 9 bus outside the school and get **off** next to the bridge.'

## Unit 23: Past simple tense of verb 'to be'

1. (a) He **was** a policeman
   (b) We **were** very happy
   (c) **Were** you busy?
   (d) They **weren't** interested in it.
   (e) I **was** at school.
   (f) It **wasn't** expensive.
   (g) **Was** she your teacher?

2. Interviewer: 'What **was** it like during the First World War, Bill?'
   Bill: 'It **was** a terrible time. I **was** a young man, so I **was** in the army. We **were** in France.'
   Interviewer: 'Where **were** your wife and children?'
   Bill: 'They **were** in London. That **was** dangerous too. There **were** bombs and there **wasn't** a lot of food. The children **were** very young and they **were** very frightened.'

3. (a) **False – Bill wasn't an old man during the First World War.**
   (b) **True**
   (c) **False – Bill wasn't in Poland**
   (d) **False – Bill's wife and children weren't in France**
   (e) **True**
   (f) **False – There wasn't a lot of food in London.**
   (g) **False – The children weren't very old**
   (h) **True**

4. (a) **How old was Bill during the First World War?**
   (b) **Was Bill in the army?**
   (c) **Where was Bill?**
   (d) **Where were Bill's wife and children?**
   (e) **Was it dangerous in London?**
   (f) **Were there bombs?**
   (g) **Was there a lot of food?**
   (h) **How old were the children?**
   (i) **Were the children frightened?**

---

## Unit 24: Past simple tense

| Down | | | Across | | |
|---|---|---|---|---|---|
| 1. | Bring | **brought** | 3. | Take | **took** |
| 2. | Rise | **rose** | 5. | Sing | **sang** |
| 4. | Drink | **drank** | 6. | Begin | **began** |
| 6. | Blow | **blew** | 7. | Know | **knew** |
| 8. | Write | **wrote** | 9. | Steal | **stole** |
| 9. | Stand | **stood** | 10. | Be | **was** |
| 11. | Swim | **swam** | 13. | See | **saw** |
| 12. | Hate | **hated** | 14. | Think | **thought** |
| 15. | Give | **gave** | 16. | Make | **made** |
| 17. | Eat | **ate** | 18. | Ride | **rode** |

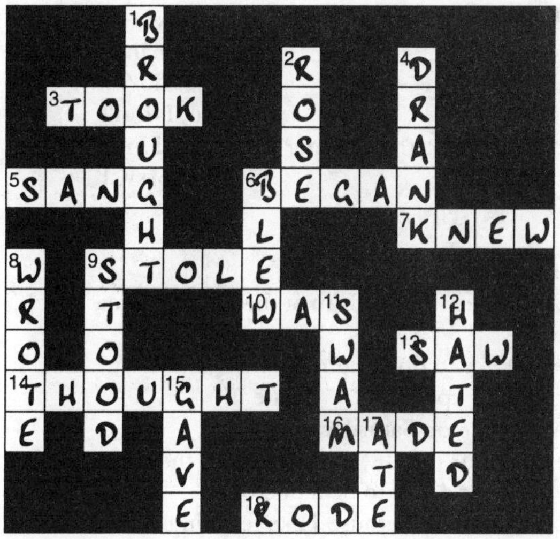


2. Carl Benz (invent) **invented** the petrol engine. Another German, Daimler, **designed** a car with an engine. This **was** the start of the modern car. At first, there **weren't** many cars. In England, a man **had** to walk in front of every car with a red flag. Then, in America, Henry Ford **built** a cheaper car, **called** the Model T. Ford, which ordinary people **could** buy.

3. George Stephenson **invented** the first steam train, **called** 'Locomotion'. Steam engines **burnt/burned*** coal and **heated** water. The hot water **produced** steam and the steam **made** the wheels go round. Railways **became** very popular. Trains **travelled** faster. They **carried** passengers, parcels, letters and food.

* Some irregular verbs have *two* possible forms. Another example is 'dream' = 'dreamt' or 'dreamed'

## Unit 25: Past simple auxiliary

1. (a) **Did Victoria have any brothers or sisters?** **No, she didn't**
   (b) **Did she go to school?** **No, she didn't**
   (c) **Did she speak French and German?** **Yes, she did**
   (d) **Did William IV die in 1837?** **Yes, he did**
   (e) **Did Victoria and Albert get married in 1840?** **Yes, they did**
   (f) **Did she love her husband?** **Yes, she did**
   (g) **Did they have ten children?** **No, they didn't**
   (h) **Did she die in 1861?** **No, she didn't**

2. (a) Where **did Victoria** study? At home
   (b) When **did she** have lessons? Every day from 9.30–5.00
   (c) What **did she** collect? Dolls
   (d) How many dolls **did she have?** 132
   (e) When **did** William IV **die?** When Victoria was 18
   (f) When **did** Victoria **become** Queen? In 1837
   (g) When **did she marry** Albert? In 1840
   (h) How many children **did** they **have?** Nine
   (i) When **did** Albert **die?** In 1861

3. (a) **True**
   (b) **Victoria didn't go to school**
   (c) **True**
   (d) **Victoria didn't speak Chinese**
   (e) **Victoria didn't have 200 dolls**
   (f) **Victoria didn't become Queen when she was twelve**
   (g) **Victoria and Albert didn't get married in 1845**
   (h) **True**
   (i) **Victoria and Albert didn't have five sons**
   (j) **True**
   (k) **Victoria didn't die in 1861**

---

## Unit 26: Would like

1. (a) Do you like tea? 4. Yes, I do/ No, I don't
   (b) Would you like a cup of tea? 2. Yes, please/ No, thanks
   (c) Do you like going to the cinema? 1. Yes, I do/ No, I don't
   (d) Would you like to go to the cinema? 3. Yes, I'd love to/Sorry, I can't

2. (a) **Would you** like a coffee? Yes, please
   (b) **I'd** like to go and see the new film at the *Roxy* Cinema this weekend
   (c) What **would you** like to do tonight?
   (d) **Do you** like getting up early? No, I hate it!
   (e) **I** like getting up late on Saturdays
   (f) **Do you** like London? It's OK, but it rains all the time!
   (g) When he's older, **he'd** like to be a doctor
   (h) Why are you a teacher? Because **I** like teaching!
   (i) **Would you** like to go out to dinner? Yes, I'd love to.

3. (a) Would you like (go) **to go** to the beach?
   (b) Do you like **playing** tennis?
   (c) What do you like **doing** on holiday?
   (d) I really like **lying** on the beach and **doing** nothing! My wife likes **sightseeing**
   (e) I like **cooking** but I don't like **doing** the washing up.
   (f) I'd like **to see** *Macbeth* tonight. I really like **going** to the theatre.
   (g) Would you like **to dance?** No, sorry, I don't like **dancing**

4. A: 'What **would** you **like to do** today?'
   B: 'Well, I think **I'd like to go swimming** in the sea. It's a lovely day. So, what **would you like to do** today, then?'
   A: '**I'd like to visit** the Castle.'
   B: 'But it's so hot! Why don't we go to the castle later?'

   A: 'Do you **like playing** tennis?'
   B: 'No, not much.'
   A: 'What sports do you **like?**'
   B: '**I like running.**'
   A: 'Oh, good! Would you **like to go** running with me this evening?'
   B: 'Sorry, I can't. I'm going to the cinema.'

## Unit 27: Requests and permission: can/could/may

1. (a) Can you tell me the time, please?
   (b) Could you spell that, please?
   (c) Can I sit here?
   (d) May I smoke?
   (e) Can I borrow your pen, please?
   (f) Could you give me a lift, please?
   (g) Can you pass me the salt?
   (h) May I go to the disco, Mum? /Mum, may I go to the disco?

2.

| REQUESTS | ASKING FOR PERMISSION |
|---|---|
| Can you tell me the time, please? | Can I sit here? |
| Could you spell that, please? | May I smoke? |
| Could you give me a lift, please? | Can I borrow your pen, please? |
| Can you pass the salt? | May I go to the disco, Mum? |

3. (a) Could you/Can you open the window, please?
   (b) Can I sit here, please?
   (c) Could you/Can you say that again, please?
   (d) Coul you/Can you spell that, please?
   (e) Can I/May I leave early, please?
   (f) Can you/Could you help me, please?

4. Manuel: 'Can I/May I use the kitchen?'
   Mr Jackson: 'Yes, you can.'
   Manuel: 'May I/Can I invite my friends round?'
   Mr Jackson: 'Yes, of course, but can/could you ask us first?'
   Manuel: 'Can/could you give me a key to the house?'
   Mr Jackson: 'Yes, but can/could you be quiet if you come in late?'
   Manuel: 'May I/Can I smoke in my room?'
   Mr Jackson: 'No, I'm sorry. This is a non-smoking house.'

---

## Unit 28: Ability (Can/could)

1. (a) A teacher can write on the board
   (b) A teacher can explain grammar
   (c) A teacher can help students
   (d) A politician can make a speech
   (e) A politician can understand politics
   (f) A waiter can take orders
   (g) A waiter can serve food
   (h) A waiter can add up a bill
   (i) A secretary can type fast
   (j) A secretary can answer the phone
   (k) A secretary can take dictation

2. (a) Can Sarah take dictation? Yes, she can
   (b) Can John answer the phone? Yes, he can
   (c) Can Sarah use a computer? Yes, she can
   (d) Can John type 100 words a minute? Yes, he can
   (e) Can Sarah answer the phone? Yes, she can
   (f) Can John write shorthand? Yes, he can
   (g) Can Sarah type 100 words a minute? No, she can't
   (h) Can John take dictation? Yes, he can
   (i) Can Sarah take dictation? Yes, she can
   (j) Can John use a computer? No, he can't

   Who do you think should get the job? – Perhaps John - he can do more than Sarah.

## Unit 29: Obligation (have to)

1. (a) The teacher has to be friendly.
   (b) The students have to work hard.
   (c) The teacher has to give some homework.
   (d) The students have to do their homework.
   (e) The teacher has to help the students.
   (f) The students have to be on time.
   (g) The teacher has to speak clearly.
   (h) The students have to speak English in class.

2. When Jane was a secretary
   (a) She **had to** type letters (+)
   (c) She **didn't have to** travel a lot (-)
   (e) She **didn't have to** work at the weekend (-)
   (f) She **had to** work from 9.00–5.00 (+)
   (h) She **had to** work hard (+)

   Now Jane is a salesperson
   (b) She **doesn't have to** type letters (-)
   (d) She **has to** travel a lot (+)
   (e) She **has to** work at the weekend (+)
   (g) She **doesn't have to** work from 9.00–5.00 (-)
   (i) She still **has to** work hard (+)

3. I am a teacher. I work in the centre of London but I live in the Southeast, quite a long way from the school. So every morning I **have to** get up at 7.00. There are no buses so I **have to** walk to the train station. I get a train to Victoria Station and then I usually go on the Underground. The school is quite near so I **don't have to** go on the Underground – if the weather is good, I sometimes walk. I **have to** be at work at 8.45 because classes start at 9.00.

   Yesterday was terrible because there was a train strike, so there were no trains to Victoria. I **had to** get up at 6.00 and walk a long way to catch a bus. When I got to the bus stop the buses were all full so I **had to** wait a long time. Luckily a friend gave me a lift home at the end of the day so I **didn't have to** walk or wait for a bus again.

4. (a) What time does she have to get up? — 7.00
   (b) Why does she have to walk to the train station? — There are no buses
   (c) Does she have to go on the underground? — No, she doesn't
   (d) What time does she have to be at work? — 8.45
   (e) What time did she have to get up yesterday? — 6.00
   (f) Why did she have to wait a long time? — The buses were all full
   (g) Did she have to walk at the end of the day? — No, she didn't

---

## Unit 30: Advising (should/shouldn't)

1. (a) You should read in English.
   (b) You should write vocabulary in a notebook.
   (c) You shouldn't try and translate every word you read.
   (d) You should listen to the radio in English.
   (e) You shouldn't speak your own language in your English class.
   (f) You shouldn't forget to do your homework.
   (g) You should watch English films.
   (h) You should study hard!

2. Jonny: 'I'm really worried about my exam, Jackie.'
   Jackie: '**You shouldn't worry**. You'll be OK.'
   Jonny: 'Yes, but I've got too much work to do!'
   Jackie: '**You should plan your time**.'
   Jonny: 'I know, but I don't have much time. I'm going to a party on Saturday.'
   Jackie: 'Well, **you shouldn't go to the party!**'
   Jonny: 'But I need to relax sometimes.'
   Jackie: 'Yes, well, **you shouldn't work all the time**. You can work on Sunday.'
   Jonny: 'I'm going skiing on Sunday.'
   Jackie: 'I think **you should work harder!**'

3. He should give up smoking.
   They should speak English in class.
   They shouldn't drink so much.
   He should buy a new car.
   She should exercise more.
   She should spend less money.
   He shouldn't eat so much chocolate.
   She should be careful!

## *Unit 31: Possibility (may/might)*

1. (a) The Princess may not make a decision.
   (b) The Princess may not want to be rich.
   (c) The Princess mightn't like Prince Humphrey better.
   (d) Her father may not like Prince Alfred better.
   (e) Prince Alfred may not love someone else.
   (f) Prince Humphrey mightn't love someone else.

2. (a) I might marry Prince Humphrey or I might marry Prince Alfred.
   (b) I might decide this week or I might decide next year.
   (c) I might travel the world or I might write a book.
   (d) I might live here or I might live abroad.

3. (a) The Princess may marry me.
   (b) We may live in my castle.
   (c) She may not like that.
   (d) We may live with her father.
   (e) Her father may not like me.
   (f) I may build a new castle in her country.
   (g) They may not like that.
   (h) She may not marry me.

4. (a) The Princess might dance with Prince Humphrey
   (b) Prince Humphrey might ask the Princess to marry him
   (c) The Princess might say 'No'
   (d) Prince Humphrey might be sad
   (e) Prince Alfred might be successful
   (f) Then Prince Humphrey might be angry
   (g) Prince Humphrey might hit Prince Alfred
   (h) The Princess might be very angry
   (i) She might not marry either of them
   (j) She might not get married at all.

---

## *Unit 32: Past continuous*

1. At 8.00am in Britain
   Susan was having breakfast
   But, in Australia
   Joe was leaving work

   At 12.00pm in Britain
   Susan was having lunch

   Joe was having a beer.

   At 10.00pm in Britain
   Susan was going to bed
   But in Australia
   Joe was getting up

   At 11.00pm in Britain
   Susan was reading in bed

   Joe was going to work.

2. Joe: 'Hi, Susan?'
   Susan: 'Joe! I tried to telephone you yesterday but you were never at home. What were you doing?'
   Joe: 'What time did you ring?'
   Susan: 'Well, first I rang at 8.00am – that's 5.30pm in Australia.'
   Joe: 'I was leaving work.'
   Susan: 'Then I rang at 12.00pm – that's 9.30pm in Australia.'
   Joe: 'Oh, I was having a beer with my friends.'
   Susan: 'Then I rang at 5.00pm – oh dear, that's 2.30am in Australia!'
   Joe: 'Yes, I was sleeping – or I was *trying* to sleep!'

3. (a) Tim was talking to Lisa
   (b) John and Stuart were having an argument
   (c) Jane was having a hamburger
   (d) Mary and Louisa were dancing
   (e) Pete was drinking a beer
   (f) Tim and Stuart were smoking
   (g) Tim and Lisa were sitting on a bench
   (h) Joe's friends were having a good time

4. (a) Was Tim talking to Louisa? No, he wasn't.
   (b) Was Jane drinking a beer? No, she wasn't
   (c) Were Mary and Louisa dancing? Yes, they were
   (d) Were Tim and Lisa eating? No, they weren't
   (e) Was Tim smoking? Yes, he was
   (f) Was Lisa standing up? No, she wasn't
   (g) Were Joe's friends having a good time? Yes, they were

## Unit 33: Past simple and continuous

1. .....I explained that I was twenty four hours late because there was a railway strike.
'Sorry, sir, he said, 'Rules are rules – £40 please.'
I was so angry that while **he was writing** the ticket for the fine **I went** to my car and **took out** my steering wheel lock and **locked** his steering wheel. 'Right,' I said. 'Now I can't move my car and you can't move your van!'
'I'll call the police!' he said. 'No, I will.' I replied and so we both called them.
But while we were waiting for the police to arrive **he said**, 'OK, you win.' and **he took** the clamp off my car. So I took off the steering wheel lock. I got in my car but as I was leaving **the police arrived** and I had to stop and explain the whole story. They couldn't stop laughing. I don't know what they thought was so funny!

2. Last night I **was feeling tired**. I **was sleeping** when this man **woke me up**. He was really angry because his car had been clamped. While he **was shouting** at me I tried to tell him he had to pay a fine of £40. As I **was writing** the ticket he **went** to his car and came back with a steering wheel lock and he locked my steering wheel! I couldn't believe it! I called the police – and so did he. While we **were waiting** for the police he got angrier and angrier. I felt quite scared so I decided to let him go. He **was driving** away when the police **arrived** but he stopped to talk to them. For some reason the policemen thought the story was really funny.

3. (a) He drove away when the police arrived.
(b) He was driving away when the police arrived.

Sentence **b** means he started driving *before* the police arrived.
Sentence **a** means he started driving *at the same time* as the police arrived.

(c) I was feeling really tired and annoyed when I arrived home.
(d) I felt really tired and annoyed when I arrived home.

Sentence **c** means he started feeling tired and annoyed *before* he arrived home.
Sentence **d** means he started feeling tired and annoyed *at the same time* as he arrived home.

4. **I was driving home when I saw an accident.**
**It was raining when I arrived.**
**I was reading when the phone rang.**
**We were dancing when the electricity went out.**
**They were robbing a bank when the police arrived.**
**She was shopping when she met him.**

---

## Unit 34: Prepositions of place (in/on/next to)

1.

| | | | | | |
|---|---|---|---|---|---|
| (a) quiet | **noisy** | (e) cold | **hot** | (i) short | **tall***|
| (b) expensive | **cheap** | (f) good | **bad** | (j) happy | **sad** |
| (c) rich | **poor** | (g) difficult | **easy** | (k) old (people) | **young** |
| (d) boring | **exciting** | (h) slow | **fast** | (l) old (things) | **new** |

* The opposite of short for *people* is tall, for things (eg a film) the opposite is long.

2 & 3.
(a) The children are very **noisy** today. (2)
(b) He bought a **new** car. It was very **expensive**. (1 & 2)
(c) The weather was **cold** today. (2)
(d) I love **hot** weather! (1)
(e) This TV programme is really **exciting**. (2)
(f) This is a **difficult** exercise. (1)
(g) My aunt is really **young**. (2)
(h) He wrote a really **good** essay. (1)
(i) The train is really **fast**. (2)
(j) My brother is quite **short**. (2)
(k) He bought me a **small** present. (1)

4. The weather **is really beautiful**.
Brighton **is an exciting town**.
but it **is quite expensive**.
Yesterday I went to see **a great play** at the theatre.
The actors **were very good**.
Today I'm going shopping. There are some **wonderful shops**.
I want to buy **a new dress**.
Then tomorrow we're going on a boat-trip – if **the sea is calm**.

## Unit 35: Comparatives

1.

| -er | -ier | more....... | irregular |
|---|---|---|---|
| old<br>nice<br>cheap<br>warm<br>quiet<br>tall<br>fast | easy<br>sunny<br>noisy<br>lucky<br>heavy | important<br>exciting<br>expensive<br>comfortable | good<br>bad<br>far |

2. (a) Rio is hotter than Brasilia
(b) Brasilia is smaller than Rio
(c) Correct
(d) Brasilia is sunnier than Rio
(e) Correct
(f) Correct
(g) Rio is nicer than Brasilia
(h) Brasilia is drier than Rio

3. (a) Manchester is bigger than York
(b) Manchester is nearer London than York
(c) The train ticket from York to London is more expensive than from Manchester to London
(d) Manchester is dirtier than York (look at the picture!)
(e) York is smaller than Manchester
(f) York is further from London than Manchester
(g) The train ticket from Manchester to London is cheaper than from York to London
(h) York is cleaner than Manchester. (look at the picture!)

4. (a) (big) Oporto is bigger than Faro
(b) (small) Faro is smaller than Oporto
(c) (sunny) Faro is sunnier than Oporto
(d) (cloudy) Oporto is cloudier than Faro
(e) (hot) Faro is hotter than Oporto
(f) (cool) Oporto is cooler than Faro
(g) (rainy) Oporto is rainier than Faro
(h) (dry) Faro is drier than Oporto

---

## Unit 36: Superlatives

1. (a) beautiful the most beautiful
(b) delicious the most delicious
(c) cheap the cheapest
(d) safe the safest
(e) dangerous the most dangerous
(f) hot the hottest
(g) boring the most boring
(h) good the best
(i) large the largest
(j) small the smallest
(k) relaxing the most relaxing
(l) expensive the most expensive
(m) clean the cleanest
(n) bad the worst
(o) near the nearest

2. (a) Recife is (expensive) the most expensive holiday.
(b) Hotel Boa Viagem is the nearest to the Beach.
(c) Recife is the longest holiday.
(d) Hotel Thai is the furthest from the beach.
(e) Hotel Thai is the biggest hotel.
(f) Phuket is the shortest holiday.
(g) Key West is the cheapest holiday.
(h) Palm Hotel is the smallest hotel.

3. Jon: Well, I think (a) (good) the best place to go is Thailand. It's certainly (b) the cheapest country and it's got (c) the most beautiful beaches. The weather is wonderful – Bangkok is (d) the hottest city in the world.
Rebecca: But Brazil has beautiful beaches too and I think it's (e) the most relaxing place.
Jon: Relaxing!! It's (f) the most dangerous! We'll probably get shot!
Rebecca: Rubbish! The United States is (g) the worst. Florida is really dangerous for tourists.
Jon: So, let's go to Thailand. Its (h) the safest. It's (i) the most interesting place too – a completely different culture. And the food is (j) the most delicious in the world.
Rebecca: Well, yes, American food is probably (k) the most boring – all hamburgers and steaks and it's (l) the most expensive place to go too.

4. (a) Brazil is the furthest place.
(b) French food is the best in the world.
(c) Correct
(d) Madame Tussauds is the most interesting thing to see in London.
(e) Are you the oldest in your family?
(f) I sat in the most comfortable chair.

5. (a) Tokyo is the biggest city in Japan.
(b) Jonny is the noisiest student in the class!
(c) Correct
(d) The fastest car won the race.
(e) Jane and Sue are both thin but Mary is the thinnest
(f) Who is the busiest person in the office?

## Unit 37: Adverbs II: manner

1. (a) bad **badly**
   (b) good **well**
   (c) easy **easily**
   (d) careful **carefully**
   (e) angry **angrily**
   (f) quiet **quietly**
   (g) noisy **noisily**
   (h) slow **slowly**
   (i) silent **silently**
   (j) violent **violently**

2. 'I'm really looking forward to our holiday.' she said, **happily**
   'Er, do you think we have enough money to go on holiday, darling?' he asked, **nervously**
   'Of course we do!' she said, **confidently**
   'But, have you forgotten we've got to pay for the new car?' he asked, **quietly**
   'I thought you did that last month!, she shouted, **angrily**
   'No, we had to pay for your new clothes last month – £500!' he replied, **crossly**
   'Oh, well, no holiday, then' she said **sadly**

3. (a) He did it **accidently**.
   (b) He laughed **wickedly**.
   (c) He speaks English **fluently**.
   (d) She behaves **politely**.
   (e) They dress **differently**.
   (f) He sings **well**.
   (g) He won **easily**.
   (h) She laughed **happily**.

4. Driving in London is not (a) **easy**. The traffic moves very (b) **slowly** in central London – about 12km per hour. You also need to drive (c) **carefully** because some drivers are very (d) **impatient** and drive (e) **dangerously**. Another problem is finding a place to park. Car-parks are very (f) **expensive**. It is often better to leave your car outside the city centre and then you can (g) **easily** travel into the centre on public transport. The buses and underground are very (h) **good**.

   There are lots of (i) **excellent** restaurants in London and – if you have the money – you can eat very (j) **well**. Some people think that the British cook very (k) **badly** but in London you can eat Indian, Thai, French, Chinese food....everything!

---

## Unit 38: Present tenses for future use

1. (a) The plane (leave) **leaves** at 8.00 on 16th June.
   (b) Mr Brown **is meeting** Mr Kuhato at 3.00pm on 17th June.
   (c) He **is having** lunch with the Directors at 1.00 on 18th June.
   (d) On 19th June he **is visiting** a textile factory.
   (e) On 20th June he **is going** to a concert.
   (f) The concert **starts** at 8.00pm.
   (g) On the 21st June he **is having** dinner with Jane Faifax.
   (h) On the 22nd June he **is playing** golf with Mr Kuhato.
   (i) The plane back to London **leaves** at 20.20 on the 23rd June.

2. (a) **What time does the plane leave London?**
   (b) **Who is he meeting on 17th June?**
   (c) **What is he doing on 18th June?**
   (d) **Where is he visiting on 19th June?**
   (e) **What time does the concert start?**
   (f) **When is he having dinner with Jane Fairfax?**
   (g) **What is he doing on 22nd June?**
   (h) **What time does the plane back to London leave?**

3. (a) **leaves**
   (b) **am staying**
   (c) **Correct**
   (d) **am meeting**
   (e) **Are you visiting**
   (f) **Correct**
   (g) **Correct**
   (h) **lands**

## Unit 39: Going to/will – I

1. (a) She's going to lie on the beach.
   (b) She's not going to take her mobile phone.
   (c) She's going to sleep late every day.
   (d) She's not going to take her lap-top computer.
   (e) She's not going to telephone her office every day.
   (f) She's going to eat delicious healthy food.
   (g) She's going to go scuba diving.
   (h) She's going to have a really good time.

2. (a) 'I feel hungry.' 'I'll have something to eat.'
   (b) 'The sun's really hot.' 'I'll go in the shade.'
   (c) 'I feel thirsty.' 'I'll have something to drink.'
   (d) 'I think I'm burning.' 'I'll put on some suncream.'
   (e) 'The sea looks wonderful.' 'I'll go for a swim.'
   (f) 'I'm bored.' 'I'll read a book.'

3. Mary: What are you going to do next week Fiona?
   Fiona: Didn't I tell you? I'm going [to go] on holiday.
   Mary: You lucky thing! Where are you going [to go]?
   Fiona: Sri Lanka. Are you going [to go] anywhere this year?
   Mary: I don't know yet. Maybe we will visit friends in Wales.
   Fiona: Well, I'll send you a postcard!
   Mary: Thanks!

4. Dear Mary,
   Having a lovely time in Sri Lanka. Tomorrow I'm going to visit an old palace in the jungle but today it's really hot so I think I'll just lie on the beach. It's so relaxing! I'll ring you when I get back, OK?
   Love, Fiona.

   Dear Mum and Dad,
   I'm really enjoying my holiday in Sri Lanka. I'm going to stay here three weeks and really relax. Next week I'm going (to go) on a trip into the jungle. – Don't worry! I'll be very careful!
   Love, Fiona.

---

## Unit 40: Going to/will – II

1. (a) the train/come — The train is going to come
   the hero/rescue her — The hero will rescue her
   (b) they/fight — they're (they are) going to fight
   one of them die — one of them will die
   (c) they/fall in love — they are going to fall in love
   they get married — they'll (they will) get married
   (d) he/fall — he's going to fall
   he/die — he'll die
   (e) he/ask her to marry him — he's going to ask her to marry him
   she/say 'Yes' — she'll say 'Yes'
   (f) he/give her flowers — he's going to give her flowers
   she/be happy — she'll be happy

2. (a) Is the train going to come?
   Will the hero rescue her?
   (b) Are they going to fight?
   Will one of them die?
   (c) Are they going to fall in love?
   Will they get married?
   (d) Is he going to fall?
   Will he die?
   (e) Is he going to ask her to marry him?
   Will she say 'Yes'?
   (f) Is he going to give her flowers?
   Will she be happy?

3. Director: 'OK, in this scene the villain (kidnap) is going to kidnap the heroine and he is going to tie her to the train tracks. She is going to scream very loudly and, before the train comes, the hero is going to hear her screaming and rescue her.'
   Actor: 'Are they going to fall in love?'
   Director: 'Yes, but first the hero and the villain are going to fight.'
   Actor: 'Is the hero going to win?'
   Director: 'Of course!'

4. (a) The hero will kill the villain.
   (b) The villain will apologise and the hero won't kill him.
   (c) The heroine will be very happy.
   (d) The hero and heroine will get married.
   (e) They'll live happily ever after.
   (f) They'll have two children.

## Unit 41: Present perfect I: experience

1.
(a) be – **been**
(b) break – **broken**
(c) buy – **bought**
(d) come – **come**
(e) cut – **cut**
(f) drink – **drunk**
(g) drive – **driven**
(h) eat – **eaten**
(i) fall – **fallen**
(j) forget – **forgotten**
(k) get – **got***
(l) give – **given**
(m) go – **been** or **gone**
(n) have – **had**
(o) know – **known**
(p) make – **made**
(q) meet – **met**
(r) read – **read**
(s) see – **seen**
(t) speak – **spoken**
(u) steal – **stolen**
(v) take – **taken**
(w) think – **thought**
(x) wear – **worn**
(y) write – **written**

*American English 'gotten'

2.
(a) **Has** George ever **eaten** snails?
**Yes, he has**
(b) **Has** Jane ever **read** Shakespeare?
**No, she hasn't**
(c) **Have** Philip and Sue ever **met** the Queen?
**Yes, they have**
(d) **Has** George **driven** a lorry?
**Yes, he has**
(e) **Has** Jane **been** to Australia?
**Yes, she has**
(f) **Have** Philip and Sue **eaten** snails?
**No, they haven't**

3.

| | | |
|---|---|---|
| (a) You/eat/snails? | **Have you (ever) eaten snails?** | Yes, I have |
| (b) Where/you/eat them? | **Where did you eat them?** | In France |
| (c) Philip and Sue/meet the Queen? | **Have Philip and Sue met the Queen?** | Yes, they have |
| (d) When/they/meet her? | **When did they meet her?** | Last year |
| (e) George/read/Shakespeare? | **Has George read Shakespeare?** | Yes, he has |
| (f) What/he/read? | **What did he read?/has he read?** | Hamlet |
| (g) Jane/drive/a lorry? | **Has Jane driven a lorry?** | Yes, she has |
| (h) When/she/drive it? | **When did she drive it?** | A few years ago |
| (i) You/meet the Queen? | **Have you met the Queen?** | Yes, I have |
| (j) Where/you/meet her? | **Where did you meet her?** | At Buckingham Palace |

4.
(a) Have you **been** to China?
(b) I **went** there last year.
(c) I have never **eaten** sushi.
(d) **Has** she been to France?
(e) They **have** travelled all over the world.

---

## Unit 42: Present perfect II: time up to now

1.
(a) John **has been** in England **since** March.
John **has been** in England **for** three months.
(b) Jack and Mary **have known** Peter **since** 1995.
Jack and Mary **have known** Peter **for** two years.
(c) I **have had** a cat **for** a year.
I **have had** a cat **since** last year.
(d) She **has lived** in Peru **since** 1993.
She **has lived** in Peru **for** four years.
(e) Terry **has been** 21 **for** two weeks.
Terry **has been** 21 **since** 16th November.
(f) We **have worked** in London **since** January.
We **have worked** in London **for** three months.

2.
(a) **How long has John been in England?**
(b) **How long have Jack and Mary known Peter?**
(c) **How long have you had a cat?**
(d) **How long has Sheila lived in Peru?**
(e) **How long has Terry been 21?**
(f) **How long have you worked in London?**

3.
(a) **He hasn't been married long.**
(b) **We haven't lived in England long.**
(c) **They haven't worked here long.**
(d) **I haven't been a teacher long.**
(e) **She hasn't had a car long.**
(f) **He hasn't known her long.**
(g) **You haven't been married long.**

4. Jan **has been** a teacher for ten years. She **became** a teacher when she left university in 1987. She likes travelling and **has been** all over the world. Last year she **went** to China.

My wife and I **got married** in 1976, so we **have been married** for more than twenty years now. When we got married we **lived** with my wife's mother but we **bought** this house fifteen years ago and since then we **have lived** here.

## Unit 43: Present perfect III: present result

1. (a) hurt **hurt**
   (b) break **broken**
   (c) burn **burnt/burned**
   (d) drink **drunk**
   (e) sprain **sprained**
   (f) catch (measles) **caught**
   (g) watch **watched**
   (h) cut **cut**
   (i) bump **bumped**

2. (a) **He has bumped** his head.
   (b) **He has watched** too much television!
   (c) **He has drunk** poison by accident.
   (d) **They have caught** measles.
   (e) **He has sprained** his ankle.
   (f) **He has sprained** his arm.
   (g) **He has cut** his leg.
   (h) **She has burnt** her finger.
   (i) **She has hurt** her back.

3. Choose simple past or present perfect.
   (a) **I've lost** my keys – I can't get into my house!
   (b) **I've broken** my leg, but it's OK again now.
   (c) **I have eaten** too much. I feel sick.
   (d) **He has fallen** over – help him to stand up!
   (e) **I've won**. Shall we play again?
   (f) Duncan **arrived** early but he's gone now.
   (g) Why are you wet? **Have you been** swimming?

4. (a) **'Have you eaten enough?'**
   'Yes, thanks. It was delicious.'
   (b) 'Why is the dog barking?'
   'Because the post **has arrived**.'
   (c) 'Oh no! It's raining and **I've forgotten** my umbrella!'
   (d) 'She **dyed** her hair purple but her mother didn't like it so she **has dyed** it brown again now.'
   (e) 'She **missed** the train so she caught a bus instead.'
   (f) 'Your shoes look new. **Have you cleaned** them?'
   (g) 'I **felt** terrible this morning but now my headache **has gone**.'

---

## Unit 44: Present perfect IV: 'yet' and 'already'

1. (a) **They've already seen the Old Town.**
   (b) **They've already had lunch at Ariel's.**
   (c) **They've already gone shopping.**
   (d) **They've already visited the Sukiennice.**
   (e) **They've already heard the Chopin Concert.**
   (f) **They haven't eaten at Staropolska Restaurant yet.**
   (g) **They haven't visited Wawel Castle yet.**
   (h) **They haven't had lunch at the Cafe Jama Michalika yet.**
   (i) **They haven't been on a trip to Wieliczka Salt Mines yet.**

2. (a) **Have they seen the Old Town yet?** **Yes, they have.**
   (b) **Have they been shopping yet?** **Yes, they have.**
   (c) **Have they visited Wieliczka yet?** **No, they haven't.**
   (d) **Have they seen the Wawel castle yet?** **No, they haven't.**
   (e) **Have they heard the Chopin concert yet?** **Yes, they have.**
   (f) **Have they had dinner at the Staropolska yet?** **No, they haven't.**

3. (a) **I've already seen the museum.**
   (b) **Have you been to Prague yet?**
   (c) **They haven't eaten pierogi yet.**
   (d) **I've already taken lots of photos.**
   (e) **I haven't spent much money yet.**
   (f) **We've already been to the Castle.**
   (g) **She hasn't crossed the bridge yet.**
   (h) **Has Lisa visited Bratislava yet?**

## Unit 45: Question Revision 1

1. (a) Is he a Portuguese builder?
   (b) Are they dancing?
   (c) Were you late?
   (d) Can Peter dance really well?
   (e) Are they going to the seaside?
   (f) Was your computer very expensive?
   (g) Would you like to go?
   (h) Is he coming home by train?
   (i) Could she swim?
   (j) Are you feeling better?

2. (a) How long have you lived here?
   (b) Can you pass the salt?
   (c) Was he happy?
   (d) What will you do?
   (e) Where is he going?
   (f) Can I help you?
   (g) Who are you going to marry?
   (h) How long was the film?
   (i) Where is your bag?
   (j) Where were they going?

3. (a) Where **are** you from?
   (b) **Can/May** I use the phone?
   (c) Where **are you going** on holiday?
   (d) What **would you** like to eat?
   (e) How old **were** you in 1975?
   (f) **Have** you ever **eaten** squid?
   (g) Where **are** you going?
   (h) **Have** you finished yet?

---

## Unit 46: Questions Revision 2

1. (a) Where **did the poor woman and her children live?**
   (b) What **colour hair did Snow White have?**
   (c) When **did the Bear knock on the door?**
   (d) What **did he say?**
   (e) What **did they give the Bear?**
   (f) Who **did they see in the forest?**
   (g) What **did the Dwarf find in the tree?**

2. (a) What **did Snow White take out?**
   (b) What **did she cut off?**
   (c) What **did he pick up?**
   (d) When **did they see him again?**
   (e) What **did he say?**
   (f) What **did the Bear explain?**
   (g) Who **did Rose Red marry?**

3. (a) Did the Bear kill the Dwarf?
   (b) Did the Bear hit the Dwarf?
   (c) Did they try to help him?
   (d) Did the Bear fall asleep by the fire?
   (e) Did he come back every day?
   (f) Did he walk off?
   (g) Did the Dwarf steal the treasure?

4. (a) Does Snow White have some scissors?
   (b) Where do the family live?
   (c) Does the Bear eat people?
   (d) Does the Dwarf steal the Prince's gold?
   (e) Does the Dwarf like fishing?
   (f) Do Snow White and Rose Red love their husbands?

# Appendix 6: Key to further-practice exercises

## *Part one: (Units 1–4): Talking about people, places and objects*

### *(Units 1 & 2)*

1. (a) I **am** an engineer.
   (b) My brother **is** called Richard.
   (c) **Is** she Chinese?
   (d) **Are** we in France?
   (e) They **are** both very intelligent.
   (f) It **is** a lovely day.

2. (a) Are you a student?
   (b) Is your teacher English?
   (c) Is English easy?
   (d) Is the Eiffel Tower in France?
   (e) Where is your friend?
   (f) What's your name?

### *(Unit 3)*

3. **This is** my dog. **That** dog **is** dangerous.

   **This is** my son.

   **Those** shoes **are** too high. **These are** more comfortable.

   John! **Those** flowers **are** dead!

   What **is this** called? It's a rose.

   Who **are those** girls?

   What **is that**?!

   **These are** my babies.

### *(Unit 4)*

4. (a) This person is English
   (b) The factory is very noisy
   (c) The bus is always late!
   (d) My key is on the table
   (e) This is my child
   (f) Where is the man?

5. (a) holidays
   (b) cats
   (c) babies
   (d) daughters
   (e) churches
   (f) women
   (g) classes
   (h) girls
   (i) houses

## *Part two: (Units 5–7): Talking about routines and habits*

### *(Unit 5)*

1. Sheila **is** a dentist. She **likes** her work but she **lives** a long way from her surgery so she usually **gets up** quite early. She **has** three children so she **helps** them get dressed and **makes** them breakfast. They **walk** to school, it isn't far. Then she **leaves** the house at about 7.30. She **goes** to work by train and then **catches** a bus. She usually **arrives** at about 8.30, **has** a cup of coffee and **sees** her first patient at 9.00.

2. Jane **works** in a cinema. She **starts** work at 3.00 in the afternoon, when the first film is on, and **finishes** about 11.00 at night. She **loves** her job because she **watches** all the new films free! But she **goes** to bed very late. So, in the mornings, she **stays** in bed until 10.00 or 11.00.

### *(Unit 6)*

3. (a) What does Alfredo do? — He's a disc-jockey
   (b) Does he work in Rome? — No, he doesn't
   (c) What time does he start work? — 7.00
   (d) Does he go to bed late? — No, he doesn't
   (e) Does he think his job is interesting? — Yes, he does
   (f) Does he like getting up early? — No, he doesn't
   (g) When do his friends see Alfredo? — At the weekends
   (h) Do his friends listen to him on the radio? — Yes, they do

4. (a) No, he doesn't work in Madrid
   (b) No, he doesn't start work at 9.00.
   (c) No, he doesn't go to bed late.
   (d) No, he doesn't hate his job.
   (e) No, he doesn't like getting up early.
   (f) No, his friends don't see Alfredo every day.

*(Unit 7)*

5. (a) Alfredo always gets up early.
   (b) Alfredo never sees his friends during the week.
   (c) Sheila is rarely late for work.
   (d) Jane usually enjoys her job.
   (e) Sheila always has a cup of coffee in the morning.
   (f) Sheila's children are often naughty.
   (g) Alfredo is usually tired.
   (h) Jane never gets up early.
   (i) Alfredo's friends often listen to him on the radio.
   (j) Jane always watches new films first.

## *Part three: (Units 8–12): Referring to people, places and objects*

*(Units 8–10)*

1. Many people know Shakespeare's play Romeo and Juliet, but this film 'William Shakespeare's Romeo and Juliet' is something new. The Director sets the story in modern day America. Romeo meets Juliet at a party and (a) **he** falls in love with (b) **her** immediately. (c) **She** also loves (d) **him**. But there's a problem. (e) **His** family hate (f) **hers** and (g) **her** family hate his. Unfortunately (h) **their** love affair cannot work. Everybody is against (i) **them**.....

2. Hi! How are (a) **you?** (b) **I** am very busy at the moment. (c) **We** are moving house next week and there is a lot to do. Now we have two children (d) **our** old house is very small and (e) **we** need more space. The new house has four bedrooms and (f) **it's** much nicer. The children are very excited because (g) **they** will have (h) **their** own bedrooms. (i) **I** hope (j) **their** bedrooms will be tidier now (k) **they** have more space.

*(Unit 11)*

3. (a) **A** policeman is walking past (b) **a** house when he hears a shout. 'Michael! Don't kill me!' (c) **The** policeman rushes into (d) **the** house and he sees (e) **a** dead body on the floor. There are three people standing near (f) **the** body – (g) **a** doctor, (h) **a** lawyer and (i) **an** engineer.
   (j) **The** policeman arrests (k) **the** engineer. How does he know who (l) **the** murderer is? (answer: the doctor and lawyer are *women*)

*(Unit 12)*

4. (a) Feijoada is something which/that people eat in Brazil
   (b) A baker is someone who makes bread and cakes
   (c) A watch is something which/that tells the time
   (d) A fork is something which/that people use to eat with
   (e) An air steward is someone who works on an aeroplane
   (f) A playwright is someone who writes plays
   (g) Yorkshire Pudding is something which/that people eat in England for Sunday dinner.

## *Part four: (Units 13–17): Amounts*

*(Unit 13)*

1.

| | |
|---|---|
| Estate Agent: | 'I've got the perfect house for you, sir!' |
| Customer: | '**Has** it **got** three bedrooms?' |
| Estate Agent: | 'Well, in fact, it**'s got** four.' |
| Customer: | 'Is it expensive? I **haven't got** much money.' |
| Estate Agent: | 'No, it's very reasonable. Only £53,000.' |
| Customer: | '**Have** you **got** the keys? Can I go and see it?' |
| Estate Agent: | 'Certainly. I think I**'ve got** some free time this afternoon, if you like.' |

*(Unit 14)*

2. (a) **some** milk
   (b) **some** paper
   (c) **a** newspaper
   (d) **some** rain
   (e) **some** mushrooms
   (f) **some** yoghurt
   (g) **a** tomato
   (h) **some** bread
   (i) **some** money
   (j) **some** toast
   (k) **some** soap
   (l) **a** cup of tea
   (m) **some** coffee
   (n) **some** cheese
   (o) **some** chocolate

*(Unit 15)*

3. (a) Have you got **any** orange juice?
   (b) There aren't **any** potatoes
   (c) I haven't got **any** money
   (d) There are **some** eggs in the fridge
   (e) I'd like to listen to **some** music
   (f) Have you got **any** cigarettes?
   (g) He usually meets **some** friends at the weekend
   (h) Why doesn't he have **any** friends?
   (i) Sorry, we don't have **any** milk today

*(Unit 16)*

4. (a) How **much** does it cost?
   (b) How **many** times a week do you go swimming?
   (c) How **many** bedrooms has your house got?
   (d) How **much** chocolate do you eat in a week?
   (e) How **much** cake would you like?
   (f) How **many** hours do you work?
   (g) How **many** people do you know?
   (h) How **much** water is there?
   (i) How **many** sandwiches are there?
   (j) How **much** bread is there?

*(Unit 17)*

5. The weather is **too** hot.
   My flat isn't warm **enough**
   The hours are **too** long
   There's **too much** noise!
   I've eaten **too much** chocolate
   It's **too** wet.
   There **aren't enough** people.
   I haven't eaten **enough**

## Part five: (Units 18–19): Talking about now

*(Unit 18)*

1. (a) **It's snowing**
   (b) **The children are throwing snowballs**
   (c) **They are wearing hats**
   (d) **They are playing in the snow**
   (e) **The sun is shining**
   (f) **Two children are carrying bags**

*(Unit 19)*

2. Sean **is** a doctor
   He **works** in a hospital
   He **is playing** football
   He **is wearing** shorts
   At work he **wears** a white coat.

   Roger and Lisa **are** teachers
   They **teach** English
   They **are having** dinner
   They often **eat** in restaurants
   They **like** good food!

   Jimmy **is** 26
   He **is driving** his new car.
   He **is listening** to music
   He **likes** rock music
   He **cleans** his car every Saturday.

   Jose **is** Spanish
   She **lives** in Barcelona
   She **likes** Barcelona because the sun always **shines**
   Unfortunately, today it **is raining.**

## Part six: (Units 20–22): Prepositions

*(Unit 20)*

1. (a) **It's under the newspaper**
   (b) **It's behind the plant**
   (c) **It's next to the flowers**
   (d) **It's in front of the radio**
   (e) **They're on the chair**
   (f) **It's in the sink**
   (g) **They're near the bread**
   (h) **It's opposite the cat**
   (i) **It's under the table**
   (j) **They're near the table**
   (k) **They're in the fridge**
   (l) **It's next to the clock**

2. (a) **The toy car is on the hi-fi**
   (b) **The radio is behind the telephone**
   (c) **True**
   (d) **The bananas are in the saucepan**
   (e) **True**
   (f) **The plant is in front of the book**
   (g) **True**
   (h) **The bread is near the keys**

*(Unit 21)*

3. (a) **On** Monday morning **at** 9.00 Louise has got a meeting.
   (b) She's got another meeting **at** 3.00 **on** Tuesday.
   (c) John's birthday is **on** Wednesday and they're having dinner **in** the evening.
   (d) **At** noon **on** 13th April, she's having lunch with the Directors.
   (e) **In** the morning **on** Saturday she's playing tennis.
   (f) **On** Easter Sunday **in** the afternoon she's visitng her grandmother.
   (g) **Next week** is her parents' wedding anniversary.
   (h) She isn't working **at** the weekend.
   (i) On Friday she finishes her job. **In** the future she won't work so hard!

*(Unit 22)*

4. A: Excuse me, how do I get **to** the post office **from** this hotel?
   B: Well, go **out** of the hotel, **across** the road, **over** the bridge, **up** the hill, **through** the park, **down** the hill, **past** the supermarket, **along** the road, **round** the roundabout, **under** the railway bridge and **into** the shopping centre. The post office is on the left.
   A: That sounds complicated. Is there a bus?
   B: Yes, get **on** a number 29 and get **off** next to the swimming pool.

## *Part seven: (Units 23–25): Talking about the past I*

*(Unit 23)*

1. (a) Where **was** the hotel? In the Old Town
   (b) **Was** it nice? Yes, lovely.
   (c) **Was** the weather good? Not bad. It rained a bit.
   (d) **Were** the museums good? Yes, very interesting
   (e) What **was** the food like? Delicious. I ate so much!
   (f) **Were** you on your own? No, I went with David.

2. (a) The weather **wasn't** very good
   (b) The Old Town **wasn't** very crowded
   (c) The museums **weren't** expensive
   (d) I **wasn't** very tired at the end of the day
   (e) David **wasn't** very interested in the museums
   (f) We **weren't** in Prague for very long – just a week.
   (g) The other guests in the hotel **weren't** very friendly.

*(Unit 24)*

3. (a) Susie **made** her own wedding dress.
   (b) I **flew** to Paris because it's quicker than the train.
   (c) She **sang** really well
   (d) Roger **threw** a stone and **broke** the window!
   (e) I **wrote** to her about a week ago.
   (f) Last night I **went** to a party and **lost** my umbrella. I think someone **stole** it.
   (g) He **drank** six cups of coffee and didn't sleep all night!
   (h) I **built** this house myself. It **took** me six years.
   (i) She **paid** the bill and **left**.

4. (a) I really **enjoyed** the film.
   (b) He **carried** the heaviest bag.
   (c) The car **stopped** at the traffic lights.
   (d) He **studied** really hard to pass his exam.
   (e) I **tried** to walk but it was too far.
   (f) They **planned** to go to Buenos Aires but in the end they couldn't.

*(Unit 25)*

5. (a) **Why did you go there?**
   (b) **Where did you teach?**
   (c) **Did you teach children?**
   (d) **Did you enjoy it there?**
   (e) **Did you learn Czech?**
   (f) **Did you make Czech friends?**
   (g) **What did you do in your spare time?**

6. (a) **Yes, he did**
   (b) **No, he didn't**
   (c) **Yes, he did**
   (d) **No, he didn't**
   (e) **Yes, he did**
   (f) **No, he didn't**
   (g) **Yes, he did.**

## Part eight: (Units 26–31): Adding meaning

### (Unit 26)

1. (a) **Would you like** a drink? No, thanks.
   (b) **Would you like** to sit down?
   (c) I think **I'd like** a cup of tea – I'm thirsty
   (d) He **likes** listening to very loud music. I hate it!
   (e) It's raining. **Would you like** to borrow my umbrella?
   (f) I **don't like** swimming much. It's usually too cold in England.
   (g) My parents **would like** to meet you. Shall I introduce you?

2. (a) A: **Would** you **like to go** (go) to the cinema next week? There's a new thriller on
   B: Well, I **like going** to the cinema but I hate thrillers! I **like seeing** comedies better.

   (b) A: Do you **like eating** out in restaurants?
   B: Yes, I love it! I really **like eating** Indian food
   A: **Would** you **like to go** out for an Indian meal tonight?
   B: Yes, please!

   (c) A: **I'd like** you **to meet** my friends. Why don't we all go out for a drink next week?
   B: Oh, I'm really shy. I don't **like meeting** new people

### (Unit 27)

3. (a) **Can I borrow some gloves please?**
   (b) **Can/May I borrow a pen?**
   (c) **Could/Can you close the door?**
   (d) **Can I pay by cheque?**
   (e) **Could/Can you lend me 10p?**
   (f) **Can/May I turn on the television?**
   (g) **Can/Could you telephone me later?**

4. (a) A: **May/Can** I use the phone?
   (b) B: Well, **could/can** you give me a lift?
   (c) B: Wait....**could/can** you lend me a pen?
   (d) A: **Can/may** I read that magazine when you've finished with it?
   (e) A: **Can/Could** you tell me the time please?
   (f) A: **Can/may** we sit here?

### (Unit 28)

5. (a) **She can play the guitar**
   (b) **She can drive**
   (c) **She can play chess**
   (d) **She can use a computer**
   (e) **She can ski**
   (f) **She can swim**
   (g) **She can speak French**

6. (a) **She could play the guitar**
   (b) **She couldn't drive**
   (c) **She could/couldn't play chess** (What do *you* think?)
   (d) **She could/couldn't use a computer** (What do *you* think?)
   (e) **She could/couldn't ski** (What do *you* think?)
   (f) **She could/couldn't swim** (What do *you* think?)
   (g) **She could/couldn't speak French** (What do *you* think?)

### (Unit 29)

7. (a) In a cinema **you have to buy a ticket**
   (b) In a library **you have to be quiet**
   (c) At the traffic lights **you have to wait until the light turns green**
   (d) In an expensive restaurant **you have to wear a tie** (if you're a man!)
   (e) On roads in England **you have to drive on the left**
   (f) In many swimming pools **you have to wear a hat**
   (g) In the bank you often **have to wait in a queue**

8. When Jim was at school
   (a) He **had to** do homework (+)
   (c) He **didn't have to** get up very early (-)
   (e) He **didn't have to** work on Saturdays (-)
   (g) He **had to** study French (+)
   (i) He **had to** wear a uniform (+)

   Now he's working in a supermarket
   (b) He **doesn't have** to do homework
   (d) He **has to** get up at 6.00 (+)
   (f) He **has to** work on Saturday mornings (+)
   (h) He **doesn't have to** study French (-)
   (j) He *still* **has to** wear a uniform! (+)

### (Unit 30)

9. (a) **You should take out insurance**
   (b) **You should write your address on your luggage**
   (c) **You shouldn't take very heavy luggage**
   (d) **You should buy a guidebook**
   (e) **You shouldn't carry too much cash**
   (f) **You should learn to speak a little of the language.**

10. You (a) **shouldn't listen** to your 'friends'. They are being very cruel. But you (b) **should try** to take more exercise. You (c) **should walk** to school rather than take the bus and you (d) **should eat** more fruit and less chocolate.

I think you (e) **should tell** your friend that she (f) **should stop** smoking. Obviously it is making her ill. Tell her that if she wants to be healthy and able to run fast she (g) **shouldn't smoke** at all.

Your parents (h) **shouldn't make** you eat meat if you want to be vegetarian but you (i) **shouldn't expect** them to cook two meals every night. You (j) **should cook** your own dinner.

*(Unit 31)*

11. (a) **she might/may be on holiday.**
(b) **He mightn't/may not like me.**
(c) **He might/may pass the exam.**
(d) **They might/may live in Scotland.**
(e) **I might/may go out tonight.**
(f) **I might/may stay at home.**
(g) **He might be a doctor.**
(h) **They might/may speak Swahili.**
(i) **She mightn't/may not speak English.**
(j) **They mightn't/may not live here.**
(k) **We might/may be lost.**

## *Part nine: (Units 32–33): Talking about the past II*

*(Unit 32)*

1. **At 9 am Elaine was having breakfast and John was driving to work.**
**At 10am Elaine was visiting an exhibition and John was writing letters.**
**At 12.30pm Elaine was having lunch and John was having a meeting with a Director.**
**At 3pm Elaine was meeting clients and John was doing the accounts.**
**At 6pm Elaine was have dinner with the Director of the Dublin office and John was driving home.**

*(Unit 33)*

2. (a) **It was raining when she left the hotel.**
(b) **She was driving to the airport when the taxi broke down.**
(c) **She was standing in the check-in queue when someone stole her handbag.**
(d) **She was talking to the police when the plane left without her.**
(e) **She was sitting on the plane when she spilt her drink.**
(f) **She was waiting for her luggage when someone told her it was lost.**
(g) **She was feeling tired and annoyed when she got home.**

3. 'The journey home was terrible. First it (rain) **was raining** when I left the hotel, so I got wet. The taxi **broke down** on the way to the airport. Then, while I was waiting in the check-in queue someone **stole** my handbag so I had to go to the police. And then I **missed** my plane because I was talking to the police for so long! I was really angry. Then, I finally got on another plane. I **was beginning** to relax a bit when I spilt my orange juice everywhere! We got to London at last and I **was waiting** for my luggage when a man came and told me it was lost!. 'It might be in Rome.' he said. So you can understand why I **was feeling** unhappy and tired when I got home!'

## *Part ten: (Units 34–37): Describing*

*(Units 35 and 36)*

1. (a) **The Amazon is longer than the Thames**
**The Nile is the longest**
(b) **A motorbike is faster than a bicycle**
**A car is the fastest**
(c) **Gold is more precious than silver**
**Platinum is the most precious**
(d) **An orange is bigger than a grape**
**A grapefruit is the biggest**
(e) **England is hotter than Norway**
**Thailand is the hottest**
(f) **Fruit-juice is healthier than coca-cola**
**Water is the healthiest**
(g) **A magazine is more expensive than a newspaper**
**A book is the most expensive**

2. (a) What is **the newest** national TV Channel in Britain? **Channel Five (4)**
(b) Which is **the** second **biggest** city in Britain? **Birmingham (3)**
(c) Which restaurant in London is owned by three of **the most famous** American film stars? **Planet Hollywood (5)**
(d) What is **the youngest** age you can marry in Britain? **16 (6)**
(e) What is Britain's **most popular** tourist attraction? **Blackpool Beach (2)**
(f) When was **the worst** fire in the history of London? **1666 (1)**
(g) Which is **the most expensive** hotel in London? **Claridges (7)**

*(Units 34 and 37)*

3. Large **adjective** new **adjective** poor **adjective** slowly **adverb** patiently **adverb** angry **adjective** magic **adjective** comfortable **adjective** immediately **adverb** angrily **adverb**

4. Once upon a time there was a very **poor** fisherman and his wife. One day the fisherman caught a fish which spoke to him. 'Let me go, fisherman.' it said, 'I am a **magic** fish.' So the fisherman let him go. He returned home to his wife but when he told her the story she was very **angry** 'Why didn't you ask him to give us a **large** house instead of this small hut we live in?' she asked, 'Go back and ask him for a house.' So the fisherman went back to the lake, called the fish and told him what his wife had said. 'Go home' said the fish, 'she has it already'. When the fisherman got home his wife was in a lovely **new** house. But two week later his wife said, 'This house is very small and not very **comfortable**. Go and ask the fish for a castle.' The fisherman didn't want to but he went back to the fish and asked him for a castle. 'Go home,' said the fish, **patiently** 'she has it already.'
When the fisherman got home his wife was very happy with her new castle but the next day she said, 'Now I live in a castle I want to be Queen. Go and ask the fish.' The fisherman went to ask the fish. 'Go home', said the fish, 'She is Queen already.' But when the fisherman got home his wife was watching the sun **slowly** going down. 'Why can't I do that?' she asked. 'Go back to the fish **immediately** and tell him I want to be Master of the Universe!' The fisherman went back to the fish and asked him but the fish said **angrily** 'Go home. Your wife is back in her small hut.'

## *Part eleven: (Units 38–40): Talking about the future*

*(Unit 38)*

1. A: 'When (meet) **are** you **meeting** Mr Johnson?'
B: 'At lunchtime. We **are having** lunch in Quaglino's'
A: 'Lucky you! **Are** you **meeting** him at the restaurant?'
B: 'No, he**'s coming** here. He **is giving** me a lift.'
C: 'What time **does** the train **leave**?'
D: 'Twelve o'clock. So hurry up!'
C: 'Where **are** we **meeting** the others?'
D: 'On the platform.'
E: 'When **are** you **going** back to University?
F: 'Well, term **starts** on October 3rd but **I'm going** back a few days early'
E: 'Why?'
F: '**I'm moving** in to my new flat on September 30th.'

*(Unit 39)*

2. (a) **She's going to type some letters.**
(b) **She's going to pay the teachers.**
(c) **She's going to telephone the Director.**
(d) **She's going to check the registers.**
(e) **She's going to check how many students there are in each class.**

3. Teacher 1: 'Ola? **Are** we **going to** get paid today?'
Ola: "Yes, I**'m going to** pay you all this afternoon, don't worry.'

Teacher 2: 'Ola? How many students are there in class B501?'
Ola: 'Can I tell you later? **I'm going to** check how many students there are this afternoon. OK?'

Teacher 3: 'Ola? Those plants look almost dead!'
Ola: 'Oh! OK. **I'll** give them some water.'

Teacher 4: 'Ola? Is the Director coming here today?'
Ola: 'No, but **I'm going to** ring him later. Do you want me to pass on a message?'

Teacher 5: 'Ola! The phone's ringing. Shall I answer it?'
Ola: 'No, it's OK. **I'll** answer it.'

Ola: 'Have you completed your registers properly?'
Teacher 6: 'Er....'
Ola: 'Well, **I'm going to** check them this afternoon..........'

*(Unit 40)*

4. (a) They're going to dance (b) They're going to rob a bank (c) She's going to answer the phone
(d) It's going to rain (e) He's going to fall in (f) She's going to miss the bus

5. Gypsy: 'You (have) **will have** a long and happy life.'
Client: 'When **will** I **get married**?'
Gypsy: 'Oh, you **won't marry** early. You **will meet** your husband when you are about thirty.'
Client: 'What **will** his job **be**?'
Gypsy: 'He **will be** a businessman.'
Client: '**Will** we **have** any children?'
Gypsy: 'Yes, you **will have** six children.'
Client: 'Six?!'

## *Part twelve: (Units 41–44): Connecting the past and the present*

*(Unit 41)*

1. (a) Dick has climbed Mount Everest
(b) Sandra has never been on television.
(c) Julie and Dave have never climbed Mount Everest
(d) Dick has never written a book
(e) Sandra has met Prince Charles
(f) Julie and Dave have been on television
(g) Dick has had an accident
(h) Sandra has written a book
(i) Julie and Dave have never met Prince Charles

2. (a) Has Dick ever met Prince Charles? No, he hasn't
(b) Has Sandra ever been on television? No, she hasn't
(c) Have Julie and Dave ever written a book? No, they haven't
(d) Has Sandra ever had an accident? No, she hasn't
(e) Has Dick ever been on television? Yes, he has
(f) Have Julie and Dave ever had an accident? Yes, they have

*(Unit 42)*

3. (a) He's been married for ten years
He's been married since 1987
(b) He's lived in Ecuador for twelve years
He's lived in Ecuador since 1985
(c) They've been teachers since 1989
They've been teachers for eight years
(d) I've had a computer for a year
I've had a computer since 1996
(e) She has played the piano for eleven years
She has played the piano since she was six
(f) I've spoken Japanese for three years
I've spoken Japanese since 1994
(g) It has been sunny for a week
It has been sunny since last week
(h) The shop has been open for two years
The shop has been open since 1995
(i) We have been at University for three years
We have been at University since 1994

4. (a) How long has he been married?
(b) How long has he lived in Ecuador?
(c) How long have they been teachers?
(d) How long have I/you had a computer?
(e) How long has she played the piano?
(f) How long have you spoken Japanese?
(g) How long has it been sunny?
(h) How long has the shop been open?
(i) How long have we/they been at University?

*(Unit 43)*

5. (a) He's shaved his beard
(b) He's grown his hair
(c) He's put on weight
(d) He's got older
(e) He's started wearing a tie
(f) He's bought some new clothes
(g) He's stopped wearing an earring
(h) He's got married
(i) He's become smarter

6. (a) Has he cut his hair? No, he hasn't
(b) Has he grown a moustache? No, he hasn't
(c) Has he put on weight? Yes, he has
(d) Has he started wearing a tie? Yes, he has
(e) Has he lost weight? No, he hasn't
(f) Has he got married? Yes, he has
(g) Has he shaved his beard? Yes, he has

*(Unit 44)*

7. (a) He's already posted the letters.
   (b) He's already paid in the cheque
   (c) He's already taken out some cash
   (d) He's already bought some bread and milk
   (e) He hasn't got any petrol for the car yet
   (f) He hasn't taken the dog to the vet yet
   (g) He hasn't paid the electricity bill yet
   (h) He hasn't bought any aspirin yet

8. (a) Has Paul posted the letters yet? Yes, he has
   (b) Has Paul paid in the cheque yet? Yes, he has
   (c) Has Paul taken out some cash yet? Yes, he has
   (d) Has Paul bought some bread and milk yet? Yes, he has
   (e) Has Paul got some petrol for the car yet? No, he hasn't
   (f) Has Paul taken the dog to the vet yet? No, he hasn't
   (g) Has Paul paid the electricity bill yet? No, he hasn't
   (h) Has Paul bought some aspirin yet? No, he hasn't

# Index